112

Hitler's Armada

Hitler's Armada

The German Invasion Plan, and the
Defence of Great Britain by the
Royal Navy, April–October 1940

GEOFF HEWITT

Pen & Sword
MARITIME

First published in Great Britain in 2008 by
PEN & SWORD MARITIME
an imprint of
Pen & Sword Books Ltd
47 Church Street, Barnsley, South Yorkshire, S70 2AS

Copyright © Geoff Hewitt, 2008

ISBN 978-1-84415-785-3

A CIP catalogue record for this book is
available from the British Library

Typeset by Concept, Huddersfield, West Yorkshire
Printed and bound in England by Biddles Ltd

Pen & Sword Books Ltd incorporates the Imprints of
Pen & Sword Aviation, Pen & Sword Maritime, Pen & Sword Military,
Wharncliffe Local History, Pen & Sword Select,
Pen & Sword Military Classics and Leo Cooper

For a complete list of Pen & Sword titles please contact
PEN & SWORD BOOKS LIMITED
47 Church Street, Barnsley, South Yorkshire, S70 2AS, England
E-mail: enquiries@pen-and-sword.co.uk
Website: www.pen-and-sword.co.uk

Keep then the seas about in special;
Which of England is the round wall,
As though England were likened to a city
And the wall environ were the sea.

Libelle of Englyshe Polycye, 1436

The best method of dealing with a German
invasion of the Island of Britain was to drown
as many as possible on the way over and knock
the others on the head as they crawled ashore.

Winston Churchill to General Maxime Weygand,
11 June 1940

Contents

List of Maps

Preface

Hitler's Armada is the culmination of many years of personal interest in the Second World War, and more specifically in the early war years of 1940 and 1941. Its conclusions have been reached following considerable research, involving the study of literally hundreds of books, articles and documents relevant to the period. As a result of this analysis, it has become apparent that the conclusion drawn at the time, and largely still accepted to the present day – that the victory of Fighter Command in the Battle of Britain made a German invasion impossible – cannot be justified.

Numerous books discuss the summer and autumn of 1940 purely in terms of aircraft losses, in some cases on a day-by-day basis, the understanding being that German success in the Battle of Britain would have made an invasion inevitable, with the invading troops being ferried across the Channel under a vast air umbrella, against which no defending force could prevail. By and large, the possibility that air superiority was not the only, or even the crucial, factor governing the success or failure of this operation was not even considered. The major events leading up to the Battle of Britain, the collapse of the Anglo-French armies in May 1940 and the subsequent evacuation of most of the British Expeditionary Force were portrayed as a military disaster followed by, at least from the British viewpoint, a miraculous deliverance brought about by a combination of German error (the order to halt on 24 May) and the valiant efforts of the Little Ships. The fact that Dunkirk, and the now largely forgotten post-Dunkirk evacuations, were successes achieved by a Royal Navy operating in the face of heavy air attack, with at best intermittent support from Fighter Command, has been largely ignored, presumably because it did not fit the myth.

The nineteenth-century English historian and scholar James Spedding wrote that, when faced with a statement of fact, the historian should ask 'Who first said so, and what opportunities had he of knowing it?' When this wise maxim is applied to many of the events of 1940, many long-cherished assumptions are found wanting, and one inescapable conclusion becomes clear – that a successful German invasion of Great Britain was never a realistic possibility.

In simple terms, Germany in 1940 lacked both suitable vessels to transport a landing force in adequate numbers, and a surface fleet with anything like the capacity to provide a viable defence for the improbable barge flotilla that was eventually assembled. The idea that the Battle of Britain did not necessarily bring about the salvation of the United Kingdom in 1940 may be anathema to many, but surely a romantic myth should not continue to obscure the more prosaic reality.

There are those who, when this suggestion is put to them, simply retreat into the 'look what happened to the *Prince of Wales* and *Repulse* off Malaya' argument. The relevance of this view is difficult to understand. The fact of the matter is that these two capital ships were sunk by eighty-five aircraft from the Japanese Genzan, Kanoya and Mihoro Air Corps. Of these, fifty-one were armed with torpedoes and thirty-four with bombs. Nine bombers encountered the old destroyer *Tenedos* on her way back to Singapore and attacked her (and all missed), whilst fifty of the fifty-one torpedo aircraft launched their torpedoes, scoring eleven hits. Each capital ship was hit by one bomb – *Repulse* early in the action by a 250kg bomb, and *Prince of Wales*, when already crippled, by a 500kg bomb. Both bombs exploded against the armoured deck of the vessel concerned and did minimal damage. The two ships were disabled and sunk by torpedoes, not by bombs.

In view of this, the number of torpedo aircraft available to the Luftwaffe at the time of Operation Sealion must be regarded as highly relevant. Disappointingly for the supporters of this argument, the fact is that in 1940 the Luftwaffe possessed no torpedo aircraft at all! The first use of torpedoes in action by the Luftwaffe did not take place until 1 May 1942, when at 0540 hours (hrs) four Heinkel He 111s armed with this weapon attacked vessels of convoy PQ15 en route to Russia.

The German Navy did, however, operate a small number (around two dozen) of slow and rather clumsy Heinkel He 115 floatplanes capable of carrying torpedoes, and on 23 August 1940 several of these attacked convoy OA203 in the Moray Firth, sinking two merchantmen, the *Makalla* and the *Llanishen*. Intriguingly, such was the rivalry between the German Navy and the Luftwaffe that subsequently, on 26 November 1940, Göring actually succeeded in having naval aircraft operations of this nature stopped, and production of the Navy's aerial torpedo (the LTF-5b) suspended! For all practical purposes, therefore, the aerial torpedo did not even exist as a weapon in the German arsenal at the time of Sealion.

Consequently, therefore, those who seek to maintain this argument are in fact claiming that the Luftwaffe would have overwhelmed the Royal Navy in the Channel in September 1940 because fifteen months later two ships of a type which the Royal Navy would almost certainly not have committed against Sealion were destroyed by means of a weapon which the Luftwaffe did not even possess, operated by aircrews highly skilled in the use of that very weapon. Frankly, this view is surely less than convincing.

Many accounts written of the Battle of Britain seem to accept that, if Fighter Command failed, then invasion would automatically have followed. *Hitler's Armada* attempts to look at the actual events of the spring and summer of 1940 without any preconceptions. Where possible, it has also sought to examine the events surrounding Sealion and the Battle of Britain from the German perspective, as all too frequently in the past this point of view has been neglected. It should also be stated, in passing, that many of the quotations from German sources included in what follows refer to 'England' when they ought properly to refer to 'Britain'. These references have not been amended, but hopefully any Welsh, Scots or Irish readers will not be too offended!

The conclusion reached is that, in 1940, the Luftwaffe was simply not able to sink or disable Royal Navy warships in sufficient numbers by day to protect an invasion force from destruction, and at night would have been unable to sink any warships at all. Furthermore, the German surface fleet, such as it was, would have been wholly incapable of providing any meaningful protection.

As the Battle of Britain developed, both air forces came to see their own, 'private' conflict more and more as an end in itself. The Luftwaffe never really sought to obey the instructions in Directive

16 to attack British harbours, but after failing to destroy Fighter Command resorted to the theory propounded by Douhet, which will be examined later, and supported by many senior airmen of the time, that heavy bombing of population centres would break civilian morale.

Eventually, it became clear that, whatever the outcome of the Battle, the fate of any attempted invasion would depend not on the skies above the Channel, but on the surface of the Channel itself. Air power could only bring about the defeat of Great Britain if its advocates were correct in their claims that bombing alone could break the will of a nation to resist by destroying the morale of the civilian population. Not for the last time in the Second World War, subsequent events proved this not to be the case.

In simple terms, for an opposed invasion, whilst control of the air was desirable, control of the sea was essential, and this remained firmly in the hands of the Royal Navy throughout. Despite this, however, the importance of the Royal Navy in the events of 1940 has never received its due recognition, and what may perhaps be called 'The Mystery of the Missing Fleet' has almost become a case worthy of an investigation by Sherlock Holmes!

Anyone with even a vague knowledge of modern British history, if asked to describe the events of 1940, would probably know of the German blitzkrieg which conquered the Low Countries and France. They would then no doubt explain that the British Army, trapped at Dunkirk, was rescued, without its equipment, by a host of little ships. After that, they would probably describe how Britain lay defenceless for the rest of the summer, but was saved from invasion and certain defeat by a handful of RAF fighter pilots, who defeated the German air force and thus made invasion impossible. If they were then asked to describe what the Royal Navy was doing whilst these momentous events were unfolding, they would probably be unable to answer. In truth, the legend of 1940 has no place for the Royal Navy. As Churchill said, in stirring words ringing down the years: 'Never in the field of human conflict was so much owed by so many to so few.'

Thus, a mystery unfolds: where was the Royal Navy, which after all was still the biggest in the world in 1940? Was it really absent at the time of Britain's greatest peril? Before visiting the great consulting detective, perhaps it is worthwhile looking a little deeper into the matter. In 2005, in *The Things we Forgot to Remember – Mers-el-*

Kebir, broadcast on BBC Radio 4, a Battle of Britain veteran, Air Commodore Peter Brothers, gave the answer to the puzzle, whilst explaining how the German invasion was prevented:

> The navy couldn't have done it, dive bombers would have sunk them, I'm afraid. Narrow waters to operate, they'd have no room to manoeuvre in the Channel. The Stuka boys, the dive bombers, they were good and they had overwhelming numbers. It didn't matter how many the navy shot down, there were still plenty more left. The navy took a long time to learn the lesson and I think it finally struck home when the Japanese sank the *Prince of Wales* and *Renown* (sic). They hadn't got air cover and they were just decimated by Japanese air attack. That's why the navy were kept out of the way up at Scapa Flow. I'm afraid I know the navy find this very disheartening but they had their day at Trafalgar. (BBC Radio 4, 2005)

There it is then, no need to visit 221b Baker Street – in 1940 the Navy was in the Orkney Islands, presumably dreaming of past glories and being kept safely 'out of the way'. Other sources support this: the 1969 film *Battle of Britain* seems unaware that there even was a Royal Navy, while the BBC GCSE Bitesize SOS Teacher website (17 January 2006), in answer to the question 'What were the causes of the Battle of Britain?' explains the Dunkirk evacuation and goes on to say 'Germany was then preparing to invade Britain (known as Operation Sealion). They would have to move their troops across the channel and it was only the RAF who would be able to stop them.' Distinguished historians from A.J.P. Taylor to Sir John Keegan have said much the same, if not quite so plainly or in such simple terms.

In the light of such popular and academic unanimity, it seems churlish to refer to those events which took place during the period between 26 May and 4 June 1940 when, under fairly constant attack from the 'Stuka boys' and their colleagues in Heinkel He IIIs, Dornier Do 17s and Junkers Ju 88s, the Royal Navy, in 680 vessels of all sizes – ranging from destroyers, motor torpedo boats, personnel ships, minesweepers, trawlers, drifters and yachts, to private motor boats and barges – and supported by 168 Allied (mainly French, but including Belgian, Dutch and Polish) vessels, lifted over a third of a million men from the east Mole and the beaches of Dunkirk, in doing so making it possible for Britain to remain in arms against a triumphant Third Reich. It would perhaps be even more insensitive to suggest that for the rest of the summer that same Royal Navy held the Channel secure, whatever the outcome of the Battle of Britain.

In view of the vital role that the Royal Navy played in the defence of the United Kingdom during this period, it is surely odd that this was not recognized at the time, or even acknowledged after the event, but there appear to have been two basic reasons for this omission. Firstly, there were the emotional and political needs of the time, and secondly, the widely held assumption that air power had eclipsed sea power.

Emotionally, the victory of the underdog has always had a strong appeal, be it David defeating Goliath or St George slaying the Dragon. The success of Fighter Command in overcoming the Luftwaffe, and in so doing apparently preventing invasion, is as dramatic as the siege of the Alamo, except that, unlike the Texans, the embattled and outnumbered defenders won. Newspapers of the time reported the wildly inaccurate aircraft losses almost as if they were the latest cricket score, with the home team recovering splendidly after being required to follow on. The phrase 'wildly inaccurate' is used advisedly – after the War, when Luftwaffe archives became available, they revealed that the British had overestimated German aircraft losses between 10 July 1940 and 31 October 1940 by 55 per cent. To put this into perspective, however, the Germans overestimated British losses by 234 per cent. The actual figures show that the British, claiming 2,698, actually shot down 1,733 aircraft, whereas the Germans, claiming 3,058, actually shot down 915 (Richards 1974).

Nevertheless, the corrected figures still demonstrate a clear victory for Fighter Command, and after the disasters of the first half of 1940, a victory was what the British public badly needed. The fact that this success in the air fighting was not the real underlying reason for Sealion not being attempted was never really appreciated. The vapour trails over the South-East could be seen; the nightly naval patrols which secured the Channel could not.

Winston Churchill was well aware that, without immediate financial and military aid from the United States, the future for Great Britain was bleak. His attempts to secure such support were hindered, however, by the political situation in America, where

Franklin Roosevelt was seeking the Democratic nomination for a third term, and the Convention in Chicago was not to take place until July.

In May 1940, an opinion poll in the United States had shown only 7 per cent of Americans in favour of going to war in alliance with Britain and France. Additionally, the United States' Ambassador to Britain, Joseph Kennedy, was convinced that Britain could not survive and made Roosevelt fully aware of his views. Any weapons the United States might send to Britain would be lost or, even worse, taken over by Germany, when Britain was forced to capitulate. Against this background, Churchill needed to demonstrate to the sceptics in the United States that Britain had no intention of doing such a thing, and was capable not only of surviving, but also of fighting back effectively. The victory in the Battle of Britain provided the necessary evidence, and by linking it with the prevention of invasion, he could prove that Britain would remain as a secure base from which resistance to the Third Reich would continue – US aid would not, therefore, be wasted or lost.

Whether Churchill himself really believed that the defeat of Fighter Command would inevitably lead to a German invasion is open to doubt – despite his public pronouncements. At a critical time in the Battle of Britain, he not only permitted but actually encouraged the despatch of three armoured regiments, totalling 154 tanks, together with forty-eight anti-tank guns, twenty anti-aircraft guns and forty-eight field guns to be sent as reinforcements to British forces in the Middle East. These reinforcements enabled the Western Desert Force to launch an offensive, Operation Compass, which culminated in a major victory over the Italian Army at Beda Fomm in February 1941. The three armoured regiments were 7th Royal Tank Regiment (with Matilda Mark II Infantry tanks), 2nd Royal Tank Regiment (with A9, A10 and A13 Cruiser tanks) and 3rd Hussars (with Mark VI Light tanks). As the Matildas represented half the total number of this armoured fighting vehicle operational in the United Kingdom at the time, and as in France it had proved itself to be the most battleworthy British tank, the date the convoy (codenamed Apology) sailed is surely significant. It was 22 August 1940, almost a month *before* what tradition maintains was the crucial day of the Battle of Britain, 15 September. If the link between the Battle of Britain and Operation Sealion is to be maintained, therefore, it must be accepted that, when the very survival of

Britain herself was in doubt, her political leadership sent a considerable proportion of her most modern weapons off to a distant theatre of war where they could not make a contribution to her defence.

Aside from the political and propaganda needs of the time was the widespread belief that sea power had become irrelevant in the face of growing air power. Had this been so, if the Luftwaffe had secured air superiority over the Channel, any anti-invasion forces deployed by the Royal Navy would have been impotent – sunk or driven back in the face of massed bombing.

To understand how this view came about, it is necessary to go right back to the last days of the First World War, when the Royal Air Force came into being, and follow the arguments put forward by its creators in order to enable it to survive as an independent force in the changed circumstances of the post-war world. These arguments influenced the way in which the events of 1940 were perceived, especially in the United Kingdom, and will be considered in some depth in a later chapter.

It has often been said that history is written by the winners, and it is certainly true that much of the information on Operation Sealion from the German point of view is not readily available. The structure of this book, therefore, has attempted to remedy this, and consists of three distinct, if unequal, sections.

The first section examines the way in which the Sealion invasion plan evolved and the details of the final document – such as which particular German units were intended to land at which point, and how they would be transported. Most important of all, however, it will consider the compromises the planners were obliged to make in an attempt to overcome what was in reality a fatal weakness: the lack of an adequate surface fleet.

The second section begins with a consideration of between-the-wars perceptions of the relative roles of air and sea power, but consists mainly of an assessment of the strengths and weaknesses of the Royal Navy of 1939–1940, and an examination of how well or badly it had fared in the period leading up to the time of the Sealion threat; from this it is possible to assess whether the threat to it from the Luftwaffe was really as great as has been generally assumed.

Finally, section three deals with the Battle of Britain, both in legend and in reality, and a description of what the accumulated evidence of the previous chapters suggests would actually have happened to Sealion had the barges put to sea in late September 1940.

Chapter 1, therefore, will examine the circumstances surrounding the rebirth of the German Navy after 1918, and explain the events and decisions which resulted in it being totally inadequate for the task which was imposed upon it in 1940.

Acknowledgements

I would like to express my gratitude to a number of individuals, some of whom encouraged me to write *Hitler's Armada*, whilst others were of great assistance in enabling me to complete the research which made it possible to see the project through to completion.

Andy Holborn, a friend since schooldays, has tolerated for more years than he or I would care to admit my sometimes long-winded expositions of my opinions and theories – his suggestions and constructive criticism have been invaluable, despite his distressing unwillingness to acknowledge the undoubted merits of Field Marshal Sir Claude Auchinleck during our many other discussions on the North African campaign! Another friend, Gordon Small, was also helpful with advice on the layout of the manuscript and his diligent proofreading of the first draft.

Amanda Stokes, of Lancashire County Council Library Services, was kind enough to locate and make available to me copies of some of the less easily available books and documents which I required at various stages.

The staff of the Photographic Archives at the Imperial War Museum, and at the Royal Naval Museum at Portsmouth, were of enormous assistance in identifying suitable photographs. I was determined to illustrate the work with photographs showing vessels in their 1940 state, and I was largely able to achieve this aim, although I believe that by summer 1940 the battleship *Revenge* had been painted with an experimental dazzle camouflage.

I must also acknowledge the tolerance of my long-suffering wife Paula, my son Martin and daughter Eleanor, who have had to put up with my 'obsession' with Operation Sealion for many years, and who as a result are doubtless better informed on the events of the early war years than they ever expected to be.

Finally, I must grudgingly thank the many bowlers from the Chorley and District Amateur Cricket League, and more recently the Palace Shield Cricket Competition, who over the years have kindly exposed my technical shortcomings as a batsman, thus giving me valuable free time on Saturday afternoons in summer to ponder in detail the final structure of *Hitler's Armada*!

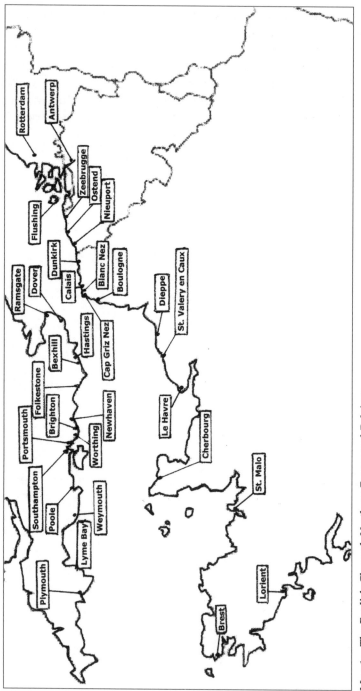

Map 1. The English Channel, Northern France and Belgium.

Chapter 1

The German Surface Fleet

The surface forces are so inferior in numbers and strength that they
can do no more than show that they know how to die gallantly.
Grand Admiral Erich Raeder, 3 September 1939

The starting point for any serious evaluation of Operation Sealion must be consideration of the strength of the German surface fleet. Whatever the anti-shipping capabilities of the Luftwaffe may have been in 1940, the fact was that the invasion force would need to be both transported and protected by surface vessels. In order to understand how the German Navy had reached the position in which it found itself in the summer of 1940, it is necessary to go back some twenty years, to the end of the First World War and the Treaty of Versailles.

The navy of Kaiser Wilhelm II no longer existed, and the victorious Allies, although they had not gone so far as to impose complete demilitarization, had imposed severe restrictions on the German armed forces in general, and the Navy in particular. Article 181 of the Treaty of Versailles restricted the surface fleet to six armoured ships, six cruisers, twelve destroyers and twelve torpedo boats. Construction of submarines was forbidden, as was the possession of military aircraft. Furthermore, Article 190, which regulated the replacement of obsolete ships, decreed that battleships and cruisers should only be replaced after twenty years service, and destroyers and torpedo boats after fifteen. Additional restrictions were placed on the displacements of any replacement vessels, so that new armoured ships could not exceed 10,000 tons, cruisers 6,000 tons, destroyers 800 tons and torpedo boats 200 tons.

To give some idea of how severe these restrictions were, the final design for the Royal Navy G3 battlecruisers of late 1921 envisaged a displacement of 48,400 tons, and the N3 battleships of the same time 48,500 tons, although the Washington Naval Treaty of 1921–2 (involving Great Britain, the United States, Japan, France and Italy) eventually restricted the displacements of future battleships to 35,000 tons, and of cruisers to 10,000 tons. As part of this Treaty, it was agreed that there would be no new battleship construction for ten years, except for two new British battleships, *Nelson* and *Rodney*, which were completed in 1927 and displaced around 33,500 tons. As the major naval powers also produced cruisers displacing 10,000 tons, and the first new Royal Navy destroyer, *Ambuscade*, constructed in 1926, displaced 1,200 tons, the severity of the restrictions imposed by the Versailles Treaty on future German naval construction is clear.

In the event, Germany retained six elderly pre-dreadnought battleships, and a number of equally antiquated Gazelle class light cruisers. The first new warship, the cruiser *Emden*, was launched early in 1925, and was basically a development of the last light cruisers built during the First World War, with eight 15cm (5.9-inch) guns in single mountings. Twelve new torpedo boats, six each of the Möwe and Wolf Classes, were also constructed between 1926 and 1929. Again, these were developments of the wartime torpedo boats of the Imperial Navy, although they were officially classed as destroyers in order to conform to the Versailles Treaty restrictions. In fact, their actual displacements exceeded the 800 tons limit by around 125 tons.

The first new designs (as opposed to developments of First World War types) were the three cruisers of the 'K' Class, *Konigsberg*, *Karlsruhe* and *Köln*, which were constructed between 1926 and 1930, and with nine 15cm guns in three triple turrets, director fire control and cruising diesels as well as turbines, compared well with the Leander Class light cruisers being introduced into service with the Royal Navy in 1931–3. Subsequently, two more light cruisers developed from the 'K' design were to appear: *Leipzig*, launched in 1929, and *Nurnberg*, launched in 1934.

The replacement of the six antiquated pre-dreadnought battleships which Germany was allowed to retain after the First World War was a difficult challenge. The intention of the 10,000 tons restriction for armoured ships imposed by the Treaty of Versailles was clear enough. New vessels could be either well armoured but slow and short range, effectively coastal-defence ships (the type actually favoured by Raeder himself, when in command of the Baltic station), or faster but more lightly armed and armoured, more akin to a cruiser. The head of the German Navy between 1924 and 1928, Admiral Zenker, eventually recommended the latter, resulting in a vessel capable of 26 knots, armour capable of resisting 8-inch shellfire and armed with six 28cm (11-inch) guns in two turrets. Such a vessel should be able to outfight the typical 'Washington cruiser' of 10,000 tons displacement and a main armament of eight 8-inch guns, which would be some five knots faster and outrun any battleship which it encountered.

At the time, German military thinking believed that any future war would be against Russia or France and the 'armour-clads', as they were called by the German Navy, would be particularly suitable for deployment against French trade routes in the eastern Atlantic – with the added benefit of drawing French naval strength into this area and away from the north Atlantic routes used by German shipping. In addition, of course, if Great Britain was not involved, then the three Royal Navy battlecruisers which could catch and sink an armour-clad – *Hood*, *Renown* and *Repulse* – would be out of the picture.

Admiral Raeder, as previously stated, had himself preferred the coastal-defence ship which would have been more suited for operations in the Baltic, but when he became head of the German Navy on 1 October 1928, he made no attempt to change the design, and construction of the first three armour-clads (or 'pocket battleships' as they came to be called) – *Deutschland*, *Admiral Scheer* and *Admiral Graf Spee* – began in February 1929, June 1931 and October 1932 respectively.

Thus, when Adolf Hitler became Chancellor in January 1933, the German Navy consisted of four light cruisers with a fifth under construction, one old light cruiser suitable for training purposes only, twelve small destroyer/torpedo boats, and one pocket battleship about to commission with two more under construction. Initially, Hitler held to the 'Conversion Plan' of November 1932, which envisaged a total of six pocket battleships, and in 1934 two were authorized for construction. Hitler had already said in 1933 that it was his wish never to go to war with Britain, Italy or Japan, and he was eager to conclude a naval agreement with Britain.

The imminent appearance, however, of the French battleships *Dunkerque* and *Strasbourg*, the first of which was already under construction, had already demonstrated to Raeder that something more powerful than the pocket-battleship design was essential. In June 1934, therefore, he urged that the new ships be more heavily armoured and be fitted with a third triple 28cm turret. Hitler authorized an increase in size to 19,000 tons displacement, but instructed Raeder to refer only to 'improved 10,000 tons ships'. Construction work on both vessels began in 1935 and they eventually emerged as the 32,000-ton battleships *Scharnhorst* and *Gneisenau*.

By the time work on these vessels commenced, the Anglo-German Naval Agreement, which Hitler described to Raeder on 18 June 1935 as 'the happiest day of my life', had been signed. This permitted Germany to build naval forces up to 35 per cent of the Royal Navy in each category of ship, other than submarines where 45 per cent was allowed, with the opportunity to increase submarine strength to parity at a later date. The significance of this agreement to the German Navy was that it seemed to rule Great Britain out as a future naval adversary. Even in Britain, Earl Beatty (commander of the Battlecruiser Fleet at Jutland and subsequently commander of the Grand Fleet) claimed in the House of Lords that there was at least one country in the world with which Britain need not fear an arms race.

The signing of this agreement and the earlier repudiation of the Treaty of Versailles now made it possible for Germany to commence naval expansion. The battleships *Bismarck* and *Tirpitz*, each displacing some 42,000 tons, were laid down in 1936, work on the first of five heavy cruisers of the Hipper class began, and between 1937 and 1939 twenty-two large destroyers of the Leberecht Maass and the Von Roeder Classes were constructed.

The Anglo-German Naval Agreement was eventually repudiated by Hitler in April 1939, but during the almost four years it existed it exercised significant influence over German naval planning. In an order of the day of 15 July 1935, the Chief of Naval Staff, Rear Admiral Guse, stated that the agreement made a repeat of the former naval rivalry between Britain and Germany impossible, and Admiral Raeder himself did not permit even theoretical studies into naval operations against Great Britain. Provisional battle orders given to the German Navy on 27 May 1936 (ironically five years to the day before the sinking of the *Bismarck*) omitted any contingency

4

for war with Britain. Despite what must surely have been clear evidence to the contrary, Raeder seems to have remained convinced that war with Britain would not take place, at least in the immediate future.

It must therefore have been a dramatic development for him when in late May 1938 he was summoned to a meeting with Hitler, who told him that Britain must be reckoned as a probable enemy and a major expansion of the Navy was required. In order to ascertain what form this expansion should take, the strategic role of the new fleet needed to be determined and Raeder took two immediate steps. Firstly, one of his youngest staff officers, Commander Heye, was given the task of devising a plan of action against Britain, and secondly, a planning committee of senior admirals under the chairmanship of Guse (by now promoted to Vice Admiral) was to draw up proposals on the strategy the Navy should follow, and consequently what types and numbers of ships would be required.

The first meeting of the committee took place on 23 September 1938 and the plan of action put forward by Heye must have caused a considerable stir. His argument was that even a powerful battle fleet operating out of the German Bight could not make significant inroads into the overall strategic position at sea. In other words, a second Jutland, even if favourable to Germany, would serve no purpose. The proper course, he argued, would be to provide a striking force to wage war against the shipping lanes upon which Britain depended, rather than to seek a confrontation with the British battle fleet. However, in order to carry out this attack, Germany needed both the right kind of ships and the ability to break out of the North Sea into the North Atlantic, and it was in the breakout element of the argument that Heye was vulnerable. When asked how he envisaged that the breakout would be achieved, his response was that high speeds and a great deal of luck would be needed, which would require light forces rather than heavily armoured capital ships. In common with most naval opinion at the time, Heye placed little reliance in submarines, believing that improved anti-submarine techniques and the use of sonar (known by the British as asdic) had significantly reduced their effectiveness.

The admirals on the planning committee immediately identified the flaws in the case put forward by Heye. A breakout could only be achieved, they argued, by utilizing powerful capital ships, and Guse

5

summed up by expressing the view that whether these heavy ships themselves should be the striking force, or whether they should be used to effect the breakout of the striking force, did not need to be decided at that time. This in itself was a remarkable statement in that it seemed to propose that the actual role the heavy ships were to fulfill could be decided after they had been built!

The final conclusions of the planning committee were put to Raeder on 31 October 1938, and between 1 November 1938 and 29 January 1939 Raeder presented these recommendations to Hitler. In his post-war memoirs, Raeder stated that he put forward two alternatives: a force of submarines and pocket battleships, which could threaten the sea lanes to Britain and be constructed comparatively quickly; or a much more powerful fleet, with a nucleus of heavy capital ships, which, though it would take longer to build, would not only threaten the sea lanes but could also challenge the British battle fleet itself. If the alternatives were indeed expressed in these terms (and German Admiralty records seem to suggest that the submarine/pocket battleship option was never seriously even considered), then it was not difficult to deduce which Hitler would choose. Raeder claims to have been reassured by Hitler that the longer building time would not be a problem as the fleet would not be required before 1946.

In this way, on 29 January 1939, the idea of the Z Plan Fleet (Z standing for Ziel, or 'Target') came about, and three months later Hitler repudiated the Anglo-German Naval Agreement. For the record, Cajus Bekker, in *Hitler's Naval War*, states that the numbers of warships to be constructed by 1947 were as follows:

Ship type	Number
Battleship – 56,000 tons type	6
Battleship – *Gneisenau/Bismarck* types	4
Battlecruiser – 21,000 tons	10
Pocket Battleship	3
Aircraft Carrier	4
Heavy Cruiser	5
Light Cruiser	12
Scout Cruiser	20
Destroyer	58
Torpedo Boat	78

U-Boat – Atlantic type	162
U-Boat – Coastal type	60
U-Boat – Special-Purpose type	27

Of the ships of cruiser size and above, *Gneisenau* and *Scharnhorst* were complete, as were the three pocket battleships. Three of the heavy cruisers were in the early stages of construction, whilst the battleships *Bismarck* and *Tirpitz* were still around two years from completion. The existing light cruisers do not actually appear in this list as, together with some of the older torpedo boats, they were to be relegated to training purposes from 1942.

Although the Z Plan proposals look impressive, they were a fantasy, to all intents and purposes. Aside from the ambitious aim of producing six 56,000-ton 'super battleships' before the teething troubles of the much smaller *Gneisenau* class had been ironed out, let alone the *Bismarck* and *Tirpitz* completed, there were other more practical problems. On 31 December 1938, even before the plan was officially accepted, a marine architect from the naval ordnance department had produced a report titled 'The Feasibility of the Z Plan', pointing out the organizational problems involved in such an immense undertaking, whilst the requirements in materials and manpower were such that it appeared that the German Navy high command must have assumed that virtually the whole of German industry was at its disposal. Given the expansion of the German Army and the Luftwaffe taking place at the same time, this would clearly not have been the case. In the event, only one of the large ships, the aircraft carrier *Graf Zeppelin*, was even launched and work on her ceased in 1942.

The feelings of Admiral Raeder when the British Admiralty radioed the two words 'Total Germany' in an uncoded signal to British ships at sea, on 3 September 1939, can be guessed at. The Z Plan Fleet, which he had been informed would not be required until 1946, existed only on paper, and the few available surface vessels would, in his words, 'just about be able to show that they could die with dignity!'

The months between September 1939 and July 1940, when Raeder must somehow produce a workable plan for Operation Sealion, had not been kind to his surface fleet. The ships which he had had available at the start of the War, and their status by August 1940, were as follows:

Gneisenau

Torpedoed off Trondheim on 20 June 1940 by HM Submarine *Clyde*. Left Trondheim on 25 July 1940 to return to Kiel in company with the cruiser *Nurnberg*. On the following day the torpedo boat *Luchs*, part of her escort, was torpedoed and sunk by HM Submarine *Swordfish*. Repairs on *Gneisenau* were estimated to be completed by early November 1940, but her next operation did not commence until 22 February 1941.

Scharnhorst

On 8 June 1940, together with *Gneisenau*, encountered and sank the aircraft carrier *Glorious* and her escorting destroyers *Ardent* and *Acasta*, 300 miles west of Narvik. *Acasta*, though crippled, managed to score a torpedo hit on *Scharnhorst* which ripped open her side near her aft gun turret. She returned to Trondheim, and subsequently to Kiel, for repairs which were expected to complete in late October 1940. Her next operation took place in company with her sister ship in February 1941.

Deutschland

Was at sea when war was declared, having left Wilhelmshaven on 24 August for operations in the North Atlantic. She was soon recalled to Germany, having achieved little, and passed through the Denmark Strait on 8 November, arriving in Kiel on 15 November 1939. She was immediately renamed *Lützow*, to avoid the potential propaganda benefits to the Allies should she be lost under her original name. She took part in Operation Weserubung (the German occupation of Norway) and on 11 April 1940, shortly after leaving Oslo, she was hit in the stern by a torpedo from HM Submarine *Spearfish*. Her damage was severe (her stern was almost broken off) but she was returned to Kiel. Repairs were not expected to be completed until April 1941.

Admiral Scheer

Refitting in Danzig and not expected to be completed until mid-September 1940. She actually left Danzig on 23 October 1940 on a commerce-raiding operation from which she returned in April 1941.

Admiral Graf Spee

Was at sea when war was declared, having left Wilhelmshaven on 21 August for the mid and South Atlantic. On 13 December 1939 she was engaged by one of the hunting groups searching for her (the 8-inch gun cruiser *Exeter* and the 6-inch gun cruisers *Ajax* and *Achilles*) at the Battle of the River Plate. She took shelter in Montevideo, Uruguay, and was scuttled off Montevideo on 17 December 1939.

Admiral Hipper
Although rammed and damaged by the destroyer HMS *Glowworm* on 8 April 1940, she was still able to take part in the invasion of Norway. She subsequently refitted in Wilhelmshaven but was operational by mid-September 1940. She did, however, in common with the other ships of her class, have a sophisticated high-pressure boiler system which, although when working enabled her to operate at high speed (in the region of 32 knots), was highly unreliable and frequently broke down.

Blücher
Took part in Operation Weserubung when not fully worked up. On 9 April 1940 she was hit by torpedoes and shellfire from Norwegian shore batteries in Oslofjord and sank.

Emden
Had taken part in the invasion of Norway and was operational in August 1940. She was, however, the oldest and weakest of the light cruisers and was normally only used as a training ship.

Köln
Operational in August 1940.

Karlsruhe
Torpedoed and sunk by HM Submarine *Truant* whilst en route from Kristiansand, Norway, back to Germany on 9 April 1940.

Konigsberg
Damaged by Norwegian shore batteries on 9 April 1940, and dive-bombed and sunk in Bergen harbour by Fleet Air Arm Skua dive-bombers operating at extreme range from Hatston in the Orkneys on the following day.

Leipzig
Torpedoed and severely damaged by HM Submarine *Salmon* on 13 December 1939 in the North Sea whilst operating, together with

9

Nurnberg and *Köln*, as a covering force for five destroyers which had laid mines off Newcastle. The damage was so severe that she was never fit for use again as anything other than a training ship.

Nurnberg

Torpedoed at the same time as *Leipzig*, she was less badly damaged. On 25 July 1940 she accompanied *Gneisenau* on her return from Trondheim to Kiel and was fully operational in August 1940.

Destroyers

Although twenty-two destroyers were in service with the German Navy at the outbreak of war, two were sunk north-west of Borkum by a German bomber on 22 February 1940, and ten were lost in the first and second Battles of Narvik on 10 and 13 April 1940. In August 1940 three more were undergoing refits not due to complete until late September/early October 1940. One new destroyer, Z23, actually commissioned on 15 September 1940, but would obviously need some considerable time to work up to an operational state, especially as she was the lead ship of a new class.

Torpedo Boats

Of the twelve pre-war torpedo boats of the Wolf and Möwe Classes, one (*Tiger*) had been rammed and sunk by the German destroyer Z3 on 25 August 1939, and a second (*Luchs*) was torpedoed and sunk by HM Submarine *Swordfish* whilst escorting *Gneisenau* and *Nurnberg* on 26 July 1940. *Möwe* was undergoing repairs in Wilhelmshaven which were due to complete early in October 1940.

A new class of torpedo boat, the Elbing Class, had also begun construction in late 1936, and twelve had commissioned (though not all were properly worked up) by August 1940. As with the Hipper Class cruisers, their high-pressure boilers and turbines were a constant source of trouble and they proved to be poor seagoing vessels. They carried a powerful torpedo armament, but only one 105mm (4.1-inch) gun. Very little use was made of them until much later in the war, although T1, T2 and T3 each took part in one, and T5, T6, T7 and T8 in three minelaying operations in the Dover Straits and North Sea areas between 1 and 16 September 1940.

The German surface fleet at the time of Sealion, therefore, consisted of one heavy cruiser with unreliable engines, two light cruisers and one training cruiser, seven or eight destroyers and nine torpedo boats. There were, of course, the elderly battleships – two (*Schliesen* and *Schleswig-Holstein*) were still in use, and the latter had fired the first shots of the Second World War when bombarding at point-blank range the Polish garrison of the Westerplatte at Danzig on 1 September 1939 – but as warships they had been obsolete for over thirty years, and their involvement in Sealion would have been inconceivable, especially as both had been largely stripped of their crews to release men for the Sealion fleet.

Neither was there much comfort in the progress of new warships under construction. *Bismarck* and *Tirpitz* were still either fitting out or completing construction, as was the heavy cruiser *Prinz Eugen*. None would be available until well into 1941. In the event, other than these three, no new ship bigger than a destroyer was to be completed for the German Navy in the whole of the war.

Thus, as the above demonstrates, the German surface fleet in the summer of 1940 was in a parlous state. The invasion of Norway, however successful in strategic terms, had deprived the naval planners of the ability to provide anything more than a token escort for an invasion fleet. The next chapters, dealing with the genesis and evolution of the Sealion plan, reveal only too clearly how the German Navy struggled to overcome this insurmountable problem.

Chapter 2

Meetings and Memoranda

Early invasion proposals, up to the production of Directive 16

We may therefore be sure that there is a plan, perhaps built up over several years, for destroying Great Britain.

Winston Churchill, 14 July 1940

In contradiction to the view expressed by Winston Churchill and quoted above, the possibility of an invasion of the British Isles had not received serious consideration by the German naval staff in the years prior to the Second World War. The Anglo-German Naval Agreement of 1935 had apparently demonstrated that Great Britain would not be an enemy, at least in the near future, Hitler had named Great Britain in 1933 as one of the countries with which he never intended to go to war, and Raeder had forbidden his staff to undertake even theoretical studies into the strategy to be employed in the event of such a conflict. As late as 27 May 1936, provisional battle instructions given to the Navy had ignored Great Britain. It was only late in May 1938 that Hitler began to talk of Britain as an enemy, and even in 'Battle Instructions for the Navy' issued in May 1939, no reference was made to landing operations.

Nevertheless, when the Polish campaign was completed and planning underway for Operation Yellow (the invasion of the Low Countries and France) which was originally scheduled to take place in autumn 1939, Raeder began (as a precautionary measure, in case Hitler suddenly asked for a plan – according to his testimony at Nuremberg) to put his mind to the possibility that an invasion would be required. This may have been an attempt by a courtier to improve his status at court (Operation Yellow was always going to be an army and Luftwaffe campaign, with the Navy out of the picture), but a more charitable view would be that it was an attempt to ensure that the Navy was not caught unawares if Operation Yellow was a complete success, and committed to a hazardous enterprise beyond its limited capabilities.

Whatever the reason, on 15 November 1939, Raeder instructed his staff to investigate the possibility of invading Great Britain. Within a fortnight, his planners had concluded that a sea-borne assault 'on a grand scale' across the North Sea was possible, and had provided a list of requirements which would make feasible a landing on the east coast. The Army was consulted, making several suggestions which the Navy could not accept, and the Luftwaffe were sceptical about the whole thing. Hitler and OKW (Armed Forces Supreme Command) were not consulted and the whole study was shelved.

By 10 May 1940 (when Operation Yellow actually began), the German Navy had become committed to the invasion of Norway, which had been urged upon Hitler by Raeder himself. Strategically, his reasoning was sound. Germany required some fifteen million tons of iron ore annually, of which some eleven million came from Scandinavia, almost half of this being transported by sea down the Norwegian coast from Narvik and Kirkenes. If the Allies were to lay mines to halt this traffic, or were even to occupy Norway itself, then this would be lost. Raeder would almost certainly have read *Maritime Strategy of the Great War*, written by Vice Admiral Wegener, which argued that Germany should have occupied Norway in 1914, as this would have given the High Seas Fleet a base from which to operate against British shipping in the North Atlantic.

In any event, Raeder duly produced a plan (Operation Weserubung), which involved the surprise transportation of German troops to Norway by virtually all the operational major surface warships of the German Navy. This invasion commenced on 9 April 1940 and Norway was entirely in German hands by 8 June, when the last Allied evacuation convoy sailed. In the later stages, the occupation of Norway was overshadowed by the success of Operation Yellow, but from the point of view of an invasion of Great Britain, the study previously undertaken by the German Navy was now totally out of date.

The issue was raised again by Raeder at a meeting with Hitler on 21 May 1940, the same day that German forces reached the French coast. Quite why he brought the matter up at this time is not clear – the earlier planning had now been overtaken by events, the German Navy had suffered heavy losses during the Norwegian campaign, and both the Army and the Luftwaffe had expressed serious misgivings. Perhaps, as was probably the case when he had previously raised the matter in the autumn of 1939, he was concerned that the Navy should not be committed to a last-minute gamble over which it had little control, and for which it was ill-prepared and inadequately equipped, as his Nuremberg statements seem to suggest; or perhaps it may have been a real attempt to put before Hitler a potentially war-winning strategy. It may even have been intended to encourage Hitler to direct the Luftwaffe into action against the Royal Navy.

Whatever the reason, Hitler was not interested at that time. The invasion of France was under way, General Halder, OKH Chief of Staff (OKH was Oberkommando des Heeres, Army High Command), recorded in his diary on the same day that 'the big battle is in full swing', and the discussions between Hitler and Raeder were not even mentioned to OKH. It may well be that if Hitler had ordered even preliminary planning to commence after this meeting then the plan would have been less flawed than it eventually was; at the very least, the major difficulties to be resolved would have become clear at an early stage. However, this did not happen, and when Raeder met Hitler again on 4 June 1940, nothing further was said on the matter. On the same day, at 1423 hrs, the Admiralty signal terminating Operation Dynamo, the Dunkirk evacuation, was made.

Between then and the next meeting, on 20 June, the German victory in France had been total. Paris had fallen on 14 June and three days later the French Government asked for an armistice. This would be signed on 22 June, humiliatingly for French pride in the same location that the 1918 ceremony had taken place, a railway carriage in the Forest of Compiègne. Already, on 15 June, OKH had been instructed to reduce the size of the Army to 120 divisions, a reduction of some 20 per cent, in order to release men back into the economy. Halder concluded from this that the war against Britain would now be conducted by the Navy and Luftwaffe, as the Army had successfully completed its task. On 17 June, General Warlimont, Deputy Chief of Operations Staff at OKW, noted that Hitler had not expressed any intention to undertake an invasion of Britain, as he was aware of the unusual difficulties involved and that, therefore, 'even at this time, no preparatory work has been carried out at OKW.'

At the meeting of 20 June, which was also attended by Keitel (Head of OKW) and Jodl (OKW Chief of Staff), Raeder again raised the subject of invasion, reporting on a number of topics, including landing sites, available shipping (estimating that the Navy could assemble forty-five barges within two weeks) and minelaying. He urged that the Luftwaffe be committed to air attacks on British naval bases in order to delay repairs to damaged warships and to hinder the construction of new ones, and requested that the Army look into the composition of the divisions required for the operation. Hitler was non-committal about the whole thing, preferring to discuss a project for settling Jews on the island of Madagascar, and listening politely as Raeder explained the utter impossibility of a plan which Hitler had previously asked him to produce for the invasion of Iceland! Up to this time, the Army, as previously stated, had never taken the idea of an invasion of Great Britain seriously, but the fact that such a discussion had taken place at a conference involving the Führer must have caused a few alarm bells to ring, and Army High Command began to take a serious interest in the project.

Thereafter, things must have moved quickly. As early as 22 June, Halder was making references in his diary to 'preparations against England', although he still seems to have regarded them as intended to be a threatening gesture rather than an actual determination to invade. A week later, however, the German naval staff were given, no doubt to their dismay, an outline of what OKH had in mind. This was a dawn landing, on a 200-mile front between Ramsgate and Lyme Bay, of thirteen divisions (over 250,000 men), followed by a second wave less than ten days later. This proposal came some nine days after Raeder had told Hitler that the Navy could assemble forty-five barges within the next two weeks! Suddenly, the Army seemed to view the prospect of invasion with enthusiasm, although the Luftwaffe seemingly did not – on 25 June an officer on the Luftwaffe general staff had a paper he had presented to Göring's Chief of Staff (General Jeschonnek) on the possible role of parachutists and airborne troops in a Channel crossing returned with a note stating that Hitler had no such plan in mind.

On 30 June, Jodl produced a memorandum some six pages in length on what should be done if the British Government did not appreciate how desperate their position really was. If politics failed and force was required, then he listed three possibilities, these being:

1. The use of sea and air power to impose a blockade on Great Britain.
2. Terror bombing attacks against the civilian population.
3. A landing 'with a view to occupying the country'.

Jodl himself seems to have been convinced that the Navy and Luftwaffe would reduce Britain to such a degree that an invasion itself would be the final act in the conquest of an already beaten enemy, in effect a symbolic act akin to the recent ceremony at Compiègne, although he did insist that the landing plan itself should be thoroughly prepared.

On 2 July, a Führer Directive ('The War against England') was issued, signed by Keitel. It stated that Hitler had decided that 'A landing in England is possible', provided that air superiority was obtained and certain other necessary conditions fulfilled. No date was fixed and, although preparations were to begin immediately, these were upon the understanding that the invasion was a plan, not yet a definite decision. The Directive stated that the landing should be on a broad front, and involve twenty-five to forty divisions, which must be highly mechanized. The Navy was to provide information on available shipping.

On the following day, the British Force H (the battleships *Valiant* and *Resolution*, the battlecruiser *Hood*, the aircraft carrier *Ark Royal*, two cruisers and eleven destroyers), attacked the French Flotte de Raid in Mers-el-Kebir, the French squadron at Alexandria was deactivated peacefully and French warships in British ports were seized. Had the French Navy fallen into German hands, it could have posed a potent threat, but in the event it was neutralized in a ruthless and, at Mers-el-Kebir, bloody manner. Perhaps the British did not realize they were beaten, after all.

Raeder had over a week to digest the full implications of the 'War against England' Directive, and presumably marshal his arguments against the sheer impossibility of the proposals, before his next meeting with Hitler at the Berghof on 11 July. In the event, he argued in favour of economic blockade, with the invasion as a last resort, and only then with air superiority. The full impact of the War should be brought home to the British people by means of heavy air attacks on larger cities, especially London, rather than small-scale attacks on lesser targets, which he described as 'pin pricks'. For what it was worth, during the course of the meeting Hitler authorized new battleship construction, although this was irrelevant to the matter at hand, and never actually took place.

Perhaps Raeder thought he had made his case, but on the following day Jodl produced another memorandum, expressing the view that an invasion in the form of a river crossing on a broad front might succeed, provided that the Luftwaffe took on the role of artillery, the Navy made the Straits of Dover an 'impenetrable sea lane' and the assault forces were very strong. A day later, on 13 July, Halder and his superior, von Brauchitsch, the head of OKH, arrived at the Berghof with the OKH plan. This proposed a surprise crossing on a broad front stretching from Ramsgate to the Isle of Wight, whilst at the same time suggesting that each of the three services consider whether a preliminary operation such as the occupation of the Isle of Wight or Cornwall would be beneficial. Initially, thirteen divisions would land in three days, six between Ramsgate and Bexhill, four between Brighton and the Isle of Wight, and three in Lyme Bay. The first ten divisions would be from Army Group A, and the three in Lyme Bay from Army Group B. These divisions would subsequently be reinforced by a further twenty-eight divisions. The plan then described the initial bridgehead to be established and the advances the Army Group would make once reinforced. Once Southern England was secured, the rest of the country would fall within a month.

In order to facilitate this, effective opposition from the Royal Air Force must be eliminated, the routes for the invasion vessels must be swept of mines, both flanks of the Straits of Dover and the western approaches to the Channel must be secured by impassible minefields, and heavy coastal guns must dominate the entire coastal front area. The Royal Navy was to be pinned down in the North Sea and ('by the Italians') in the Mediterranean, whilst the Army carried out this 'mighty river crossing' on 15 August 1940.

The plan was ambitious in scope and revealed a total lack of understanding by the high-ranking professional soldiers of OKH of the problems peculiar to amphibious operations. Nevertheless, it

17

was accepted by Hitler and was issued as Directive 16 ('Prepara-
tions for the Invasion of England') three days later on 16 July. An
English translation of the text, taken from *Silent Victory* by Duncan
Grinnell-Milne, reads as follows:

Directive 16
Preparations for the Invasion of England

As England, in spite of the hopelessness of her military position, has so far shown herself unwilling to come to any compromise, I have therefore decided to begin to prepare for, and if
necessary to carry out, an invasion of England. This operation is
dictated by the necessity of eliminating Great Britain as a basis
from which the war against Germany can be fought and, if
necessary, the island will be occupied.

I therefore issue the following orders:

1) The landing operation must be a surprise crossing on a broad
front extending approximately from Ramsgate to a point west
of the Isle of Wight. Units of the Air Force will do the work of
the artillery and units of the Navy the work of engineers. I ask
each of the fighting services to consider the advantage from
their respective points of view of preliminary operations such
as the occupation of the Isle of Wight or the Duchy of Cornwall
prior to the full-scale invasion, and to inform me of the result of
their deliberations. I shall be responsible for the final decision.
The preparations for the large-scale invasion must be concluded by the middle of August.

2) The following preparations must be undertaken to make a
landing in England possible: (a) The British Air Force must be
eliminated to such an extent that it will be incapable of putting
up any substantial opposition to the invading troops. (b) The sea
routes must be cleared of mines. (c) Both flanks of the Straits of
Dover, and the Western Approaches to the Channel approximately on a line from Alderney to Portland, must be so heavily
mined as to be completely inaccessible. (d) Heavy guns must
dominate and protect the entire coastal front area. (e) It is
desirable that the English fleets both in the North Sea and in the
Mediterranean should be pinned down (by the Italians in the
latter instance) shortly before the crossing takes place; with this

aim in view, the naval forces at present in British harbours and coastal waters should be attacked from the air and by torpedoes.

3) Organisation of the Commands and of the preparations. The Commanders-in-Chief of the respective branches of the armed forces will lead their forces, under my orders. The Army, Navy, and Air Force General Staffs should be within an area of no more than 50km. from my Headquarters (Ziegenberg) by 1st August. I suggest that the Army and Navy General Staffs establish their headquarters at Giessen. The Commander-in-Chief of the Army will nominate an army group to lead the invasion forces. The invasion will be referred to by the code name *Sealion*. During the period of preparation and execution of the landings, the armed forces will carry out the following measures: (a) *Army* – Will draft a plan for the crossing and operations of the first wave of the invading force. The necessary anti-aircraft batteries will remain under the command of the individual army units until such time as their tasks can be divided into the following groups: support and protection of the land troops, protection of the disembarkation ports, and protection after their occupation of air bases. The Army will allocate landing craft to the individual units and determine, in conjunction with the Navy, the points at which the embarkation and the landings will take place. (b) *Navy* – Will provide and safeguard the invasion fleet and direct it to the individual points of embarkation. As far as possible, ships belonging to defeated nations are to be used. Together with aircraft patrols, the Navy will provide adequate protection on both flanks during the entire Channel crossing. An order on the allocation of commands during the crossing will follow in due course. The Navy will further supervise the establishment of coastal batteries, and will be responsible for the organisation of all coastal guns. The largest possible number of heavy guns must be installed as soon as possible to safeguard the crossing and to cover both flanks against enemy interference from the sea. For this purpose, anti-aircraft guns mounted on railway bogies (supplemented by all available captured guns) with railway turntables will be used. The Todt Organisation will be entrusted with the technical side of the organisation. (c) *Air Force* – Will prevent all enemy air attacks, and will destroy coastal defences covering the landing points, break the initial resistance of the enemy land forces, and annihilate reserves behind the front. The accomplishment of these tasks will require the closest co-operation between all individual units of the Air Force and the invading Army units. In addition, roads used for troop movements will be attacked and approaching enemy naval vessels engaged before they can reach the embarkation and landing points. I invite suggestions concerning the use of parachute and airborne troops, and in particular as to whether it would be advisable to keep the parachute and airborne troops in reserve for use only in case of necessity.

4) The necessary preparations for the installation of signals communications between France and England are being undertaken by the Signals Corps. The armoured under-sea cables are to be laid in co-operation with the Navy.

5) I hereby order the Commanders-in-Chief to provide me with the following information: (a) The plans drawn up by the Navy and Air Force for providing the above basic conditions necessary for the Channel crossing (see **2**). (b) A detailed survey of the location of the naval coastal batteries. (c) An estimate of the shipping space necessary and of the methods of preparation and equipment. Will civilian authorities be asked to co-operate? (*Navy*). (d) The organisation of air defence in the areas in which the invading troops and vehicles are concentrated (*Air Force*). (e) The plan for the Army crossing and operations; the organisation and equipment of the first wave. (f) Details of the measures planned by the Navy and Air Force for the execution of the crossing itself, its protection, and the support of the landing operations. (g) Suggestions concerning the use of parachute and airborne troops, and the organisation of the anti-aircraft artillery, once the spearhead troops have advanced sufficiently on English soil to permit their use (*Air Force*). (h) Location of Army and Naval Headquarters. (i) Are the Army, Navy, and Air Force Commanders of the opinion that the invasion should be preceded by a preliminary small-scale landing?

(*signed*) Hitler
(*initialled*) Keitel
(*initialled*) Jodl

Chapter 3

Compromise and Criticism

Inter-Service discussions after the issuing of Directive 16

Raeder must have read Directive 16 with total disbelief. Less than a month earlier, on 20 June, he had advised Hitler, Keitel and Jodl that the Navy had no landing craft, but that they could prepare about forty-five seaworthy barges within a fortnight. To naval eyes the sheer amateurishness of the proposals was astonishing, and it was clear that, whilst Raeder could hardly disobey a Directive from the Führer, he could not possibly leave it unchallenged. Accordingly, he composed a long memorandum to OKW detailing a whole host of difficulties which it seemed the planners had either not considered or of which they had been ignorant.

Among these were the weather, British land defences, lack of artillery support, the danger from mines and the certainty that the Royal Navy would intervene decisively. If the Luftwaffe could not prevent this, then even if the first wave got ashore it might well be cut off and annihilated. An additional problem, a factor which OKW seemed completely to have overlooked, was whether shipping in the quantities that would be required could even be made available and assembled within the timescale.

The plan proposed that around 260,000 men and 600 tanks, together with supplies, vehicles and some 55,000 horses, would land in the first wave. (It is often forgotten that the German Army, whilst it had a kernel of highly mechanized Panzer and motorized divisions, still depended to a considerable degree on the horse. Although ten panzer divisions had led the breakthrough in France,

21

the forces following them, over 110 divisions, brought with them a vast number of horses. At full establishment, a German infantry division contained 17,000 men, 900 vehicles and over 5,000 horses). The Navy estimated that this force would require just over two million tons of shipping. The table which follows, reproduced from *Silent Victory* by Duncan Grinnell-Milne, clearly demonstrates how woefully short of this figure the German shipping resources actually were:

Total Tonnage of German Merchant Shipping, 1939	4,500,000 Tons
(Less Tonnage of Inland Shipping)	(1,000,000 Tons)
Total Seagoing Tonnage, 1939	**3,500,000 Tons**

After one year of war, however, this figure had been significantly reduced, and some of the remaining tonnage was unsuited to the needs of Sealion, as follows:

Blockaded in Foreign Ports	1,000,000 Tons
Scuttled or Captured	350,000 Tons
Lost during the Norwegian Campaign	50,000 Tons
Converting to Merchant Raiders	50,000 Tons
Retained for Baltic & Scandinavian Trade, or to supply Norway	1,250,000 Tons
Fishing Fleet	50,000 Tons
Large Liners & Other Unsuitable Vessels	200,000 Tons
Total Tonnage Therefore Unavailable	**2,950,000 Tons**
Balance of Shipping Therefore Available	550,000 Tons
Shipping Captured in Dutch & Belgian Ports	200,000 Tons
Total Shipping Available for *Sealion*	**750,000 Tons**

This, therefore, represents a shortfall of at least 1,250,000 tons, based on the naval staff estimates.

Keitel and Jodl duly passed Raeder's memorandum on to Hitler, who summoned him to a Commanders-in-Chief conference in Berlin, to take place on 21 July. Any comments Raeder may have made during the course of the meeting have not survived. He was asked the extent to which the Navy could defend the invasion forces and opined that on a narrow front, in the Dover or Beachy Head area, some protection could be given, but that the proposed broad front could not be safeguarded at all. Only in the Straits could the three necessary conditions (air superiority, minefields and heavy coastal guns) be satisfied. Even so, the shortage of shipping and lack of port facilities meant that it would take at least ten days to ferry the first thirteen divisions of the first wave across – without any heavy artillery.

His concerns must have been allayed somewhat by many of Hitler's remarks. On the face of it, he was sympathetic to the problems Raeder had described in his memorandum. The invasion would be an exceptionally daring undertaking – it was not just a river crossing, but the crossing of an enemy dominated sea, 'in the face of a prepared and utterly determined enemy'. Hitler still ended the meeting by saying that forty divisions would be required. On the following day, the Army made a concession. Its preparations could not be completed by 15 August, but could certainly be ready a month later. The Luftwaffe, for its part, was confident that its efforts alone would have eliminated Britain as an enemy by mid-September in any case.

Raeder next met Hitler on 25 July and asked for priority for the requisitioning of shipping throughout Germany and Western Europe, together with shipyards in which the necessary modifications could be carried out. Even when the Army later agreed to a compromise and the plan was scaled down, the requirements were enormous, involving some 3,500 vessels of all types, but mainly coasters, motor boats, tugs, trawlers and barges. The barges were essential, as they would transport most of the troops, and they would need to be modified. For assault barges, the bows would require to be removed and replaced by ramps for the use of troops or tanks. Those intended to carry tanks or motor vehicles would have concrete floors poured in. Most of the canal barges had carrying capacities ranging from 500 to 800 tons, and river barges up to twice that, but very few were self-propelled, so over 400 tugs would be needed. Furthermore, when loaded, the average barge would be low in the water, which might not have been of particular concern on the inland waterways and rivers of Europe, but most certainly would be in the choppy waters of the English Channel.

The modifications would not have helped the seaworthiness of the typical barge and a large wave would probably swamp it. On the night of 10/11 September, for example, an anti-invasion patrol by the destroyers *Malcolm* (commanded by Captain (D) 16th Destroyer Flotilla, Captain T.E. Halsey), *Veteran* and *Wild Swan*, encountered one such barge off Ostend and sank it. In his subsequent report, Halsey described the barge in the following terms:

> It appeared to be rather less than the length of a destroyer, with a slightly raised bow and low freeboard of two or three feet. It is thought to have been self-propelled and under way at slow speed on a parallel course to *Malcolm*. This barge was engaged and hit by each destroyer in turn, *Veteran* reporting it awash and sinking when she had passed.

This, then, was the type of vessel which would form the backbone of the invasion fleet. Raeder pointed out how much strain the loss of all these vessels from the German economy would place upon it, but the necessary authority was granted and requisitioning began.

Three days after this conference, the Navy sent a further memorandum to OKH. This repeated the estimate of ten days for transportation of the first wave, and was received with anger by Halder. His response ('If that is true we can throw away the whole plan of invasion.') was understandable and demonstrated the insurmountable flaw in the whole Sealion concept. In truth, both Army and Navy had valid cases. The Navy said it could land three divisions on a 50-mile front between Folkestone and Beachy Head. The Army required a broad front.

Consequently, OKH made a few compromises: they would accept the lack of heavy artillery and a reduction in motor transport (because of the further transport problems that large stocks of fuel would entail) but, for sound military reasons, they stood firm on the broad front landing.

On 31 July, a further conference took place. On this occasion, as well as Raeder, Keitel and Jodl from OKW, von Brauchitsch and Halder from OKH were present. Raeder was able to report on the progress made so far and presented a whole series of objections to the plan as it stood. If his record of the conference is correct, then the impression is of an experienced sailor telling ignorant landsmen the facts of life regarding amphibious operations. The Army wanted a dawn landing, but the varied and unwieldy vessels being used would be hard enough to organize in daylight. The small navy units marshalling and escorting them would in any case need some light in order to navigate. Furthermore, it would only be possible to commence the attack if the sea was calm.

Then there were the tides: a landing at high tide would leave the landing vessels high and dry for almost twelve hours; a landing before high tide would cause the vessels to move about, leading to further confusion. Therefore, the landing needed to be about two hours after high tide, at the beginning of the ebb tide. There were two occasions when moonlight and the tides might suit, 20 to 26 August and 19 to 26 September.

The next problem was the Royal Navy. It could be assumed that, in addition to the local flotillas and squadrons, further units from as far north as Rosyth would intervene, and the Luftwaffe could not oppose them in darkness. The alternative of a day crossing would ease the navigational and organizational problems, and air reconnaissance would be able to locate the whereabouts of British naval forces. Encouragingly for his listeners, he then pointed out that the operation could be aborted if necessary.

He did not, presumably because he dare not, say that Sealion was impossible, but he ended by proposing a cancellation until May 1941. Hitler, however, was unmoved, still insisting that preparations for a broad front landing, on 15 September, be continued. The Luftwaffe air offensive was due to begin on 5 August, and the final decision whether Sealion should be confirmed or postponed could be made after this had been in progress for a week. All this was duly confirmed in an OKW order issued the following day, although the margin for assessment of the effects of the air offensive was increased to eight to fourteen days.

Also on 1 August, Hitler issued Directive 17, 'For the Conduct of Air and Naval War against Britain', which read as follows:

Directive 17
For the Conduct of Air and Naval Warfare against Britain

In order to establish conditions favourable to the final conquest of Britain, I intend to continue the air and naval war against the British homeland more intensively than heretofore.

With this in mind, I issue the following orders:

1) The Luftwaffe is to overcome the British Air Force with all the means at its disposal and in the shortest possible time. The attacks are to be directed primarily against the aircraft themselves, against their ground installations and their supply organizations, also against the aircraft industry, including plants producing anti-aircraft material.

2) After we have achieved temporary or local air superiority, the air war is to be carried on against harbours, especially against establishments connected with food supply, and also against similar establishments in the interior of the country. Attacks on the harbours of the south coast are to be undertaken on the smallest scale possible, in view of our intended operations.

3) On the other hand, air attacks on enemy warships and merchantmen may be diminished, unless particularly advantageous targets offer themselves ...

4) The intensified air war is to be carried out in such a manner that the Luftwaffe can be called upon at any time to support naval operations against advantageous targets in sufficient strength. Also it is to stand by in force for *Operation Sealion*.

5) I reserve for myself the decision on retaliatory terror attacks.

6) The intensified air war may commence on or after August 5th ...

The Navy is authorized to begin the projected intensified naval warfare at the same time.

(*signed*) Hitler   August 1st, 1940

The intensified air war was to commence on or after 5 August. It actually commenced on 13 August. Perhaps an opposed landing might not be necessary after all. The German naval staff would subsequently complain that the loose wording of the Directive not only failed to make clear that air attacks on those naval ports where the British destroyer forces were based were essential, but actually discouraged such attacks in paragraph 2. The Luftwaffe, by contrast, could, and did, interpret the Directive as authorization to continue waging a private war against Fighter Command, with the needs of Sealion very low on the list of priorities.

Given the nature of the decision made on 31 July, it is not surprising that relations between army and navy staffs should have been strained. The Army clung tenaciously to its demand for a broad front landing, and after the two staffs had exchanged memoranda for a week, OKW called a meeting of the two Chiefs of Staff, Halder and Admiral Schniewind, at Fontainebleau. The Navy's narrow front argument was examined in some detail, until an exasperated Halder remarked with some heat, 'From the point-of-view of the Army I regard the proposal as complete suicide. I might as well put the assault troops straight through a sausage machine!' A further memorandum expanding on this theme was sent to the Navy, to which Schniewind replied on 14 August to the effect that British naval power meant that the broad front army plan was equally suicidal. Both men, from the viewpoints of their own services, were right; the Army could not successfully land on a narrow front, and the Navy could not hope to protect a broad front from the forces the Royal Navy might commit.

The day before Schniewind produced this reply, he and Raeder met Hitler again at the Berghof. By now, the date for Sealion was only a month away and the differences between the Navy and the Army had reached a virtual impasse. Raeder consequently asked for a definite decision on the nature of the landing in order that appropriate preparations could continue. His own view was that, in view of the limited shipping resources available, Sealion should be seen as a last resort, only to be undertaken if Britain could not be persuaded to sue for peace any other way. Hitler was seemingly sympathetic to the views expressed by Raeder, but was not willing to make a decision until he met again with von Brauchitsch and Halder the following day.

On 15 August the decision was made – the operation would go ahead on 15 September, but at last a concession was made to the Navy: the Lyme Bay landing would not now take place, and dispositions were to be made so as not to exclude the possibility of a landing on a narrow front, with a possibility of an independent landing in the Brighton area. Raeder must have taken some comfort from this development – perhaps his narrow front would win the day after all, and in any case the Luftwaffe 'Eagle Attack' had commenced on 13 August. If all went well the effects of this would be the demoralization of the British people and the collapse of the Churchill government. The invasion might be nothing more than the token landing of an army of occupation.

Nevertheless, the navy staff went about the task of assembling the shipping that would be needed if any sort of landing was to happen. The effort with which they went about this must have been quite remarkable, because by the end of August they had successfully put together a fleet of 168 merchant ships and coasters, 1,900 barges, 386 tugs and trawlers, and 1,600 motor boats, and were in the process of moving them to the Channel ports. Whether the invasion was a serious aim or an enormous bluff, the German Navy had successfully assembled a fleet big enough to take the assault troops to sea. What would happen to them once they put to sea, however, was another matter.

On 27 August, Hitler made his decision known. The army broad front plan had won. True, the landings at each end (Lyme Bay and Ramsgate) had been abandoned, but the front was still 80 or so miles long (by comparison, the Allied Normandy landings in 1944 were on a front of 40 miles) and the first wave was to consist of thirteen divisions (subsequently further reduced to nine divisions plus two airborne divisions, one of which would be in the first wave) to be put ashore in two to three days.

Chapter 4

The German 'Overlord'?

The general opinion here, that an invasion will be attempted in the near future, has gained ground.
Reuters News Agency, London, Saturday, 14 September 1940

The army plan of 27 August was, as previously stated, amended once again, following further objections from the German naval staff. The first wave was now reduced to nine divisions, but an airborne division, which obviously would not depend on the resources of the Navy for transportation, was added. The first wave would be reinforced by a second and third wave of troops once the beachheads were secured.

In detail, the complete army order of battle, and the areas they would assault, as shown on Map 2, were as follows:

Folkestone–New Romney
The first landings would be made by the Sixteenth Army's XIII Army Corps, under the command of General of Panzertroops von Vietinghoff. This corps consisted of two infantry divisions, the 17th and the 35th, supported by a Luftwaffe anti-aircraft regiment. Commando teams from the Brandenburg Regiment would also land with these divisions and would attack along the coast towards Dover, knocking out British positions on the coast and along the Royal Military Canal, whilst a further unit would attack the coastal batteries around Dover and prevent the sinking of blockships in the harbour entrance.

Rye–Hastings
The first wave, also from Sixteenth Army, consisted of the two divisions (7th Infantry and 1st Mountain) of VII Army Corps,

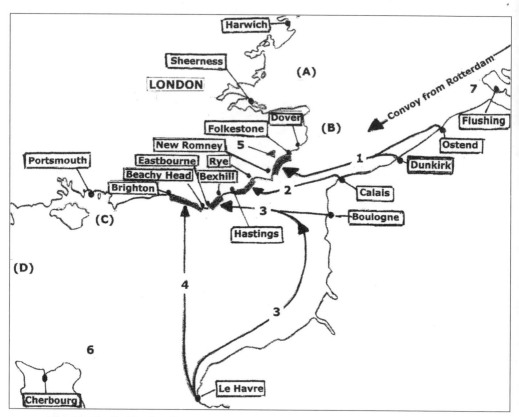

Map 2. The Sealion Landings.
(1) Leading echelons of 17th and 35th Infantry Divisions, transported in 150 barges from Dunkirk and 50 barges from Ostend. Subsequently, two convoys from Rotterdam and Ostend, totalling 57 transports and 114 barges, would bring the remaining elements of the two divisions. (2) Leading echelons of 7th Infantry and 1st Mountain Divisions, transported in 200 barges from Calais. A further convoy from Antwerp, would follow with the remaining divisional units. (3) Leading echelons of 26th and 34th Infantry Divisions, transported in 330 barges from Boulogne and 50 barges from Le Havre. (4) Leading echelons of 8th and 28th Infantry Divisions and 6th Mountain Division, in 300 motor boats from Le Havre. Two further convoys from Le Havre would subsequently bring the three divisions up to strength. (5) Landing Zone for 7th Parachute Division. The 22nd Air Landing Division would subsequently be flown into Lympne airfield, once it had been captured by 7th Parachute Division.
German Naval Protection: (6) 5 destroyers and 4 torpedo boat flotillas based at Cherbourg and Le Havre. (7) 2 destroyers and 3 motor torpedo boat flotillas based at Zeebrugge, Flushing and Rotterdam.
Royal Navy Units in the Immediate Vicinity: (A) Nore Command. 3 'Town' class cruisers and 11 MTBs in the Humber. 2 light cruisers, 24 destroyers, 4 corvettes and 11 MTBs at Sheerness and Harwich. (B) 2 MTBs at Dover. (C) Portsmouth Command. 1 light cruiser, 14 destroyers, 5 torpedo boats and 6 MTBs at Portsmouth and 2 destroyers at Southampton. (D) Western Approaches Command. 1 battleship, 1 'Town' class cruiser, 1 light cruiser and 16 destroyers based at Plymouth. There were, additionally, 25 minesweepers and 140 mine-sweeping trawlers, together with numerous auxilliary patrol vessels, operating out of Plymouth, Portsmouth, Dover, Sheerness and Harwich.

30

commanded by Colonel General von Schobert. Again, an anti-aircraft regiment was attached.

In support of the four divisions making the initial assault would be three battalions of amphibious/submersible tanks. Some 250 of these vehicles, in four battalions, were intended to support the landings, of which around fifty were amphibious Panzer IIs, the remainder being submersible Panzer IIIs and IVs. These vehicles will be discussed in more detail later, but at least one of the divisional commanders (Lieutenant General Loch of 17th Infantry Division) had never even seen one.

Bexhill–Eastbourne
The landings here were to be made by XXXVIII Army Corps, commanded by von Manstein, from Ninth Army. The Corps consisted of two infantry divisions (26th and 34th), again supported by a Luftwaffe anti-aircraft regiment. Commando teams from the Brandenburg Regiment would land with both divisions, probably in order to attack and neutralize British coastal batteries.

Beachy Head–Brighton
This was the objective of General Heitz's VIII Army Corps, again from Ninth Army, and consisted of three divisions (8th Infantry, 28th Infantry and 6th Mountain), with a Luftwaffe anti-aircraft regiment attached.

The remaining battalion of amphibious/submersible tanks was intended to support the Ninth Army landings.

Airborne Landings
7th Parachute Division, consisting of three paratroop regiments and an airlanding regiment, would support the right flank of the landings by Sixteenth Army, by capturing the high ground to the north and north-west of Folkestone, and by taking and holding Lympne airfield. Subsequently, 22nd Airlanding Division would fly in to the captured airfield.

Once the beachheads were secure, the Commander-in-Chief of Army Group A, Field Marshal von Rundstedt, and his army commanders (Colonel General Busch of Sixteenth Army and Colonel General Strauss of Ninth Army) could commit their second- and third-wave units. In the case of Sixteenth Army, these were:

31

Second Wave (Sixteenth Army)
V Army Corps (General Ruoff) – 12th and 30th Infantry Divisions. XXXXI Army Corps (General Reinhardt) – 8th and 10th Panzer Divisions, 29th Motorized Infantry Division and the SS 'Grossdeutschland' and 'Liebstandarte Adolf Hitler' Regiments.

[handwritten margin note: NOT SS!]

Second Wave (Ninth Army)
XV Army Corps (Colonel General Hoth) – 4th Panzer Division, 7th Panzer Division and 20th Motorized Infantry Division.

Third Wave (16th Army)
IV Army Corps (General von Schwedler) – 24th and 58th Infantry Divisions. XXXXII Army Corps (General Kuntze) – 45th and 164th Infantry Divisions.

Third Wave (Ninth Army)
XXIV Army Corps (General von Schweppenburg) – 15th and 78th Infantry Divisions.

In addition to these forces, all under the overall command of von Rundstedt's Army Group A, II Corps, consisting of the 6th and 256th Infantry Divisions, part of Sixth Army from Field Marshal von Leeb's Army Group C, was also held ready to embark from Cherbourg and land in Lyme Bay; further divisions under Army High Command control could be allocated as a fourth wave as and when necessary.

This, then, was the Army plan which would bring about the conquest of Great Britain, and the list of armies, corps and divisions given above is undoubtedly impressive. However, the image which is brought to mind of nine superbly equipped divisions, supremely confident following the campaign in France, and supported by airborne forces and amphibious tanks, storming ashore in the dawn and establishing beachheads into which reinforcements including Panzer divisions and regiments of SS fanatics would be poured to lead the inevitable breakout, is a false one, and is given the lie by one simple fact, which is this: the so-called 'first wave' would actually take, not the two to three days reluctantly accepted by army planners, but *eleven days* to land!

In order to achieve even this timescale, the Army planners had had to agree to reduce the number of vehicles to be transported (as

32

previously stated a typical German infantry division was 17,000 men strong, but also included 900 vehicles and more than 5,000 horses), and to accept that divisional artillery would not accompany the first wave. Even so, the German Navy estimated that the four divisions from Sixteenth Army could only expect, at best, some 6,700 men from each division to be got ashore in what might be termed 'the first wave of the first wave'. As the Army had originally called for thirteen divisions to be landed on a 200-mile front between Ramsgate and Lyme Bay in three days, had subsequently agreed to a reduction in the front to 80 miles, and had finally accepted a further reduction in the number of divisions to nine, their reaction to this timescale is not difficult to deduce.

The final plan had, therefore, at last succeeded in uniting both army and navy staffs. The Army thought the landing force too small and the speed at which it would be landed too slow for the task, while the Navy thought the width of the front still too great to defend. Nevertheless, the orders were confirmed by Keitel on 3 September: the earliest date for sailing would be 20 September, with the landing on 21 September, the go-ahead would be given ten days before and final orders at noon three days before. Cancellation would be possible twenty-four hours in advance, presumably in the event of bad weather in the Channel.

Chapter 5

Mines, Coastal Batteries and U-Boats

Up to this point, the various stages in the development of the invasion plan, the conflict between the Army and Navy high commands and the apparent indifference of the Luftwaffe to the whole idea have been examined, and the final army order of battle has been explained in some detail. It is now proposed to deal with the way in which Directive 16 sought to overcome what appeared to be, and in fact was, the fatal flaw in any plan that could be produced in 1940: the desperate weakness of what remained of the German Navy after the losses of the Norwegian campaign.

As the German Navy lacked sufficient surface warships to provide even token protection for the invasion fleet, some other method of keeping the Royal Navy at bay needed to be devised. Accordingly, Directive 16 placed considerable importance on protective minefields, heavy coastal batteries and the optimistic suggestion that 'English fleets both in the North Sea and the Mediterranean should be pinned down.' Quite how effective these measures were likely to have been is discussed below.

Mine Barriers
Once the preliminary warning order for the attack had been given, the German Navy would have ten days in which to carry out the laying of the mine barriers which would, according to the plan, protect the flanks of the invasion force from Royal Navy interference. Four barriers were to be laid, codenamed Anton, Bruno, Caesar and Dora. The first two were intended to guard the invasion route to Brighton from Le Havre, the third was to prevent Royal

Navy attacks into the Dover Straits from the North Sea and the fourth to keep out the Plymouth-based vessels.

The German Navy did have considerable expertise in minelaying, having laid the 'Westwall' mine barrier to protect the German Bight against the risk of Royal Navy assaults, and in the first winter of the war German destroyers had carried out eleven operations in the North Sea to lay mines off Newcastle-upon-Tyne (twice), Cromer (three times), the Thames estuary (four times) and the Humber (twice). These had resulted in the loss of some sixty-seven merchant ships, as well as the Royal Navy destroyers *Blanche*, *Grenville* and *Gypsy*, and six smaller naval vessels, without loss to the German warships involved although, as already described, in December 1939 two German cruisers, *Leipzig* and *Nurnberg*, had been torpedoed by the submarine *Salmon* whilst screening German destroyers returning from one of the operations off Newcastle.

Since that time, however, the bulk of the German destroyer force had been lost, but even so there seems little doubt that protective minefields could have been laid, given the time, although how long these minefields would have remained in place is questionable. Quick, undetected, hit-and-run minelaying raids were one thing – laying and maintaining the Sealion minefields was quite another, and would have exposed the minelaying vessels to an immediate response from the Royal Navy. Directive 16 may have stated the areas which were to be 'so heavily mined as to be completely inaccessible', but how the Royal Navy could have been prevented from interfering with the minelaying operations, sweeping those mines which had been laid and sinking the minelayers, was a different matter.

In fact, the ten days available would have been totally inadequate. The Royal Navy, laying the Dover barrage at the start of the war, had taken five days to lay 3,000 mines between the Goodwin Sands and the Dyck Shoal, using two specialist minelayers and two converted train ferries. A second field, of a further 636 mines, was laid at the end of September. After three U-boats were mined in the Channel in quick succession (U-12 on 8 October 1939, U-40 on 13 October 1939 and U-16 on 24 October 1939), U-boats abandoned this route out into the Atlantic.

If five days had been required to lay a field of this size between two Allied nations, unhindered by enemy action and with ample resources available, it is surely questionable how much could have been achieved in ten days by a navy to which none of these advantages applied. The most westerly of the planned minefields alone was around 60 miles in length. Hopes that the large coastal guns intended to protect the flanks of the invasion routes could also protect the minelayers soon proved illusory; in August British heavy guns near Dover (including one of the two 14-inch guns manned by the Royal Marines, and known as 'Winnie' and 'Pooh') began to fire back. If the German naval staff were to place any reliance in their own heavy guns, then they were obliged to acknowledge the threat posed by British batteries.

As a result, the later stages of the minelaying programme, which would require the ships to be working close to the British coast, would have to be carried out in darkness, when the heavy guns of both sides would be largely useless. Nor could German light naval forces contribute much of a screen. A flotilla of destroyers based at Brest or Cherbourg, accompanied by a few S-boats, and two or at most three destroyers, together with a few torpedo boats on the Calais–Dover flank, was all that could be provided.

A further problem with the defensive minefields would have been the suitability of the mines which could be employed. Three types of mines existed in 1940, the magnetic mine, the acoustic mine and the moored contact mine.

Magnetic Mines

At the start of the war, the magnetic mine was a weapon of which the German Navy expected great things. This is not to say that its workings were a mystery to the British – the Royal Navy had deployed an unsuccessful magnetic mine in the First World War, had an improved version ready for production before the Second World War and eventually commenced laying it in April and May 1940, having held back on production until they had had an opportunity to examine the German version. An Admiralty committee was, indeed, already working on means of defence against this type of mine. Nevertheless, by March 1940, German mines, laid by both destroyers and U-boats, had sunk some 128 merchant vessels, totalling 429,899 tons of Allied shipping between September 1939 and March 1940, the bulk of the losses being attributed to magnetic mines.

A successful magnetic mine had been available to Germany for some time. The first fifty had been secretly manufactured as early as 1930, and by 1935 types suitable for laying by surface vessels,

U-boats and aircraft were ready to go into production. As that was the year of the Anglo-German Naval Agreement, which apparently demonstrated that Great Britain was not to be a future enemy, the rate of production was slow (numerous other armaments programmes having priority) and by September 1939 only around 1,500 of all types were available, of which around 470 had been used by the end of the year.

Raeder had been highly impressed by their early successes, however, and by November 1939 was eager to maximize their use, by using S-boats and aircraft as well as destroyers and U-boats. As minelaying was defined as 'strategic' warfare, and aircraft used for such tasks came under the control of the Luftwaffe, he required the co-operation of Hermann Göring, the head of the Luftwaffe. Only 120 airborne magnetic mines were available and Göring was unwilling to allocate aircraft to deliver them – he wished to build up a stock of 5,000 instead and then swamp British ports with them. There was considerable logic in this, but Raeder argued that the mines should be used immediately, as once the British produced counter-measures the opportunity would be lost. In fact, the Naval staff had made a serious tactical error by using the mines at a time when they had only a comparatively small quantity available for use, instead of building up a considerable stock (mass production of mines only commenced in January 1940, with a target of 21,500 magnetic and 48,000 contact mines being aimed at by March 1942) and then deploying them en masse.

Thwarted by Göring, Raeder chose to use the few reconnaissance and air-sea rescue aircraft that he did control to carry out minelaying flights. The aircraft used, mainly Heinkel He 59 floatplanes, were obsolescent and hardly suited to the task, as each aircraft could carry only two mines. Seven mines were dropped in the Thames on 20 November 1939, and two further drops of ten mines and twenty-four mines, mainly in the Thames and off Harwich, subsequently took place. The last drop, on 22 November 1939, was a calamity for the German magnetic mine campaign, as two mines landed on a mudflat near Shoeburyness, and at low tide on 23 November both were found. A team from HMS *Vernon*, the Royal Navy torpedo and mine school at Portsmouth, consisting of Lieutenant Commanders Ouvry and Lewis, Chief Petty Officer Baldwin and Able Seaman Vearncombe, successfully dismantled both mines and the subsequent detailed examination revealed their secrets.

37

As early as 27 November, tests were carried out on the cruiser HMS *Manchester*, which demonstrated that ships could be 'de-gaussed' (i.e. their hulls demagnetized to prevent detonation of the mine) by use of powerful electric cables placed around the ship, initially externally but later internally. Smaller ships could be 'wiped' by positioning them alongside cables through which an electric current was passed, and although this process had to be repeated every few months it enabled the vast quantities of cable which would otherwise have been required to be reduced. The Admiralty ordered de-gaussing to begin on 10 December 1939 and by 9 March 1940, 321 warships and 312 merchantmen had already been treated.

Additionally, a successful method of sweeping had been devised (the LL sweep) and some Coastal Command aircraft were fitted with de-gaussing rings to trigger mines from the air. Once the secrets of the German magnetic mine had been discovered, the mine threat was significantly reduced. According to *British Vessels Lost at Sea, 1939–1945* (HMSO, 1947) mine losses for each year were as follows:

Year	Merchant vessels lost
1939 (four months)	83
1940	201
1941	108
1942	48
1943	37
1944	25
1945 (four months)	19

On 26 January 1940, Raeder was urging that the Luftwaffe deploy its stock of mines before British countermeasures became effective, but Göring still insisted on delaying until 5,000 mines were available, and on 23 February 1940 OKW ruled in his favour.

Acoustic Mines

This type of mine, which was triggered by the sound of a ship's propellers, was not part of German minelaying plans as, at this stage of the war, only a tiny number existed. The first such mines in British waters were laid in August 1940, and on 25 August the Admiralty issued a warning that mines of this type were in use. As it was necessary to determine the frequency of the sound waves which activated the mine, it was fortunate that two were recovered from mudflats in the Bristol Channel during the following month.

HMS *Vernon's* specialists were able to devise a countermeasure (which actually consisted of a pneumatic road drill striking a 19-inch diameter diaphragm made of steel 7/16th of an inch thick, originally fitted in the flooded bow compartment of converted trawlers but later deployed on a boom over the bow) known as the acoustic sweep, which came into use in November 1940, detonating three acoustic mines in the Thames Estuary on the 24th.

However, as the mine was only available in tiny numbers, it had little bearing on Operation Sealion.

Moored Contact Mines

These were what people generally think of when sea mines are mentioned. They were attached to a cable, which in turn was attached to a weight. The mines themselves had positive buoyancy and could therefore be laid so as to float at a predetermined depth. They were detonated in the 'traditional' manner (a ship needed to bump into one) and were easy to lay, with both British and German navies using converted civilian vessels as well as specialist minelayers. At the start of the war, the German Navy had over 20,000 in stock.

From the German point of view, this type of mine had a number of shortcomings. The magnetic mine, which rested on the seabed, would still be invisible at whatever state of the tide (although it became less effective the deeper the water became), whereas the contact mine was suspended from a fixed length of cable. Therefore, at high tide it could well be too deep and ships would pass over it unscathed, whilst at low tide it would be visible on the surface. Unfortunately for German plans, the tides in the Channel are fierce.

From the Atlantic, the Channel is roughly funnel-shaped, starting at around 100 miles wide, reducing to around half that by Folkestone, and down to about 20 miles at Dover. Twice each day, the powerful Atlantic tide floods into this funnel and twice a day the tide floods back in the opposite direction from the North Sea. The Straits of Dover are shallow, with numerous dangerous banks, shoals and rocks. The net result of this is that the difference between high and low tide can be as much as 18 feet or more and the currents are powerful. Given these conditions, moored mines could easily be ripped away from their cables and end up floating among the invasion barges, imperiling the very transports they were meant to protect.

The conclusion from all this is clear: countermeasures had been developed which would significantly reduce the threat of the magnetic mine, the acoustic mine was not available in any quantity and the contact mine was likely to be ineffective, or even dangerous to German forces, if deployed. On top of all this, of course, are two further points. Firstly, once German minelaying began in earnest, it clearly signposted the routes the invasion forces would take; and secondly, the Royal Navy would probably be able to sweep the mines as quickly as the German Navy could lay them.

Just as minelayers were easy to convert from civilian vessels, so could minesweepers be quickly adapted. The Royal Navy at the beginning of the War had only forty fleet minesweepers (of which seventeen were of the Halcyon Class and a further twenty-three of the First World War Hunt Class, most of which were laid up at Malta and Singapore) and four minesweeping trawlers; but the Navy also had access to a vast number of trawlers, drifters and paddle steamers, and as early as February 1940 already had some 400 operational minesweepers.

Between February and September 1940 the minesweeping force had further increased to a total of 698 vessels – and it is not difficult to deduce where a fair number of these were deployed. Additionally, many of the standard pre-war British 'A-I' Class destroyers were also fitted with minesweeping gear. Directive 16 may have instructed that 'the [invasion] sea routes must be cleared of mines' but does not seem to have grasped that the German minefields might be subjected to the same treatment.

Coastal Batteries
If the minefield barrier was likely to prove more impenetrable in theory than in practice, then perhaps heavy guns could keep the Royal Navy at bay. Directive 16 required that 'Heavy guns must dominate and protect the entire coastal front area.' As these guns were also intended to shield the minelayers from Royal Navy interference, work on constructing their emplacements began quickly, by the second half of July.

The first battery, of four 28cm (11-inch) guns, was in position in the area of Gris Nez, and ready to fire by early August. A second battery of three 30.5cm (12-inch) guns north of Boulogne was ready by mid-August, a third, of four 38cm (15-inch), positioned south of Gris Nez, was ready about a month later, and at around the same date two more 11-inch were in place between Calais and Blanc Nez. In addition to these big guns, a further thirty-five heavy and medium artillery batteries, together with seven heavy batteries captured from the French, were added towards the end of August, producing a total of over 150 medium, heavy and super-heavy guns with which to close the Straits to British shipping, protect the mine-layers, and subsequently to drive the Royal Navy away from the invasion convoys. The biggest of these guns had a range of over 15 miles. Bad light or darkness would, however, reduce the effectiveness of those batteries without radar.

The first test shelling of British coastal convoys took place on 12 August 1940, and firing became heavy on 22 August, when an eastbound convoy (CE9), consisting of twelve ships escorted by two Hunt Class destroyers (*Fernie* and *Garth*), together with trawlers and kite vessels (intended to deter aircraft), was engaged. Weather conditions were fine, visibility good and the sea calm, when three four-gun salvos were fired by the Gris Nez batteries as the convoy passed Hythe, at around 0924 hrs.

Firing ceased for about an hour but was resumed about an hour later as the convoy approached Dover. Again, the firing was initially in four-gun salvos, and subsequently in three-gun salvos as the next battery took over. The convoy had been in two columns, but although 108 rounds were fired in all, no hits were scored, some shells missing completely and landing in Dover harbour. The destroyers laid smoke during the action, but obviously this would not have had any effect on radar range finding.

This inauspicious (from the German viewpoint) beginning was typical of the performance of the heavy coastal batteries in the months and years ahead. Post-war Admiralty records state: 'No British or foreign merchant ship was sunk by enemy batteries throughout the war. No foreign merchant ship was damaged. Seven British merchant ships (of an aggregate tonnage of roughly 8,000) were damaged.' From August to December 1940, 1,880 rounds were fired, with on some occasions as many as 200 rounds per convoy. The conclusions that the German naval staff would draw from these events must have been obvious. If the batteries could not hit convoys plodding through the Straits at 5 or 6 knots, the likelihood that they could disable highly maneouvrable cruisers and destroyers

41

moving at between 25 and 30 knots would have been remote in the extreme.

The batteries subsequently had further opportunities to redeem themselves against 'proper' naval targets. On 29 September 1940, the old monitor HMS *Erebus* bombarded Calais with her two 15-inch guns. *Erebus* was an old ship, built in 1916, and was of a type specifically designed to bombard shore targets. She was shallow draught, short and wide, with a maximum speed when new of 12 knots, although by 1940 she was probably only capable of about 8 knots. In the Channel, on the night of 29 September, she was an ideal target for the Gris Nez guns. The guns duly opened fire but failed to hit her.

Later, on the night of 10/11 October 1940, the old 'R' Class battleship HMS *Revenge*, together with seven destroyers of the 5th Destroyer Flotilla and six motor gunboats, bombarded Cherbourg dockyard. The battleship fired some one hundred and twenty 15-inch shells into the assembled shipping, supported by a further eight hundred and one 4.7-inch shells from the destroyers. German shore batteries, including a heavy battery east of Cherbourg, engaged the force as it withdrew, and for half an hour fired without success.

The heavy coastal guns, which in theory were at least equal in firepower to several battleships, would in practice be totally unable to 'dominate and protect the entire coastal front area'. If mines and heavy guns could not deter the Royal Navy, perhaps U-boats could.

The Grey Wolves and the Sealion

There is just nothing about our torpedoes that is right. It is my belief that never before in military history has a force been sent into battle with such a useless weapon.

Erich Raeder

It has often been claimed that as the Royal Navy attempted to intercept the Sealion invasion convoys, the approaching vessels would themselves have been vulnerable to interception by the German U-boat fleet.

In fact, U-boats were rarely mentioned in connection with Operation Sealion. The shallow waters of the Channel were not suited to the operations of submarines, and those which had attempted to intervene during the evacuations from France had achieved little, although the type IIc coastal U-boat U-62 had torpedoed and sunk the destroyer *Grafton* off Dunkirk on 29 May. Seven boats despatched to intercept the later evacuations of Operations Cycle and Aerial had failed even to carry out attacks on the lightly screened larger vessels which undertook them.

In any case, the German Navy had very few operational U-boats at this stage of the War, and those which were available were hampered by serious faults in torpedo design. The G7a and G7e magnetic torpedoes in use by the German Navy were highly unreliable, being prone to run too deep and with magnetic detonators which often failed. After the Norwegian campaign, the German Navy estimated that twenty potential hits on Allied vessels ranging from battleships to transports had been negated by torpedo failures, and it was as late as November 1942 before these technical faults were overcome. In June 1940, the U-boat arm was even obliged to resort to contact detonators of First World War vintage.

In detail, the numbers of boats in use during the period of invasion threat were as follows (Tarrant 1989):

Month (1940)	Total Number of Available Boats	Number of Operational Boats	Number of Training Boats	Average Daily Number at Sea
June	51	27	24	18
July	53	30	23	11
August	55	27	28	13
September	61	27	34	13
October	68	30	38	12

The first U-boat to operate from a base on the French Atlantic coast was the type VIIa U-30, which arrived at Lorient to refuel and rearm after an Atlantic operation on 7 July, and within a month the same port was able to carry out repairs. The benefit of operating from the French bases was obvious, as it effectively added a week to the duration of each patrol, by making it unnecessary for the boat to return via the North Sea to a German base. Furthermore, until August 1940, B-Dienst of German naval intelligence could read Admiralty signals, and even when the Royal Navy changed its codes many Merchant Navy signals could still be read.

The conclusion, therefore, is that Sealion was of significant help to the operations of the U-boat force, by tying up many destroyers and other vessels which could otherwise have strengthened convoy escorts, and this is demonstrated all too clearly by the escalating figures of merchant ship losses from June 1940 onwards listed elsewhere. The converse, however, does not apply – the U-boat arm could not be, and was not, of any material help in the defence of Sealion.

Diversions and Distractions

The final requirement put forward in Directive 16 which would make 'a landing in England possible' was the pinning down of the Royal Navy in the North Sea and ('by the Italians') in the Mediterranean.

In the North Sea, the Home Fleet was to be prevented from intervening by means of a diversionary operation, Operation Herbstreise (Autumn Voyage), involving eleven large transport vessels and the large liners *Europa*, *Bremen*, *Gneisenau* and *Potsdam*, escorted by the last three operational light cruisers, *Nurnberg*, *Köln* and *Emden*, the gunnery training ship *Bremse*, and a small number of light units. Two days before the landing was due to take place, these vessels would approach the British east coast, suggesting that a landing was about to be attempted between Newcastle-upon-Tyne and Aberdeen. At the same time, the only operational heavy cruiser, *Admiral Hipper*, would operate in the Iceland/Faroes area.

The pinning down of substantial British naval forces in the Mediterranean when the Sealion crossing was to take place would, at least, not place further pressure on Raeder's planning staff, as this would be the responsibility of the Italian Navy – a comparison of the relative naval strengths of Italy and Britain in this theatre reveals that the Italian Navy had substantial resources available to achieve it. The following table compares British and Italian vessels in the Mediterranean theatre, illustrating the situation at the beginning of June 1940:

Vessel Type	Italian Fleet	Mediterranean Fleet
Battleship	4	4
Aircraft Carrier	0	1
Heavy Cruiser	7	0

Light Cruiser	12	9
Fleet Destroyer	57	25
Torpedo Boat	69	0
Submarine	115	12

A simple comparison of numbers, however, cannot tell the whole story. The four Italian battleships, although originally constructed during the First World War, had been extensively modernized, had main armaments of ten 32cm (12.6-inch) guns and were capable of 27 knots. In addition, they were shortly to be joined, in August, by two large new vessels, armed with nine 38.1cm (15-inch) guns and capable of 30 knots.

By contrast, only one of the four battleships of the Mediterranean Fleet, *Warspite*, had received a similar degree of modernization, and although all four mounted main armaments of eight 15-inch guns, two (*Royal Sovereign* and *Ramillies*) were capable of 21 knots at best; even *Warspite* and her partially improved sister ship *Malaya* could only achieve 23.5 knots. As the maximum range of the Italian 32cm guns was around 28,000 yards, and the maximum range of the 15-inch guns of three of the four British battleships was only 23,400 yards (*Warspite* herself, with the maximum elevation of her main armament increased to 30 degrees, in contrast to the 20 degrees of the other three, had a range of 32,200 yards), then the Italian ships could dictate the range at which a fleet action would be fought and even, with their significant speed advantage, decide whether an action should be fought at all.

This was demonstrated at an early stage in an engagement off Calabria on 9 July 1940, when Cunningham's fleet of three battleships, an aircraft carrier, five cruisers and seventeen destroyers encountered an Italian force of two battleships, twelve cruisers and three destroyer flotillas. Two of Cunningham's battleships (*Malaya* and *Royal Sovereign*) were unable to engage at all, and after *Warspite* had hit the Italian flagship *Guilio Cesare*, at a range of 26,000 yards, causing 115 casualties and putting her out of action for four months, the Italian commander was able to break off the action.

Nevertheless, it can be argued that, in terms of Operation Sealion the Italian Navy had achieved what Directive 16 had hoped it would and had compelled the Royal Navy to retain significant forces in the Mediterranean. The Royal Navy Pink List of 16 September 1940 shows that the following vessels of destroyer size and above were with the Mediterranean Fleet and Force 'H':

Vessel Type	Mediterranean Fleet	Force 'H'
Battleship	*Warspite, Malaya, Valiant, Ramillies*	*Resolution*
Battlecruiser	(none)	*Renown*
Aircraft Carrier	*Illustrious, Eagle*	*Ark Royal*
Heavy Cruiser	*Kent, York*	(none)
Light Cruiser	*Liverpool, Gloucester, Orion, Sydney* (RAN), *Calcutta, Ajax*	(none)
Destroyer	*Hyperion, Havock, Hero, Hereward, Hasty, Ilex, Imperial, Dainty, Diamond, Decoy, Defender, Jervis, Nubian, Mohawk, Juno, Janus, Wryneck, Stuart* (RAN), *Vampire* (RAN), *Voyager* (RAN), *Waterhen* (RAN), *Vendetta* (RAN)	*Faulknor, Fortune, Fury, Forester, Foresight, Firedrake.* (In addition, *Greyhound, Gallant, Griffin, Encounter, Hotspur, Vidette, Velox, Wishart* and *Wrestler* were also at Gibraltar as part of North Atlantic Command).

From the point of view of the Sealion planners, therefore, at least this part of Directive 16 seemed achievable. A substantial number of the surface units available to the Royal Navy could indeed be distracted. The problem with this, however, was that even with the need to maintain a strong Mediterranean Fleet, the need to fill the vacuum left by the collapse of France by basing a powerful squadron on Gibraltar, and the requirement for the Home Fleet to guard against a possible break-out by German heavy ships into the Atlantic, the Admiralty could still provide and maintain more than adequate anti-invasion forces.

Indeed, the Herbstreise diversion voyage would have had little or no relevance to the success or failure of Sealion, as on 20 July the Admiralty had already decided that the Home Fleet would not enter the southern part of the North Sea unless heavy German units appeared. As is now known, there simply were no serviceable German heavy units which could have operated there, and Herbstreise was, therefore, an attempt to guard against an eventuality which almost certainly would not have arisen.

At the post-war Nuremberg war trials, the last head of OKW, Field Marshal Wilhelm Keitel, said of Hitler that 'his remarkable knowledge not only of the armies, but of the navies, of the globe, amounted to genius'. Even if any credence is given to Keitel's ideas of the nature of genius, it is evident that as far as Operation Sealion was concerned Hitler's genius was seriously at fault, in that he had grossly under-estimated the ability of the Royal Navy – fortunately free at the time from the need to despatch a fleet to undertake operations against the Japanese Navy in the Far East, to provide adequate anti-invasion forces and to maintain strong Home and Mediterranean Fleets.

Chapter 6

Month of Decision –
September 1940

In England they are filled with curiosity and keep asking 'Why doesn't he come?' Be calm, be calm, he is coming.

Adolf Hitler, 4 September 1940

The previous chapter has demonstrated in some detail that the mine barriers and coastal guns which were intended to protect the invasion fleet in the absence of German surface units would, in reality, have been ineffective – and the German naval planners must surely have realized this. However, whatever doubts there must have been, the fact was that the invasion plan had been finalized by the beginning of September, and if Sealion was to sail on 20 September the instruction must be given ten days earlier in order for the Navy to commence laying the minefields which were intended to protect it.

On 5 September Hitler had ordered the Luftwaffe to begin the final assault, commencing with night and day air raids on London. The following day, Raeder and his Chief of Staff attended a meeting in Berlin with Hitler, Keitel and Jodl. Raeder, at this critical time for Sealion, gave a detailed report beginning with an account of minesweeping and minelaying operations. Some barrages had been laid along the Belgian coast, but activities in the Channel had been hampered by the weather and 'the situation in air warfare'. He moved on next to the defence of Norway, the operations of auxiliary cruisers and the performance of the U-boat arm, which had had considerable success but had suffered heavy losses.

After this preamble came the main subject, Operation Sealion. Schniewind gave a report on progress, apparently concentrating on technical aspects such as assembly of the transports, available space, personnel and fuel supplies, after which Raeder summed up. His view was that the deadline of 20 September for assembling the transports would be met. Indeed, the first-wave vessels would be in position by 15 September. After this positive news, a note of caution was added. The crossing would be difficult, and the Army should not expect the divisions to be kept together, but 'the execution of Operation Sealion appears possible if attended by favourable circumstances regarding air supremacy, weather, and so on.' The Herbstreise diversionary operation, which was supposed to distract the Home Fleet, thereby preventing it from interfering with the Sealion landings, and which has been explained in more detail previously, was described, and the meeting then veered away from Sealion into what can only be described as a general discussion on world politics.

By the end of the meeting, the situation seemed clear. The Army had received its instructions, the Luftwaffe was entering the final phase of its campaign and Sealion was ready to launch. The Luftwaffe had, however, in the view of the naval staff, lost sight of the instruction in paragraph four of Directive 17. Rather than the air attacks being in support of the wider objective – the success of Sealion – the air staff now seemed to view the destruction of the RAF and the attack on London as an end in itself. Göring himself had always believed that bombing alone would force Britain to come to terms, and now seemed intent upon proving it. Consequently, the bulk of his resources were concentrated against London, with only small-scale raids on targets more relevant to Sealion.

A heavy raid was made on Liverpool over three nights commencing on 28 August, and though it may have benefited German forces in the Battle of the Atlantic in the long term, it was of little help to the imminent invasion. The naval bases at Sheerness and Harwich, homes of the destroyers of Nore Command, had been virtually untouched. Even when on 7 September the order was given to commence the final stage of the air assault, the Luftwaffe declared on the following day that maximum resources would remain concentrated on London until her harbours, power stations and supplies were destroyed. In effect, against the overwhelming menace of British sea power, Sealion could expect little or no help from the Luftwaffe, at least in the preparatory stage.

Equally worrying for the naval staff in these last days before D-day was the growing realization that complete mastery of the air was far from being a *sine qua non* as far as assembling the Sealion fleet was concerned. The British had continued to move large quantities of shipping through the Channel each month. Losses had been inflicted by both S-boats and dive-bombers, but nevertheless the convoys continued. Surely, therefore, the German Navy should be able to assemble the invasion fleet in the Channel ports, protected by German fighter aircraft and threatened by a comparatively small British bomber force. Although Sir Arthur Harris felt able to claim in 1946 that it was the wholesale destruction caused to invasion shipping in Channel ports by Bomber Command that convinced the Germans that an invasion attempt would be futile, the facts suggest otherwise. RAF light bombers had begun attacks on invasion ports on 5 September, and heavy bombers two days later. Different sources quote different figures, but the highest estimate for losses from bombing by the end of September 1940 is given in *Operation Sealion* by Peter Fleming. This quotes the losses as:

Vessel Type	Number destroyed by Bombing
Transport	21
Barge	214
Tug	5
Motor Boat	3

To put these figures into context, a different source (*Hitler Confronts England* by the American admiral (and D-day planner) Walter Ansel) states that at the end of September, after the losses listed above, the invasion ports still contained:

Vessel Type	Number Available
Transport	159
Barge	1,859
Tug	397
Motor Boat	1,100
Command Boat	68

This suggests the destruction was not quite as wholesale as Sir Arthur subsequently claimed.

On 10 September, almost at the last moment according to the original schedule, the Navy staff presented a further report. The staff believed that the Luftwaffe had achieved air superiority over the Channel, but that little had been done to 'pin down' the Royal Navy, as Directive 16 had instructed.

In fact, none of the supposed requirements which must be fulfilled to give Sealion a reasonable chance of success depended on the Luftwaffe at all. The diversionary operation to the north, intended to draw off the Home Fleet, actually needed to be spotted by British air reconnaissance, as the decoy force would serve little purpose if no one saw it! The minesweeping and minelaying operations, and British responses to them, would all be night-time operations, the crossing would itself be made largely at night and the Luftwaffe was irrelevant to the heavy coastal gun batteries.

The last two requirements (tactical surprise and good weather) needed an element of good fortune. Given the nightly activities of the Royal Navy in the Channel, surprise was most unlikely, and the weather could easily abort the whole operation. The Navy report, indeed, remarked on the weather conditions being 'completely abnormal and unstable', and commented that they were impairing the movement of transports and affecting minesweeping operations. On the night of the 10th, these conditions did not stop Royal Navy destroyers from patrolling between Le Havre and Boulogne, and a separate force attacking trawlers and barges off Ostend. The smaller ships of the Royal Navy Auxiliary Patrol and Coastal Forces were also at sea, as usual.

The only area, therefore, where the Luftwaffe might possibly be of real assistance was, in truth, the one which really mattered. The ports where the Royal Navy forces which would confront Sealion were based could have been heavily attacked, as the Navy staff believed the loosely worded instructions of Directive 17 intended. Raeder and his staff, so late in the day, still shrank from urging this course upon the Luftwaffe and Hitler. Perhaps Göring was right after all and the systematic collapse of morale in Britain under constant air attack would make Sealion unnecessary.

As the decisive moment arrived, Hitler wavered. He was still clinging to the idea that Britain would collapse, and on 11 September he delayed giving the go-ahead for three days. Raeder, for

51

his part, by now knew that Sealion must not be attempted if the air bombardment by the Luftwaffe had not brought about a British collapse. On 12 September he received a pessimistic report from Naval Group West in Paris, listing a whole host of problems. Ostend, Dunkirk, Calais and Boulogne were not safe as night anchorages because of regular attacks by Royal Navy warships. There were too few minesweepers, too few mines, too much shelling from the Dover batteries and an increase in night bombing.

Air reconnaissance and visual sightings had already left no doubt that the Royal Navy was present in the area in considerable force – a large number of destroyers and cruisers, together with two battleships, could reach the invasion route within a few hours of the alarm being given, and the Royal Navy had numerous small patrol vessels at sea which would certainly make a surprise attack impossible. (There was actually one minor error in this assessment: there was only one battleship, HMS *Revenge*, in the area, at Plymouth. The supposed second battleship, also at Plymouth, was in fact the old target ship *Centurion*, a former First World War battleship which had long been demilitarized, but which had been fitted with dummy wooden guns to appear operational.)

On the same day, the Navy staff produced yet another report, stating bluntly their view that the Luftwaffe was not making any useful contribution to Operation Sealion. The Royal Navy was operating almost unhindered in the Channel. The main safeguard for the operation, therefore, must be the minefields, already known to be unreliable. Their conclusion was that the operation should not take place, and on the nights of 11/12 and 12/13 September the Royal Navy gave substance to the German naval staff view when destroyers, motor gunboats and motor torpedo boats from Plymouth, Portsmouth and the Nore swept the entire length of the coast from the Channel Islands to Holland, investigating Cherbourg, Le Touquet, Boulogne, Dunkirk, Ostend, the Scheldt and the Maas, and attacking targets of opportunity. No British vessels were damaged and supporting cruisers were not called upon.

On the 13th, the two most powerful capital ships in the Royal Navy, the battleships *Rodney* and *Nelson*, came south from Scapa Flow with two new cruisers and a destroyer flotilla to join the battle-cruiser *Hood* at Rosyth. The Royal Navy now had its ships fully disposed to meet the invasion and to deal with any incursion by

German capital ships into the North Sea. Even the Herbstreise diversionary operation was in danger.

As this was happening, the commanders of the German Ninth and Sixteenth armies, Colonel Generals Busch and Strauss, whose troops would lead the assault, had assured Hitler that they were having no particular problems with their preparations, but that same evening he addressed a dinner of recently promoted senior army officers, during which he stated that he would not think of taking such a great risk as to land in England. He was still confident that bombing alone would be sufficient, and said the same to Raeder the following day, at a conference of the Commanders-in-Chief. This was, incidentally, the only conference during the whole of the summer of 1940 at which all three C-in-Cs were intended to be present. Hitler generally saw each one separately, presumably on the principle of divide and rule. In the event, Göring did not even attend this meeting, but was represented by Jeschonnek, his Chief of Staff.

As a meeting of all three Cs-in-C with Hitler was such a rare event, Raeder might well have feared that it was for the purpose of giving the order for Sealion to proceed. In any event, he came armed with a short memorandum in which he explained once again the reasons why a seaborne invasion should not take place, preferring instead to emphasize the importance of air attacks on London. Hitler then announced that he believed that it would be unwise to call off Sealion altogether, as he had intended to do on the previous day, as the cancellation would be a boost to British morale at a critical time for the bombing assault.

Raeder was apparently more than a little surprised at this announcement, as he had known nothing about the proposed cancellation, but to hear Hitler apparently agreeing with the points the naval staff had been making must have been a considerable relief. Consequently, he was emboldened enough to propose a postponement until the next occasion on which the tides and moon were favourable, which was 8 or 24 October. Hitler would have none of this; he would defer the decision until 17 September, which would mean the attack might still be launched on 27 September.

Then came a dramatic development: von Brauchitsch, head of OKH, stated that the Army no longer insisted on a dawn landing, which had previously been a requirement from which they had refused to budge. Perhaps, opined Raeder, the generals in command of the assault forces themselves had finally understood the arguments his staff had been presenting all along of the chaos into which a night crossing could degenerate, and had made OKH aware of this realization. Whatever the reason, Hitler did not pursue the point, and on the evening of the 14th a new Directive was issued, continuing the air attacks on London and postponing the decision for Sealion until the 17th.

Ironically, so well had the naval and army staffs done their work that on 15 September the transports were in position, and the assault divisions ready to board. There were even sufficient surplus vessels to replace the losses caused by bombing and by naval gunfire. More to the point was the growing realization that Bomber Command could not stop Sealion. If the fleet could not seriously be harmed by British bombing when concentrated and stationary in its ports, then how much less vulnerable would it be when at sea and moving, albeit slowly?

Unfortunately for Sealion's prospects, however, this argument was double-edged. The Luftwaffe had inflicted damage on some of the British Channel convoys, but, apart from a brief period, they had not stopped them, so how could they be expected to stop fast-moving destroyer forces? Even the commander of the dive-bombers, General Wolfram von Richtofen, had voiced doubts. Furthermore, once the destroyers broke into the invasion columns, they would have been largely invulnerable to air attack in the melee which would ensue. What was needed was what the naval staff had always known was needed, a naval surface force capable of holding off, or at the very least delaying, the Royal Navy, and the last faint hope of this had disappeared when the German Navy suffered heavy losses off Norway.

The end, when it came, was almost an anti-climax. Royal Navy destroyers from Portsmouth and the Nore were patrolling the French coast on the nights of 14/15, 15/16 and 16/17 September, and on the 15th one of the 14-inch guns at St Margaret's Bay fired at Gris Nez. On the 17th, with heavy weather in the Channel, Hitler called off Sealion indefinitely. On the 19th ten vessels from the Herbstreise diversionary operation were released in order to transport supplies to Norway, as were six from the Sealion fleet. A Directive was issued to the effect that the ships should be able to return to the embarkation ports in 8–10 days if required, but the

Navy War Diary summed up succinctly why Sealion would not happen:

1) The preparations for a landing on the Channel coast are extensively known to the enemy, who is taking more counter-measures. Symptoms are, for example, operational use of his aircraft for attacks and reconnaissance over the German operational harbours; frequent appearance of destroyers off the south coast of England, in the Dover Strait, and on the Franco-Belgian coast; stationing of his patrol vessels off the north coast of France; Churchill's last speech etc.

2) The main units of the Home Fleet are being held in readiness to repel the landing, though the majority of the units are still in western bases.

3) Already a large number of destroyers (30) has been located by air reconnaissance in the southern and south-eastern harbours.

4) All available information indicates that the enemy's naval forces are solely occupied with this theatre of operations.

Late in September and into October the steady pressure continued. In addition to the nightly sweeps by destroyers, the Royal Navy introduced 15-inch guns. As previously described, on 29 September the old monitor HMS *Erebus* bombarded Calais, and on 11 October the battleship HMS *Revenge*, a veteran of Jutland, led a force to shell Cherbourg.

On 12 October, Hitler called Sealion off, and late in October the invasion fleet dispersed.

Chapter 7

Plans, Planes and Personnel
Sealion in detail and the question of air superiority

The previous chapters have attempted to explain how the final plan for Operation Sealion came about, but this was far from the whole story. The finer details of the plan, including such obvious questions as how the German naval staff, with comparatively slender resources at their disposal, intended to provide crews for their ships, are worthy of closer examination, if only to make possible a judgement as to how realistic their proposals really were.

The true extent of the problems facing the German naval staff as Operation Sealion evolved can be determined by considering the tasks Raeder laid down for the Navy at the conference with Hitler on 25 July. Not in any particular order of importance, these involved requisitioning, assembling and modifying the necessary vessels, preparing the ports from which they would sail, locating sufficient trained manpower to crew them, and determining how the various fleets would be organized. In addition, when the time came, British minefields must be cleared, protective minefields laid and maintained and the landing areas reconnoitered. Finally, the heavy coastal gun batteries, which it was fondly believed (if not by the naval staff, then certainly by Hitler) would repel any effective response by the Royal Navy, must be positioned, and the diversion of British heavy units by suggestions of a dummy landing (the Herbstreise operation) on the north-east coast anywhere between Newcastle-upon-Tyne and Aberdeen must be prepared.

Nevertheless, by the end of August, a fleet of over 3,500 vessels had been assembled, which would require 24,000 men simply to crew it. According to *Jane's Fighting Ships* the German Navy consisted of some 75,000 officers and men in 1938 and, of course, it did not have access to anything like the resources of the Royal Naval Reserve and the Royal Naval Volunteer Reserve that the Royal Navy could call upon. The importance of this reserve may be demonstrated by the fact that, at the beginning of 1939, whilst the active service strength of the Royal Navy and Royal Marines totalled 131,322 officers and men, there were an additional 73,240 officers and men with the two reserve forces.

Despite the many problems facing them, however, by utilizing men from ships under repair and men standing by warships approaching completion, the German naval staff had managed to make some 4,000 men available. In addition, appeals were made for men with appropriate experience, who subsequently volunteered or were called up, but an interest in boating or canoeing was hardly a sufficient qualification to take a vessel of questionable seaworthiness across the Channel. Furthermore, the crews would be required to undertake this voyage not once, in a daring assault in favourable weather, but continuously over a period of several weeks, at a time of year when the weather would be sure to deteriorate. By comparison to these men, the barge crews with experience of negotiating the inland waterways of Europe could almost be considered master mariners!

Nevertheless, when on 3 September the final orders for Operation Sealion were confirmed by Keitel, proposing a landing date of 21 September with the final go-ahead being given ten days prior to this, the German naval staff had actually achieved most of the tasks required of it. Minelaying was intended to take place once the go-ahead had been issued, but the rest of the requirements had been fulfilled. The problem, therefore, was not whether the targets set within the plan could be achieved, but whether the plan itself was feasible, or simply the product of wishful thinking.

On paper, the Sealion plan of a landing of nine divisions on a front of around 80 miles, supported by three airborne regiments, might stand comparison with the Allied Operation Overlord, a landing of five divisions on a front of 40 miles, supported by three airborne divisions, especially as Overlord was attacking, across a greater distance, an enemy who had had considerable time to prepare defences, whilst Sealion was attacking an enemy who only three months earlier had lost most of his equipment – but in reality the two were vastly different operations. Overlord could deploy over 3,800 purpose-built landing craft and 310 landing ships for the initial assault alone, together with over 420 ships working on the PLUTO pipeline and the Mulberry artificial harbours, and a support force of 1,260 merchant vessels.

In comparison to the token German naval presence of a handful of destroyers and fast motor boats, together with twenty-seven coastal gunboats to provide artillery support across the whole 80-mile wide front, the Allies in 1944 deployed over 1,200 warships (79 per cent of which were British, 16.5 per cent American and 4.5 per cent other allies), including 30 battleships and cruisers, over 100 destroyers, and almost 450 minesweepers, frigates and corvettes to protect and support the initial assault. With total sea and air superiority, the Allies in 1944 could at least be sure that the attacking forces would reach their target beaches. In 1940, Sealion lacked any hope of such assurance. Only air superiority could (possibly) be achieved, but this alone could not protect the invasion forces. In these circumstances, it is interesting to consider firstly what was the exact situation in the air, and secondly how the German Navy actually intended to land the assault troops on the British mainland.

The question of air superiority, which traditionally has always been stated as the reason Sealion never sailed, was not in fact quite so clear cut. As has been explained previously, Sealion could only take place when the light and the tides were right. The Army required, right until the last moment, a dawn landing, and the Navy required sufficient light to have any chance of positioning the unwieldy barges correctly. In addition, the landing needed to be at the beginning of the ebb tide in order to get the barges off the beaches, rather than leave them stranded. The only suitable dates were 20 to 26 August, and 19 to 26 September. As the August dates were too early, the September ones became the target towards which German planning worked, and it is therefore important, in view of subsequent events, to look at the comparative strengths of the opposing air forces in September. If, as was subsequently claimed, the reason for the eventual cancellation of Sealion was the inability of the Luftwaffe to achieve air superiority, then this fact should surely be reflected in the figures. It is not.

By early September 1940, the Battle of Britain had reached a crucial stage. The Luftwaffe, after its initial attacks on Channel convoys starting in July, and what it perceived as its major assault, commencing on 13 August, made RAF fighter airfields in south-east England its priority targets from 24 August until 6 September. During these thirteen days, identified by the RAF as 'the critical period', six out of seven sector airfields were badly damaged, 466 RAF fighters were destroyed or damaged and only 269 new or repaired fighters were received. In addition, 231 RAF fighter pilots, out of a complement of around one thousand, were killed, wounded or missing. As September began, Fighter Command had 358 operational Spitfires and Hurricanes in the whole of Britain, whereas the Luftwaffe had just over 750 bombers and a similar number of fighters operational in France and Belgium. By the second week of September, RAF reserves had reached their lowest level, with only some 130 fighters available with storage units.

Although in the event Fighter Command was saved by a change in German tactics from 7 September, when daylight and subsequently night-time attacks on London began, it is clear that, had Sealion sailed on 20 September and the Luftwaffe been ordered to concentrate its resources over the barge trains, then Fighter Command would not only have been seriously outnumbered but would have been at a tactical disadvantage. German fighters would have been nearer to their bases and could have refuelled, rearmed and been back over the Channel extremely quickly. Although Fighter Command could have contested Luftwaffe operations in support of Sealion to a certain extent, the Royal Air Force could not itself have secured and maintained air superiority over the English Channel, or even materially interfered with the progress of the barge trains themselves.

In point of fact, much of this, despite the subsequent myth, is irrelevant. Even if the RAF fighters had evaded the large numbers of Me 109s patrolling over the various elements of the invasion force and been able to attack the invasion barges, the bullets of the eight .303-inch machine guns, each of which carried only thirteen seconds of ammunition, which was the armament of the Spitfire and the Hurricane, would not have harmed even the frailest of the barges. Indeed, such a suggestion is clearly absurd, and Fighter Command never for a moment intended or expected their aircraft to operate in this manner. In any case, the final hours of the assault would be made during the night, in order for the assault troops to land at dawn, and neither air force would have been able to make any significant contribution. Fighter Command never at any time claimed that it could prevent the invasion, and only subsequently did this idea come into being, as the Battle of Britain legend evolved.

Similar constraints also applied to Bomber Command. To attempt to attack the invasion convoys at sea in daylight would have resulted in heavy losses to the aircraft concerned from the massed German fighter escorts, from which the outnumbered RAF fighters could not have provided protection, while the likelihood of hitting targets at night was remote in the extreme. Bomber Command had struggled to inflict significant damage on the invasion fleet when it was concentrated in port, despite carrying out twenty-three night raids in September, and was well aware of its shortcomings. Admiral Drax at the Nore subsequently recorded that the RAF were reluctant to commit any aircraft to co-operate with the Navy in the event of an invasion, because '[Bomber Command's] bomber forces had done no training to fit them for naval co-operation and they therefore had to point out that if asked to help us they would be just as likely to bomb our own ships as the enemy's'.

If it is accepted that in September 1940 the RAF could not have prevented Sealion from sailing, and could not have hindered it en route, then the next subject to examine is exactly how the assault troops would have been transported.

The final Sealion plan spoke grandly of an assault by nine divisions, but how the actual landings were to be carried out was a different matter. The first point to make is that any idea of a massed landing by troops storming ashore from specially designed landing craft, in the manner of the Allies in Normandy in June 1944, should be discounted. The vast array of specialized vessels available to Overlord was totally absent from Sealion. In their place, the German naval planners intended to use barges towed by tugs or by trawlers acting as tugs.

Originally, they estimated that over 400 tugs would be required, but suitable (or even almost suitable!) vessels were in short supply and only 397 were available in late September. Fortune did smile on the German planners in one respect, however, as the efforts of Bomber Command resulted in the loss of only five of these vessels to air attack whilst in port. Over 200 barges were lost, but a considerable barge surplus, of around 700, had been assembled to replace losses.

How to get these barges across the Channel was a further problem. Most of them were not powered, and the majority of those that were lacked sufficient power to enable them to navigate the Channel unaided. Consequently, the planners determined that each tug would tow two barges, one unpowered and one powered, in line. These little formations would then form up in columns three or four abreast, with thirty or even more tug/barge combinations in each column. As the crews of the various vessels would in most cases have had little experience of towing at sea, and even less of towing at sea in convoy, it is safe to assume that they would have left as much space as possible between themselves and the vessels around them – the resultant formations would not only have covered a considerable area of sea, but would, given the shortage of power of most of the vessels concerned, have been unwieldy in the extreme, and probably only capable of moving at a brisk walking pace at best.

Even with a calm sea (and the barges could not have coped with much more) and clear moonlight, one or two parted towlines or mechanical breakdowns could have thrown the whole formation into chaos. The numbers of tugs, barges and motor boats allocated to each area of the proposed landing will be explained in greater detail later, but the actual method of getting the troops ashore from the barges is worth describing, if only to give some idea of the improbability of the whole operation.

The method was, in fact, quite simple. The lines of tugs and barges would approach their target beaches by steaming parallel to the coast, in a swept channel (assuming of course that this channel had been properly swept, which assumption the German planners had to make), and once the commander of the escort, such as it was, believed that the transports had reached their intended landing area, each tug would be ordered to turn towards the beach. Next, the tugs would tow their barges towards the shore and would then, to avoid grounding, release them to make their own way to the beach. This would have been difficult enough for the powered barges, but the unpowered ones would have been in a desperate state, presumably being helped by small motor craft or, if really fortunate, by a powered barge.

All this time, and the timescale would probably have been two hours at least, both tugs and barges would have been exposed to fire from the British coastal defences, which by now would have been thoroughly alerted. In contrast to Overlord, the assault forces would have had virtually no artillery support of their own, unless one of the twenty-seven coaster gunboats was in the vicinity, but Luftwaffe bombers would presumably have attempted to attack the defenders. Even so, the landing area was 80 miles wide and the Luftwaffe could not be everywhere at once, especially as the ground troops had no means of communicating directly with the aircraft.

The first troops to reach land would have been the men of specially selected advance detachments, 2,000 of whom were intended to be transported in fast minelayers or minesweepers to each beach. They would then transfer into small *sturmboots* and motorboats for the final assault. Each *sturmboot*, which was actually an army vessel intended for river crossings, held only eight men, so even the advance detachments would not be landed in one operation. As these tiny, fragile boats would have been horribly vulnerable to shore fire, perhaps the term 'advance detachment' would be better translated into the British military term 'Forlorn Hope!'

Finally, the Germans did have one potential trump card which might have brought some relief to the infantry struggling to establish a bridgehead in the conditions described above – some 250 tanks, organized in four battalions. Some were light tanks, which were genuinely amphibious and intended to launch from barges and 'swim' ashore, but others were Panzer III and Panzer IV medium and heavy tanks, which had been waterproofed and fitted with long flexible tubes intended to float on the surface as the tank itself drove along the sea bed. These could operate in 25 feet of water, although driving off the end of a barge and sinking to the sea bed must have called for crews with strong nerves.

Once on the sea bed, the tank was blind, and therefore unable to avoid obstacles or even be sure that currents had not caused it to reach the bottom facing in a different direction from the one intended. These tanks had actually performed successfully in trials in shallow water with a smooth sandy sea bed, but how they would behave in the unknown conditions of the English coast was a different matter, and the commander of the German 17th Infantry Division, one of the four divisions intended to attack the Folkestone–Hastings landing area, had not even seen one.

The landings proposed for the two airborne divisions (one in the first wave, and the second flying into a captured airfield) were not, of course, subject to the restrictions described above, and may therefore be considered first. Airborne troops were only committed to Sealion at the last moment and the bulk of them were intended to land north and north-west of Folkestone, mainly in gliders rather than by parachute. The main force involved, 7th Flieger Division, was intended to be landed by glider, the gliders having been released by their towing aircraft some distance from the target areas. Even if the bulk of the gliders had landed safely, their approach would almost certainly have been tracked by radar, the essential element of surprise largely lost and ground forces fully alerted.

The vulnerability of lightly equipped airborne forces to ground troops was subsequently demonstrated more than once during the course of the War. The obvious example was actually an Allied operation, Market Garden, the attempt in 1944 to capture bridges leading to the 'Bridge too Far' at Arnhem; even the apparently successful German capture of Crete in 1941 resulted in such heavy casualties among the 22,000 German airborne troops involved (almost a third were killed or wounded) that the Germans never again used such forces in a major airborne operation.

The previous paragraphs have attempted to explain in some detail how the Sealion assault forces were to get ashore once they reached their target areas, and elsewhere the areas where they were intended to land have been described. What remains is to examine the resources the German naval planners had allocated to each of the landing areas, and the schedule they would need to follow in order to achieve a dawn landing at the right stage of the tide, which for the purpose of clarity will be assumed was to take place on the morning of 21 September 1940.

The most important of the landing areas was surely that between Folkestone and Hastings. This was around 30 miles long, was the nearest to France, and was the target for four divisions from Sixteenth Army: the 17th, 35th, 7th and 1st Mountain divisions. In fact, the area was actually divided in two, with separate fleets for each, but the target itself was one continuous bridgehead. To attack this area, leading elements of the 17th and 35th Infantry divisions would embark in 150 barges, towed by seventy-five tugs or trawlers, and would leave Dunkirk on the afternoon of 20 September. These would join with a further fifty barges (towed by twenty-five tugs) which would have left Ostend four or five hours earlier. The rest of the two divisions would follow along behind from Ostend and Rotterdam, in fifty-seven transport vessels towing 114 barges. The forward echelons of this force, led by the advance detachments described previously, would hope to put ashore 6,700 men from each division in the first wave, assuming that no casualties were suffered en route, which was, frankly, a rather unrealistic assumption! The landing area for this force was nearest to the Pas de Calais bases of the Ju 87 dive-bombers of Fliegerkorps VIII, and therefore might be thought to have the best hope of air protection.

In fact, however, the commander of the Fliegerkorps General Wolfram von Richtofen, did not believe that he had the resources to protect the whole of the landing area, and proposed a reduction of the first wave to one corps only, a proposal understandably rejected with horror by the army planners.

Although this description of the first of the four invasion fleets may seem quite logical and straightforward on paper, the reality would have been very different. Dunkirk, of course, had been the scene of Operation Dynamo only three months previously, and the port was a shambles, still largely in ruins and choked with wrecks. Most of the locks between the inner harbour, where the barges were assembled, and the outer harbour were still not operational – simply getting the fleet to sea would have been a complicated and time-consuming task. Additionally, the vessels joining the fleet from more distant ports, such as the steamers and barges from Rotterdam, would have been at sea for at least two days – given the basic or even non-existent toilet facilities aboard most of the vessels, together with the probability that men would have suffered from seasickness to a greater or lesser degree, conditions would surely have been fairly squalid, and the troops hardly in prime condition to undertake an opposed landing. Similar comments would apply to all four invasion fleets.

The second fleet, heading for what may be termed the 'other half' of the Folkestone–Hastings bridgehead, actually the Rye to Hastings section, would sail from Calais, and would consist of 100 tugs towing 200 barges, transporting the forward elements of the 7th Infantry and 1st Mountain divisions. The assault force for the Bexhill–Eastbourne area was the largest individual fleet, consisting of 330 barges towed by 165 tugs, which would sail from Boulogne and form up into an unwieldy mass four rows wide. The final force, intended to assault the Brighton–Beachy Head area, would sail from Le Havre in 300 motorboats, followed by further transports, tugs and barges if the initial landing succeeded. An additional group of twenty-five vessels towing fifty barges from Le Havre would head for Boulogne in order to join the Bexhill–Eastbourne force.

The problem with the above is in the numbers involved in the initial assaults. The first landings, even if completely successful with minimal casualties, would put ashore not nine full divisions, but the leading elements of these divisions, resulting in just over 26,000 men in the Folkestone–Hastings bridgehead, 13,000 in that from Bexhill to Rye, and 20,000 between Brighton and Beachy Head. In total, this was just about the equivalent of three divisions. Furthermore, the bridgeheads could not support each other, lacked artillery support and armour (even if most of the amphibious and waterproofed tanks reached the beaches, they would be desperately thinly spread); the final plan for bringing in reinforcements estimated that eleven days would be required to bring in the remaining elements of the initial nine divisions, after which two further divisions would arrive every four days.

Even this schedule made a number of rather daring assumptions. Firstly, it assumed that the barges from the initial assault could be recovered by their tugs, towed back to their ports of origin, reloaded with reinforcements and supplies, and towed back across to the bridgeheads, not once but on several occasions. The plan did allow for barges losses and some 700 barges were held in reserve to meet this eventuality, but recovering the towlines under fire would not have been easy, and losses among the tugs and trawlers, of which there were only just enough to begin with, would have seriously dislocated this schedule. Perhaps, therefore, the solution would have been to capture a port at an early stage of the invasion. This would have greatly speeded up unloading, and would have permitted greater use of the more capacious steamers rather that the more numerous but slow and clumsy barges. Even with an operational port, however, the figures are, from the German viewpoint, not encouraging.

Unlike the Allies in 1944, who took the portable Mulberry harbours with them, the Sealion planners would be obliged to transport both supplies and reinforcements over the beaches until they were able to capture a port. The British General Staff estimated that each German division would require some 300 tons of supplies per day to enable it to remain in action – this figure was probably an underestimate, as a British infantry division would have required rather more. If, therefore, Sealion eventually managed to bring the nine infantry divisions and two airborne divisions up to full strength, then 3,300 tons of supplies would be required every day, without even considering the additional requirements of any further divisions brought over later.

The first port the invaders could realistically hope to capture would be Folkestone, which was directly threatened by the largest of the invasion forces. At best, Folkestone could probably handle around 600 tons per day, and only then after the damage caused by the retreating British (such as the destruction of port equipment and the probable sinking of blockships) had been put right. The second possible port, Dover, might be able to handle 800 tons per day. This would, therefore, mean that 1,900 tons per day would need to be delivered over the landing beaches simply to maintain the eleven divisions of the original plan.

Thus far, only the details of the invasion plan and the flaws contained within it have been considered. It has been assumed that the various fleets, comprising around 1,500 vessels, would have been able to sail and to reach the British coast undetected, or at least unmolested. This is a rather daring assumption for, in reality, the nightly patrols carried out by the Royal Navy would certainly have located the invasion convoys at an early stage. The actual dispositions the Royal Navy had made will be examined later, but before then there is another important, and frequently overlooked, aspect of Sealion to consider, and that is whether Hitler seriously intended to carry it out at all.

Chapter 8

The German Perspective

Give us ten days fine weather, and England is finished.

Joseph Goebbels

The preceding chapters have attempted to describe the evolution of the Operation Sealion plan, to examine the limiting factors, most notably the lack of a surface fleet, within which the German planners were obliged to work, and to demonstrate the shortcomings of the expedients to which they resorted in order to attempt to overcome these limitations. The reader may well assume, from the many references to the meetings and conferences between Hitler and his Army, Navy and Luftwaffe commanders, that Hitler was wholeheartedly committed to the invasion. If this was not the case, then, surely, the misgivings of Army and Navy chiefs would have led to the whole Sealion concept being abandoned at an early stage as impracticable.

There is, perhaps surprisingly, considerable evidence that this view is incorrect and this chapter proposes to examine the political, rather than military, aspects of the possible invasion, and to attempt to determine how Hitler really viewed the possibility of an invasion of Britain.

On 5 June 1940, the German offensive in France resumed with a drive south across the Somme. By then, thirty divisions, almost a third of the French Army, had been lost and only two divisions of the British Expeditionary Force remained in France. On 14 June Paris was occupied and two days later Marshal Pétain formed a new French Government, which immediately sought an armistice. When Hitler received this news, on 17 June, he actually performed a little hop of joy, which was captured by his movie cameraman; the pictures were subsequently doctored by British propagandists in order to produce the effect of a silly dance!

The following day, he travelled to Munich with Göring to meet Mussolini. The various remarks he made at this time shed considerable light on his state of mind. He said to Göring, 'I shall come to an understanding with England', whilst in his meeting with Mussolini he described the British Empire as 'a force for order in the world'. Count Ciano, who was Mussolini's son-in-law and the Italian Foreign Minister, wrote in his diary that 'Hitler is now the gambler who has made a big scoop and would like to get up from the table risking nothing more.'

As early as 2 June, Hitler had, according to General Günther Blumentritt, voiced similar views during a conversation with General von Rundstedt at Army Group A headquarters, when he had expressed his admiration for the British Empire, which, together with the Catholic Church, was, in his opinion, an essential element for stability in the world. Britain would be offered an honourable peace if she would accept Germany's position on the Continent.

The talks with Mussolini and Ciano ended on 19 June, leaving Mussolini disappointed at what he perceived to be the leniency of the proposed armistice terms – he had hoped to annex most of French North Africa and sought the surrender of the French fleet. Hitler returned to his headquarters at Bruly-le-Peche in Belgium in order to prepare for the signing of the armistice and, as has already been described, met with Keitel and Raeder on the 20th.

The armistice was signed on 22 June, with the actual ceasefire to take effect on the 25th, and then Hitler took what can only be described as a holiday. There were no meetings with senior commanders between 23 June and 11 July.

The balance of the evidence, therefore, strongly suggests that Hitler did not at this stage of the war believe that an invasion of Great Britain would be necessary. Indeed, he had never even regarded Britain (or France, for that matter) as his primary enemy. His remarks to Raeder in June 1935, that the signing of the Anglo-German Naval Agreement was 'the happiest day of my life' were probably genuine. His ambition for Germany, clearly expressed in *Mein Kampf*, was expansion in Central and Eastern Europe. The war in the West had been brought about because Britain and France had been unwilling to give Germany a free hand in the East. As Trevor-Roper wrote: 'The offence of France was its traditional policy of Eastern alliances, which had enabled it, for three centuries, to intervene in Germany. The offence of Britain was its refusal to be content with a maritime supremacy, its insistent tradition of preventing the domination of Europe by a single Continental power. But the offence of Russia was the existence of Russia.' (Trevor-Roper 1973, chapter one).

Hitler must now have believed that Britain had no reason for continuing her former policy; Poland was no longer an independent state and France was defeated. Surely, he concluded, the British would take the pragmatic, sensible course of action, and in a very few days the first peace feelers would reach him. In such circumstances, there was no need to worry about planning an invasion.

But strangely, the approach did not come. Hitler returned to Berlin and after a triumphal motorcade through the city on 6 July, met Count Ciano on the 7th. In his absence, General Halder (OKH Chief of Staff) had referred in his diary, on 22 June, to 'preparations against England' and a week later OKH had produced outline proposals for the landing of thirteen divisions across a 200-mile front. On 30 June, Jodl produced his memorandum considering what military actions could be implemented against Britain, and on 2 July a Führer Directive signed by Keitel suggested that a landing was a possibility. Finally, on 3 July, the British responded, not with peace feelers but with the ruthless neutralization of much of the French fleet.

Not surprisingly, Ciano found Hitler uncertain as to what action to take, but willing to admit that the war in the west might have to continue. Hitler still seems to have been undecided when he met Raeder on 11 July and discussed with him the peace offer he intended to make to Britain when he spoke to the Reichstag on 19 July. By the time the speech was made, however, Hitler seems to have decided that his 'appeal to reason' would fall on deaf ears, as he had already issued Directive 16 three days earlier. The clear conclusion must be that if Britain would not willingly accept the inevitable, then measures must be taken to ensure her submission.

How this was to be brought about was, however, less clear. The Army might talk confidently about a 'mighty river crossing' but the Army commanders and planners were ignorant of the perils of amphibious warfare. Indeed, the lack of even elementary knowledge of the sea exhibited by senior officers led to incidents which were both amusing and revealing. Two of these are worth recording. Firstly, there was the case of the commander of one of the two mountain divisions allocated to Army Group A. This individual took what must have seemed the sensible decision to have his men given swimming lessons, which would take place in the sea at 0900 hrs each morning. The training programme for the division had been worked out with German military thoroughness and could not easily be amended. Consequently, the soldiers would arrive on the beach punctually each morning, only to find that the sea, which was governed by tides rather than training programmes, had receded further from them each day.

The second case was that of General Erich von Manstein, commander of XXXVIII Corps, who would have crossed the Channel with Captain Lindenau from Boulogne in the naval tender *Hela*. Manstein chose to go swimming with his driver and his aide-de-camp, leaving his staff car on the beach – only by commandeering a tractor were they able to rescue the Mercedes as the incoming tide lapped around its wheels. These incidents are not described here to suggest that the officers concerned were fools. They were not, they simply lacked any knowledge of the sea, yet senior officers with similar backgrounds could happily regard crossing the English Channel as akin to crossing a large river.

Hitler, however, was not so naive. At a Commanders-in-Chief conference in Berlin he was clearly well aware of the problems, referring to the invasion of Britain as 'an exceptionally daring undertaking, because even if the way is short this is not just a river crossing but the crossing of *a sea which is dominated by the enemy* ... a defensively prepared and utterly determined enemy faces us *and dominates the sea area we must use*'. Already, on 21 July, Hitler was aware that the crux of the matter was control of the sea, and that the Royal Navy still remained supreme.

If this was the case, and Hitler appears to have accepted it at an early stage, then how else could Britain be brought to heel? The only viable alternative was a combination of attacks on the shipping lanes bringing supplies to Britain and an air offensive to break civilian morale. Attacks on shipping would not have an immediate impact, given the small number of U-boats and commerce raiders available at the time, but the air offensive was more promising, and it is here that German and British beliefs in the role of air power diverge. The traditional British view, put simply, has always been that if the Luftwaffe had destroyed Fighter Command then the invasion would have been certain. In other words, the Battle of Britain and Operation Sealion are inextricably linked. Lose the former and the latter would inevitably follow.

The German view is best expressed by Colonel Paul Deichmann, Chief of Staff of Kesselring's Fliegerkorps II: 'I personally always viewed Sealion and the air offensive as two quite independent projects.' Göring himself, at a Luftwaffe conference on 16 September, less than a week from the target date for Sealion to sail, said, 'Sealion must not disturb nor burden the Luftwaffe operations.' What these remarks demonstrate is that, to the Luftwaffe, the air fighting over Southern Britain was not part of the preparation for invasion, but had an even more ambitious objective: that of bringing about the conquest of Britain by air power alone.

Göring believed that, as Douhet had predicted, civilian morale would collapse under aerial bombardment and the British people would demand that their government sue for peace. In such circumstances, Sealion could indeed take place, but as a symbolic operation only, akin to the formal entry of German troops into Paris, against the background of a Britain brought to terms by attack from the air. As is now known, Göring was wrong, as he had been before when he undertook to destroy the surrounded British forces at Dunkirk, and as he would be again when he promised to supply Stalingrad from the air – but at the time it must have seemed to Hitler that it was, at least, worth trying.

The three German armed services seem to have viewed the idea of Sealion in different lights. The Luftwaffe, as explained above, regarded it as an irrelevance. The British would be brought to heel by aerial bombardment alone, after which the Navy could ferry an occupation force across the Channel if this was what the peace treaty required. The Army, originally sceptical, was interested for a time but became dubious when realization dawned that the river-crossing analogy was inappropriate, and that the Navy could not protect the invading force from interception and probable annihilation by the Royal Navy en route.

The German Navy, which effectively meant Admiral Raeder, was in a difficult position. Erich Raeder had been a professional naval officer since he entered the Naval Academy at Kiel in 1894, at the age of eighteen. He had fought at Jutland and subsequently became

71

Chief of Staff to Admiral Franz Hipper, probably the ablest German admiral of the First World War. Raeder had been head of the Navy since October 1928 and first met Hitler in April 1933.

For a long time thereafter Raeder believed that he could educate Hitler in the importance of sea power. Raeder was a traditionalist in naval matters, holding to the battleship-focused Tirpitz tradition, and his words at the outbreak of war ('Today the war against England and France broke out which, according to the Führer's previous assertions, we had no need to expect before 1944. The surface forces are so inferior in number and strength that they can do no more than show how to die gallantly and thus are willing to create the foundations for later reconstruction'), when the ambitious 'Z Plan' fleet existed only on paper, clearly demonstrate a sense of betrayal. Despite his confidence in his ability to educate Hitler, Raeder found himself a lone voice among those close to the Führer – the only man with a grasp of the realities of sea warfare.

When instructed by Directive 16 to produce a workable plan, Raeder could not simply point out that the operation was impossible. To say 'no' to the Führer would be dangerous both for his service and for himself. At the various conferences with Hitler, therefore, he continually sounded a note of caution, emphasizing the dangers of the operation without actually saying that it should not take place, and insisting throughout that Luftwaffe air supremacy was essential. This was a masterstroke – Raeder knew that Sealion would be a disaster for the German Navy and that air supremacy could not halt the Royal Navy, but by placing the emphasis firmly on the Luftwaffe he had found a means of escape.

If Göring was right and the British were forced to come to terms, then Sealion, if it took place at all, would be unopposed, yet if the Luftwaffe failed then he could argue that his prime requirement had not been fulfilled.

Whatever views Raeder and his senior officers may have held, however, it is clear that his naval planners certainly did take Sealion seriously. After the War, Admiral Walter Ansel of the US Navy, who had worked on the plans for Overlord, saw the final plans produced by the German Navy, and commented on the performance of the German naval staff as follows: 'To anyone acquainted with the problems that faced them – the tension of strife, the meagerness of resource in working staff, in experience and in material, and most of all in the shortness of time – these men had performed veritable prodigies of amphibious warfare planning and preparations' (Ansel 1960). Whatever the misgivings of their seniors, the fact is that the middle-ranking officers on the German naval staff had, by September, produced a workable plan and had assembled the vessels to carry it out.

In accordance with the requirements of Directive 16, therefore, both the Army and the Navy had produced their plans. The troops were ready and sufficient transport vessels had been made available to embark them. The fact that senior commanders in both services were opposed to the operation by this stage would not have stopped it if Hitler had given the order. He had ignored or overridden the advice of his professional military advisers before and been proved right. Unlike them, he had concluded that France could be defeated quickly, and his army had duly achieved in a matter of weeks and with light casualties what the army of the Kaiser had attempted unsuccessfully for four years. He might have believed the same of Sealion.

Consequently, Hitler's own views on the likelihood of a successful invasion, touched upon briefly earlier, should now be examined in more detail. The unavoidable conclusion must surely be that, apart perhaps from a short period in mid-July, he did not believe it to be a realistic possibility. His attitude to war against Britain and France has already been explained and there can be no doubt that he appreciated the real practical problems which stood in the way. The clearest expression of this doubt can be seen in the phrasing of the introduction to Directive 16 itself: 'I have therefore begun to plan for, and if necessary to carry out, an invasion of England.' When compared with subsequent directives concerning Yugoslavia ('Yugoslavia ... must be crushed as quickly as possible') and Russia ('The German armed forces must be ready to crush Soviet Russia in a swift campaign'), the language of Directive 16 is almost pusillanimous.

However doubtful Hitler had been about the chances of a successful invasion, he was faced with the fact that the elimination, or at least neutralization, of Britain was strategically essential if he was to attack Soviet Russia. He had told his generals on 23 November 1939 that 'we can oppose Russia only when we are free in the west.' Nevertheless, he seems to have taken little direct part in the planning of Sealion and certainly did nothing to suggest that he was wholeheartedly behind the operation. Von Rundstedt, commander of Army Group A, never believed that the Sealion preparations were anything other than a bluff, and as early as 21 July 1940, the head of OKH, von Brauchitsch, was briefed by Hitler to 'start dealing with the Russian problem'. Just over a week later, on 29 July, Jodl told the head of OKW's planning section, General Warlimont, that Hitler had made up his mind to prepare for war with Russia, and by 9 August Warlimont's staff were already starting work on deployment areas for troops in the East.

The evidence is therefore compelling that, at a very early stage of the Sealion preparations, Hitler had made up his mind to attack Russia, even though this contradicted his previous insistence that Germany must be secure in the West before taking decisive action in the East. Sealion preparations would continue, as Hitler may still have clung to the hope that the Luftwaffe bombing campaign would succeed, and the build-up of invasion forces would add to the pressure. In any case, as Hitler admitted on 14 September, to cancel Sealion would involve a major loss of prestige. Only on 12 October 1940 could Keitel issue a directive stating that 'preparations for Sealion shall be continued solely for the purpose of maintaining political and military pressure on England.'

At the same time, the apparent emphasis on Sealion would help maintain the secrecy of the planning for Operation Barbarossa. In a memorandum to Admiral Kurt Assmann, head of the German Naval Historical Staff, in 1944, Raeder stated that he had no idea that an attack on Russia was being planned, and Göring claimed that he knew nothing of the intention until November.

In conclusion, therefore, it is clear that after at most a brief dalliance with the idea Hitler had realized that Germany did not have, and could not in any foreseeable future expect to possess, the one factor which would have made the operation possible: command of the sea. His Luftwaffe adjutant, Nicholas von Below, was later to write of Hitler: 'In autumn 1940 the great unknown, the fairly improvised crossing over the sea, frightened him. He was unsure.'

The final words should perhaps be given to Admiral Assmann, whose staff prepared in 1944 a 'Brief Statement of Reasons for Cancellation of Invasion of England.':

As the preliminary work and preparations proceeded, the exceptional difficulties became more and more obvious. The more forcibly the risks were brought home, the dimmer grew faith in success ... just as in Napoleon's invasion plans in 1805, the fundamental requirement for success was lacking, that is, command of the sea. This lack of superiority at sea was to be compensated for by air superiority, but it was never even possible to destroy enemy sea superiority by use of our own air superiority. The sea area in which we were to operate was dominated by a well prepared opponent who was determined to fight to the utmost of his ability. The greatest difficulty was bound to be that of maintaining the flow of supplies and food. The enemy's fleet and other means of naval defence had to be considered as a decisive factor. Owing to the weakness of our naval forces there could be no effective guarantee against the enemy breaking into our area of transports, despite our mine barrages on the flanks and despite our air superiority.

After the War, when Assmann could be more candid in his remarks, he was to write:

When the time came for the final decision to be taken, none of the responsible personalities was ready, despite his knowledge of the weighty matters at stake, to take a firm hand against the operation. All, however, were inwardly relieved to be able to find, in the lack of air mastery, a sound argument which would openly justify them in abandoning the operation.

Chapter 9

Air and Sea Power

Aircraft and the U-boat have turned surface fleets into obsolete playthings.

Adolf Hitler, 1934

On land I am a hero but at sea I am a coward.

Adolf Hitler

The first section of this book has covered in considerable detail the genesis and evolution of the plan for Operation Sealion, as well as describing what may perhaps be termed the 'mechanics' of the plan itself, and the political and military situation which brought it about. The second section will deal with the force which, from the very outset, made Sealion impracticable, the Royal Navy; it will look closely at the British fleet of 1939–1940 and how that fleet had fared in the first year of the War.

Before embarking on this task, however, it is necessary to examine the arguments over the relative importance of sea and air power which raged between the wars, as these often heated debates provided the background against which the performance of the Royal Navy at this time must be assessed.

Supporters of what may perhaps be described as the traditional British view of 1940 – that, in essence, the victory of Fighter Command over the Luftwaffe made Britain safe from invasion, and that, therefore, the victory of the Luftwaffe over Fighter Command would have made invasion inevitable – might well feel at this point that most of the first section of this book totally misses the point. The shortcomings of the minefields, the inaccuracy of the coastal

76

batteries, the lack of German naval protection, the doubts of the senior commanders and the strength of the Royal Navy would all have been unimportant if the Luftwaffe had attained superiority over the Channel and the landing zones.

No doubt the Royal Navy would have attempted to intercept the invasion convoys as they crossed the Channel, or would have sought to attack them as they unloaded their troops, but this would have involved their ships coming within range of the Luftwaffe, whose medium bombers and dive-bombers would, under a protective screen of fighters, have sunk or damaged most of them. In simple, if lurid, terms, the Royal Navy would have died in the Channel and the invasion would have succeeded. After all, when the Royal Navy had previously encountered the Luftwaffe off Norway and at Dunkirk, the superiority of air over sea power had been clearly demonstrated. At least, that has always been the traditional view, and the origins of these opinions on the superiority of air power may be traced right back to the last days of the First World War and the birth of the Royal Air Force.

The Royal Air Force came into being on 1 April 1918, as a result of a recommendation made by a cabinet committee on Air Organisation and Home Defence against Air Raids (itself set up in response to the German Gotha bomber raids of mid-1917). This committee concluded that an independent third service should be created and that in the future the traditional services (i.e. the Army and Navy) might well become secondary to it. In other words, a time might come when air power alone would win wars. Consequently, the Royal Flying Corps and the Royal Naval Air Service were merged. At the time the RNAS, with some 55,000 officers and men, consisted of 100 air stations and more than 2,500 aircraft, making the Royal Navy without doubt the world leader in the field of naval aviation. However, most RNAS personnel chose to transfer to the RAF and those who remained (with joint Navy-RAF ranks) found that their careers suffered.

A miniature Fleet Air Arm came into being in 1921, but for much of the inter-war period responsibility for this was shared between the Admiralty and the Air Ministry. As a result, naval aviation was neglected in a time of economic difficulty, situated as it was between an Admiralty dominated by admirals with traditional views of the importance of the battle fleet, and an Air Ministry with total faith in the value of the strategic bomber.

Two Whitehall committees set up in the early 1920s to consider the future of the battleship and the role of air power took evidence from both sides in the argument and eventually concluded that the battleship still had a future. In 1921, the US Army Air Corps had managed to sink the former German battleship *Ostfriesland*, but due to the circumstances of the sinking (the battleship was a semi-derelict hulk at anchor and obviously without a crew able to apply damage control measures or otherwise protect, let alone manoeuvre, the ship) this was far from conclusive – other than to the supporters of the bomber.

Unfortunately, in the United Kingdom, the argument in the 1920s and early 1930s degenerated into a battle between the Admiralty and the Air Ministry over who should control carrier aviation; the situation was hardly improved by a compromise imposed by Prime Minister Stanley Baldwin that the RAF would be responsible for recruitment, training and maintenance of the Fleet Air Arm, with the Navy exercising operational and disciplinary control at sea. The RAF were to supply 30 per cent of pilots, with the remaining 70 per cent (and all observers) to be from the Navy. Responsibility for the procurement of new aircraft remained with the Air Ministry, who in the 1930s believed absolutely in the strategic bomber, with fighters a poor second and naval aviation badly neglected.

Finally, with the increase in defence spending commencing in 1936, and following further inter-departmental wrangles and numerous letters to *The Times* from supporters of both sides of the argument, control of the Fleet Air Arm (but not of shore-based maritime aircraft, which remained with the RAF as Coastal Command) returned to the Royal Navy. The harm that naval aviation had suffered during this period can be demonstrated by the fact that in 1932 the Royal Navy had six aircraft carriers (three of which were large, fast, vessels converted from battlecruisers) but only 150 obsolete aircraft, compared to the US Navy, which had three carriers and over 400 aircraft. Furthermore, the carrier-borne naval aircraft in the Royal Navy was regarded as primarily intended for reconnaissance and air defence – it was not seen as a strike weapon, other than to slow down opposing capital ships to enable the battle fleet to engage them.

Whereas the United States Navy had been carrying out exercises with carrier task forces as early as 1929, and Admiral Yamamoto in Japan was forcefully arguing the case for aircraft carriers, torpedo bombers and dive-bombers in 1935, the new Royal Navy carriers, the Illustrious Class, were designed to protect themselves from air attack not with their own aircraft, but with armoured hangars and anti-aircraft guns. Perhaps it is unfair to be too critical of this, given the parlous state to which the Fleet Air Arm had been reduced. Even in 1939, it had only 232 aircraft, of which a mere eighteen were the modern, but still obsolete, Blackburn Skua.

The decline in British manufacturing capacity between the wars was also a factor hindering naval aviation, and, indeed, the pre-war expansion of the Royal Navy in general. A comparison of the 1914 and 1939 editions of *Jane's Fighting Ships* is most revealing. In 1914, twenty major British shipyards are listed, whereas by 1939 this number has reduced to fourteen; the number of smaller yards had reduced from 111 to just nineteen. In addition, Royal dockyards, which in 1914 actually built most major warships, had largely lost this capacity by 1939.

Just as British warships took longer to build than their overseas equivalents, and in many cases parts had to be obtained from overseas (such as armour plate for the new carriers, much of which was manufactured in Czechoslovakia), so production of the Skua dive-bomber, the specification for which dated from 1934, was not expected to reach even sixteen aircraft per month by the end of 1938. Consequently, even when new aircraft reached the carriers, they were invariably obsolete and outclassed. The eight-gun Fairey Fulmar fighter, reaching the fleet carriers in mid-late 1940, was slower than most of the bombers it was intended to engage.

The result of all this was that the Fleet Air Arm entered the Second World War with aircraft that were generally inferior to those that they would expected to meet in combat, whilst the years of inter-service bickering had produced an atmosphere of mutual distrust, at least at the higher levels of the Air Ministry and the Admiralty. What should have been a responsible debate into the relative roles of warships and aircraft in combat, hopefully investigating the capabilities and weaknesses of each, and how each could complement the other, had degenerated into a battle of words between two entrenched positions.

The Air Ministry view was, in simple terms, total faith in the war-winning capability of the strategic bomber, reflecting the views originally propounded by Trenchard, and the subsequent writings of the Italian theorist Guilio Douhet. Sir Hugh (later Lord)

Trenchard, was Chief of Air Staff between 1919 and 1929, and he believed absolutely in the need for an independent Air Force, rather than one acting as a support service for the Army and the Navy. In order to justify this view, an independent strategy was required and that strategy was based around the bomber.

In simple terms, Trenchard and the Air Ministry argued that 'the bomber will always get through.' Any future war would be won by strategic bombing – the only way to defeat an enemy bomber force was by having an even larger one which would destroy the bases and the industrial centres upon which the enemy depended. Between the wars, the Air Ministry argued that the Empire could be policed by a powerful air force moving between trouble spots as needs dictated, and attempts were made to justify this belief by bombing troublesome villages in Iraq. The Army and the Navy, although not actually unnecessary, were, in the Air Ministry view, very much defensive forces – wars would be won by the Air Force. Consequently, any attempt to draw off aircraft from this primary role (such as giving control of maritime aircraft to the Navy) was anathema to the holders of such opinions.

Guilio Douhet, one of the fathers of the strategic bombing concept, was an Italian general who in 1921 wrote *The Command of the Air* and, at the end of the 1920s, *The War of 19–*, in which he described battles between French and Belgian air forces and the 'Independent German Air Force'. After the use of high explosives, incendiaries and poison gas, the story ends with the French and Belgian governments, under intense pressure from the civilian population, suing for peace after several towns are obliterated by bombing.

Although Douhet died in 1930 and *The Command of the Air* was not actually published in English until 1942, his assumptions (that civilian morale would collapse under heavy bombing and that large bomber fleets could not be stopped) were widely accepted and promoted by the supporters of the strategic bombing concept. Hermann Göring was a fervent believer, as, subsequently, was Sir Arthur Harris, the Commander-in-Chief of Bomber Command from February 1942 until the end of the War.

By the eve of the Second World War, such was the fear of the bomber that the British Ministry of Health could calculate that 600,000 people would die, with a further 1,200,000 seriously injured, in the first six months of air attack. These calculations were based on the only previous experience available, which was the effect of the

German bomber offensive on London in the First World War. As this involved the dropping of only just over 70 tons of bombs in total, then it could be argued that the calculations were perhaps rather hypothetical, but this was not the view taken at the time. Even Liddell Hart warned of around 250,000 British casualties in the first week of the War.

In the event, British civilian losses to bombing in Britain during the whole of the Second World War were 146,777 killed, missing or seriously injured. Bad enough, certainly, but nowhere near the pre-war predictions – 600,000 civilians *were* killed by bombing, but by Allied bombing of Germany, and over a period of five years. Thus, when in December 1937 Sir Thomas Inskip, as Minister for the Co-ordination of Defence, proposed that radar, together with the new eight-gun monoplane fighters, could provide a defence against the bomber, Lord Trenchard would argue in the House of Lords that acceptance of this claim by the Cabinet 'might well lose us the war', reflecting the Douhet belief that the use of aircraft for air defence, or the tactical support of armies (and, presumably, of navies), was 'useless, superfluous, and harmful'.

The relevance of all the above to the Royal Navy of 1939–40, and to Operation Sealion, is clear. If, as many believed, bombers could obliterate entire cities and slaughter their populations in hundreds of thousands, then it was surely clear that warships would have little chance of survival in their presence. To have any hope at all, the pessimists would argue, warships would need batteries of well-directed anti-aircraft guns, and the fact was that the Royal Navy was poorly equipped in this regard.

The destroyers which would constitute the cutting edge of the naval forces and would meet Sealion, mainly the 'V & W' and 'A to I' Classes, all followed the same basic pattern. Generally, they had four low-angle 4-inch or 4.7-inch guns in single mountings, and two sets of either triple, quadruple or quintuple torpedo tubes. Their purpose was to screen the main fleet from attack by enemy destroyers and to launch torpedo attacks on the enemy fleet. Although this armament would have made short work of the vessels comprising the invasion force, it provided little protection against air attack. The low-angle main armament could not engage dive- bombers, although it could contribute to a barrage over other ships in company.

For defence against air attack, the destroyers carried either two single 2-pdr anti-aircraft guns, or eight .5-inch machine guns in two four-barrelled mountings. These weapons were short range at best, and the stop-gap measure applied in 1940 to some destroyers of fitting a 3-inch or 4-inch anti-aircraft gun instead of the after set of torpedo tubes served little purpose, the gun having a restricted field of fire and being aimed by sight. Some of the 'V & W' Class had been rebuilt as 'fast escort vessels', which involved fitting a new bridge, removal of the torpedo tubes and original armament, and the installation of two twin 4-inch dual-purpose mountings. Fifteen destroyers were modified in this manner, together with one Scott Class leader, although by the end of June 1940 one had not been completed and two had been lost. The Hunt Class destroyers, which began to enter service in June 1940, were similarly armed, but with an additional four-barrelled 2-pdr anti-aircraft gun.

The rebuilt 'V & W's and the Hunts were fitted with HACS, or High-Angle Control System, in order to engage aircraft, as were larger vessels of cruiser size and above, but the choice of this equipment had, unfortunately, had a major detrimental effect on the ability of Royal Navy warships to protect themselves when under air attack. The Admiralty had underestimated the risk to surface ships from air attack, and the Navy gunnery school, HMS *Excellent*, did not have a specialist anti-aircraft department until as late as 1935.

Several years prior to this, the Admiralty had already adopted an anti-aircraft fire-control system significantly inferior to the tachymetric system selected by both the United States and German navies. This may well have been because the decline in British manufacturing capacity had also seen a commensurate decline in precision engineering. Even the less complex HACS system only belatedly went into production in any quantity in 1937, and the Admiralty had already complained late in that same year of the difficulty that had been experienced in finding firms willing to produce it. Consequently, several new cruisers entered service with no high-angle control system at all.

There were even serious bottlenecks in the manufacture of the anti-aircraft guns themselves. The King George V Class battleships were designed to carry eight 5.25-inch twin gun turrets as secondary armament, and the same turret provided the main armament of the Dido Class cruisers. This weapon could not be produced quickly enough for both and some of the cruisers entered service with four, rather than the designed five, turrets. Indeed, two were even fitted with four twin 4.5-inch mountings instead. In 1938, the Sub-Committee on Bombing and Anti-Aircraft Gunfire Experiments criticized the lack of facilities for research into Anti-Aircraft fire control, and in the previous year a radio-controlled target aircraft had circled the Home Fleet for over two hours without being hit! By the time the shortcomings of HACS had been discovered, it was too late to change to the superior tachymetric system, and, as previously stated, the skills and facilities no longer existed in Britain to produce it in any case.

Thus, at the commencement of the Second World War, a Royal Navy apparently inadequately equipped to defend itself against air attack would seem to have had small hope of operating safely within range of shore-based bombers. Perhaps the disciples of air power were right and the Royal Navy could no longer defend Britain effectively. The Norwegian campaign and the evacuation of the British Expeditionary Force from France were the first tests of this belief. The crucial question to be resolved was, therefore, whether the Luftwaffe would prove as destructive to the Royal Navy as the enthusiasts of air power believed.

The next chapters, therefore, will examine the structure, strength and role of the Royal Navy at the outbreak of war in some depth, and will then consider how its ships had actually performed against the Luftwaffe in the events leading up to the summer of 1940, i.e. the Norwegian campaign and the evacuation of the British Expeditionary Force and Allied troops from mainland Europe.

Chapter 10

The Royal Navy of 1939–1940

The English fleet had the advantage of looking back on a hundred years of proud tradition which must have given every man a sense of superiority based on the great deeds of the past.
Admiral Reinhard Scheer, commander of the
German High Seas Fleet at Jutland

To assess how well founded was the fear of British naval power which permeated the thinking of the German naval staff throughout the planning of Operation Sealion, it is necessary to look more closely at the organization and role of the Royal Navy of 1939–40, the resources available to it, and to assess what proportion of those resources could have been deployed against a German seaborne invasion.

Responsible as the Royal Navy was for the protection of a worldwide empire, at the beginning of the War its commands and vessels were widely spread. Map 3 shows the various 'stations' described below, and Map 4 the naval bases in home waters. The main fleets were the Home Fleet based at Scapa Flow and Rosyth, and the Mediterranean Fleet based at Alexandria and Malta, but there were also a number of separate stations such as the North Atlantic Station (based at Gibraltar), the South Atlantic Station (Freetown), the America and West Indies Station (Bermuda), the East Indies Station (Ceylon) and the China Station (Singapore/Hong Kong). In home waters, and therefore most directly relevant to Sealion, there were also a number of separate 'commands', these being Portsmouth, The Nore, Western Approaches, Rosyth, and Dover. In wartime some stations, such as the China Station in 1940, would obviously be

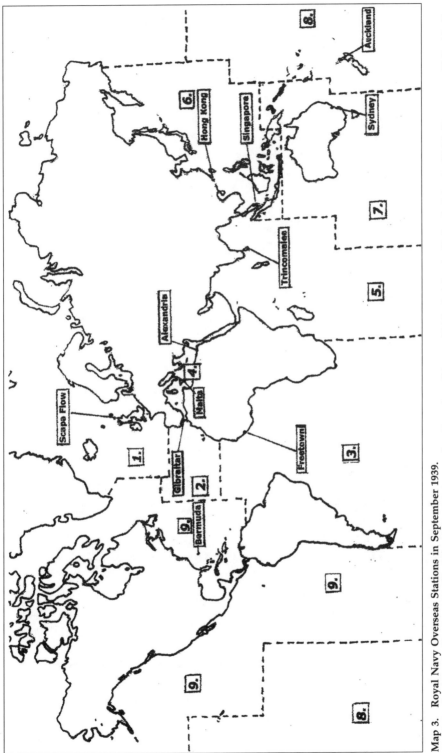

Map 3. Royal Navy Overseas Stations in September 1939.
(1) Home Commands (Portsmouth, The Nore, Western Approaches, Rosyth and Dover; (2) North Atlantic; (3) South Atlantic; (4) Mediterranean; (5) East Indies; (6) China; (7) Australia; (8) New Zealand and (9) America and West Indies.

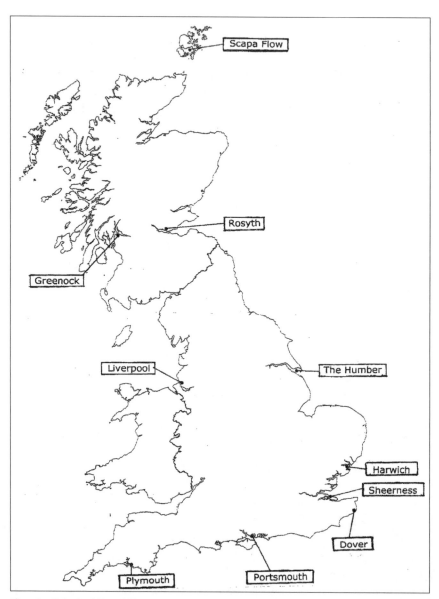

Map 4. Principal Royal Navy Bases in Home Waters, 1940.

virtually stripped of ships to reinforce others, and vessels would frequently transfer between stations and commands.

The role of the Royal Navy in the Second World War was what it had always been. It had four main duties:

1. To protect the trade routes to Great Britain. If these were severed, in simple terms, Britain would be starved into submission.
2. To close the sea routes used by the enemy.
3. To transport British (and Allied) armed forces to their theatres of operations.
4. To prevent an invasion of Great Britain.

Clearly, to carry out these various duties, the Royal Navy would need considerable resources, and in September 1939 its strength in vessels of destroyer size and above, including ships of the Royal Australian and Royal Canadian Navies, was as follows (ships operational, in reserve, or refitting):

Vessel Type	Number Available
Battleship	12
Battlecruiser	3
Aircraft Carrier	7
Fleet Cruiser	38
Small & Anti-Aircraft Cruiser	26
Destroyer & Destroyer Leader	193

This was an enormous fleet in simple numerical terms and it is easy now to forget just how big the Royal Navy of 1939 was. However, numbers can be misleading. Only two of the battleships and battle-cruisers were of post-First World War design, and of the thirteen older vessels, only four had been or were being extensively modernized. Only one carrier was new and naval aviation had been badly neglected during the years when it had been under RAF control.

Admiralty studies between the wars had estimated that a minimum of seventy cruisers were required for trade protection (the threat was believed to be from surface raiders rather than U-boats). The small cruisers of the 'C' and 'D' Classes, and the old Australian cruiser *Adelaide*, twenty-two in all, were still capable of protecting convoys from surface raiders, and seven 'C' Class had been converted into anti-aircraft cruisers for service with the main fleets, but there was a serious shortage of modern cruisers suitable for fleet operations.

Of the destroyers, eighty-one were of the standard 'A' to 'I' Classes, and thirty-two of the new 'Tribal', 'J' and 'K' Classes. There were also twelve First World War 'R' and 'S' Classes, fifty-eight 'V & W' Class and ten old destroyer leaders of the Scott and Shakespeare Classes. Most of these were fitted with a low-angle main armament of four 4-inch or 4.7-inch guns in the case of the 'V & W' and 'A' to 'I' Classes, eight 4.7-inch guns in the Tribal Class and six 4.7-inch guns in the 'J' and 'K' Classes, although a modest programme of converting nineteen 'V & W's and one Scott into fast escort vessels with four 4-inch high-angle guns had commenced in 1938.

By the middle of May 1940, the Royal Navy had successfully kept open the trade routes, inflicting heavy losses on the small German U-boat fleet. In September 1939 Germany had fifty-seven U-boats, and by the middle of May 1940, twenty-three had been lost. Even with new construction, the total U-boat fleet consisted of only forty-nine boats by May 1940.

Surface raiders had so far had little effect. Two of the three pocket battleships had sailed for the Atlantic late in August 1939, but one, *Graf Spee*, had been engaged by a British hunting group and scuttled off Montevideo in December; the second, *Deutschland*, had returned to Kiel in November. The third, *Admiral Scheer*, was refitting and would not be operational until mid to late September 1940.

The Royal Navy had also safely transported the British Expeditionary Force to France and had largely cleared the sea lanes of German shipping, much of which was either trapped in neutral ports, captured or sunk. The next four months would, however, impose enormous pressures which pre-war studies had never considered and for which the Royal Navy was ill-prepared.

Prior to the German invasion of Norway, one battleship (*Royal Oak*), one aircraft carrier (*Courageous*) and two destroyers had been lost to U-boats, three destroyers to mines, and one (*Bruce*) sunk as a target. In addition, one cruiser (*Exeter*) was under long-term repair following action damage at the Battle of the River Plate, and a second (*Belfast*) had been severely damaged by a mine. Between 8 April 1940 and 25 June 1940 (the invasion of Norway and the final evacuation of troops from France respectively), the demands placed upon the Navy had greatly increased, whilst the resources available to fulfill these demands had been seriously eroded. Evacuation of Allied troops from central Norway began as early as 30 April, and between then and 25 June three major evacuations had taken place, whilst a new enemy had emerged in the Mediterranean.

During this period, the Royal Navy evacuated 35,000 Allied troops from Norway, 338,226 troops from Dunkirk, and 191,870 troops and 35,000 civilians from other ports ranging from Le Havre right round to Bayonne and St Jean de Luz near the Spanish border. The Dunkirk evacuation, which will be described in a later chapter, was originally conceived as a two-day operation to evacuate some 45,000 men, but by its end it had involved several hundred vessels. (Winston Churchill gave a figure of 693 British vessels of all sizes, as well as 168 Allied ships, mainly French, Dutch, Belgian and Polish; Captain Roskill estimated 848 vessels in total; and L.F. Ellis 765 British vessels alone). In undertaking these evacuations, the vessels involved were frequently obliged to operate at low speed, close inshore and on occasions overcrowded with troops. Unable to use their speed and manoeuvrability, they were highly vulnerable to air attack. The actual losses of vessels of destroyer size and above suffered by the Royal Navy during the period 8 April to 25 June 1940, and the reasons for them, were:

	U-boat	S-boat	Bombing	Surface Action	Collision	Wrecking
Aircraft Carrier	0	0	0	1	0	0
Cruiser	0	0	1	0	0	1
Destroyer	1	1	9	5	1	0

On 10 June, two days after the evacuation of troops from Norway had been completed, and whilst the evacuations from southern France were still under way, Italy declared war. In 1937, when considering the possible 'worst case scenario' of war with Germany, Italy and Japan at the same time, the British Chiefs of Staff had concluded that, in the order of priorities should be the United Kingdom, the Far East (i.e. Singapore) and the Mediterranean, and that British interests in the Mediterranean must not be allowed to hinder the despatch of a strong naval force to the Far East.

Although by the middle of 1939 the need to maintain strong naval forces in the Mediterranean in the hope of deterring further German and Italian expansion had been accepted, the Chiefs of Staff still proposed that, if Japan declared war, powerful naval forces should be sent to the Far East, even though this would almost certainly hand control of the eastern Mediterranean over to Italy.

For the first nine months of the war, of course, both Japan and Italy had remained neutral, and as a result, by December 1939 the Mediterranean Fleet had been reduced to four old cruisers, five destroyers from the Royal Australian Navy, and two submarines. From March 1940, however, as the likelihood of Italy remaining neutral became increasingly doubtful, the fleet had received signifi-cant reinforcements. The Commander-in-Chief of the Mediter-ranean Fleet, Sir Andrew Cunningham, subsequently recorded in his autobiography that the fleet at Alexandria on 9 June 1940 con-sisted of four battleships, nine cruisers and some twenty-five destroyers. Within two weeks, a cruiser and a destroyer had been sunk.

One factor which even the 'worst case scenario' had not con-sidered, however, was the collapse of France, and on 17 June 1940, when this was clearly imminent, the First Sea Lord, Sir Dudley Pound, proposed abandoning the eastern Mediterranean completely and basing the Mediterranean Fleet at Gibraltar. This proposal was formally vetoed by Churchill on 23 June and a significant British naval presence would, therefore, remain in Alexandria.

Nevertheless, following the French armistice of 22 June 1940, it was clear that a strong Royal Navy force would need to be based at Gibraltar to replace the French Navy in the western Mediterranean. Force H, as this powerful squadron was known, came into being at the end of June, the first operation it carried out being the attack on the French Flotte de Raid, the warships at Mers-el-Kebir.

By the end of August, it consisted of one battlecruiser (*Renown*), one aircraft carrier (*Ark Royal*), one Town Class cruiser (*Sheffield*) and the 8th Destroyer Flotilla. A second flotilla (13th) was also based at Gibraltar under the control of Flag Officer North Atlantic.

If you add to the extra commitments above the half flotilla of old 'S' Class destroyers on the China Station, then the number of destroyers available for home defence had reduced significantly between May and July 1940. It was these vessels which, with cruiser support, would form the nucleus of the naval response to Operation Sealion, should it be launched.

Of the 193 destroyers available to the Royal Navy in September 1939, six had been lost prior to the invasion of Norway and a further eighteen between April and the end of June. The seven Royal

Canadian Navy destroyers operated in the North Atlantic, four old 'S' Class were on the China Station, and as described above, some forty destroyers were in the Mediterranean and at Gibraltar, with the Mediterranean Fleet and Force H. This left a total of around 115 destroyers in home waters, to which should be added six further destroyers of the 'Brazilian H' Class – vessels being built for the Brazilian Navy in British shipyards to the 'H' Class design, and which were taken over by the Royal Navy on the outbreak of war (one, *Havant*, had been sunk at Dunkirk) – and the first few Hunt Class escort destroyers, which were entering service from June 1940. The very flexibility of sea power, of course, makes it difficult to give precise numbers, as ships could change operating areas with great rapidity (for example, on 10 May the destroyer leader *Codrington* steamed from Scapa Flow to Dover in twenty-three hours), but at the end of June 1940 the destroyer force in home waters, including vessels refitting and under repair, and the Canadian destroyers, comprised:

Class	Numbers in Home Waters
R and S	8
V & W	49
Scott and Shakespeare	7
A to I	41
J, K and Tribal	17
Hunt	5

Immediately after the Dunkirk evacuation, however, the Royal Navy had only seventy-four undamaged destroyers operational, although most of the damaged vessels were quickly back in service. For example, of the thirteen destroyers of the 'A' to 'I' and 'J' Classes (the newer destroyers) which survived Dunkirk, all but three of the nine which sustained damage were repaired by 18 June. Of the other three, *Impulsive* completed repairs on 10 July, and *Ivanhoe* by 28 August. The last of the three, *Jaguar*, completed repairs at Immingham and joined the Mediterranean Fleet in November.

If a realistic assessment of whether Operation Sealion could have succeeded is to be made, however, then the worldwide dispositions of Royal Navy warships, and the rights and wrongs of Mediterranean strategy, are not, in the final analysis, relevant. What is critical is how those vessels which were allocated to the defence of the South Coast would have performed in the face of heavy Luftwaffe attack, assuming that when the invasion was launched German air power would have been concentrated over the Channel to protect it. The only way to reach any conclusion must surely be to examine what had happened on those occasions in the twelve months leading up to September 1940 when German air power and British sea power had come into conflict – and the first of these was the Norwegian campaign.

Chapter 11

Early Encounters and the Campaign in Norway

A fleet had been sacrificed to gain a base, but the base had little value without the fleet.
Dr S.T. Possony, United States Naval Institute Proceedings,
July 1946

In view of the known problems with the High-Angle Control System for naval anti-aircraft guns, and the obsolescent nature of the aircraft available to the Fleet Air Arm, it is perhaps understandable that the professional head of the Royal Navy, the First Sea Lord, Sir Dudley Pound, should have been pessimistic about the threat to the fleet from the air. As early as August 1939 he was writing to the Commander-in-Chief in the Mediterranean, Sir Andrew Cunningham, that he did not think the Mediterranean Fleet's aircraft carrier, *Glorious*, would last long when war came, although Cunningham took a more optimistic view, believing that 'ships moving at high speed and with full freedom of manoeuvre are not easy targets.' Pound wrote to Cunningham again in November, and once more expressed doubts about the ability even of battleships to stand up to air attack. Late in May 1940, shortly before the entry of Italy into the War, a further letter from Pound stated: 'The one lesson we have learnt here is that it is essential to have fighter protection over the fleet whenever they are within range of enemy bombers.'

Ironically, despite the pessimism with which Pound viewed the vulnerability of the Royal Navy to air attack, the first major casualty of the War, the aircraft carrier HMS *Courageous*, was lost to a submarine attack, being torpedoed and sunk on 17 September 1939 in the Bristol Channel when detached from the Home Fleet and forming, with two destroyers, a hunting group to search for U-boats. Three days earlier, HMS *Ark Royal*, as part of a second hunting group, had also been attacked by a U-boat, but the torpedoes exploded prematurely and escorting destroyers sank the U-boat. This unwise deployment of fleet carriers was abruptly terminated after the loss of *Courageous*, but of even greater concern, although unknown at the time, was the fact that the whereabouts of *Courageous* was known to U-boat command because B-Dienst of German Naval intelligence had broken the Royal Navy's codes.

Indeed, as early as the Abyssinian crisis of 1935–6, B-Dienst had been able to track the movements of the Mediterranean Fleet. After the evacuation from Norway Sir Charles Forbes was to write critically of the poor quality of British air reconnaissance, believing that German air reconnaissance had been able to track the operations of his fleet during the Norwegian campaign, when in fact much of the information came from intercepted and decoded Royal Navy signals. Only on 20 August 1940 did the Royal Navy change its codes.

Shortly after the loss of *Courageous*, on 26 September, the first significant clash between the Royal Navy and the Luftwaffe took place, when a task force including *Ark Royal* and *Hood* was sent to the Heligoland Bight to support the withdrawal on the surface of a damaged submarine, *Spearfish*. *Ark Royal* was nearly hit and *Hood* received a glancing blow from attacks by Ju 88s of I/KG 30. A second bomber force, from I/KG 26, was also sent to attack the 2nd Cruiser Squadron, which was providing close cover for the submarine, but failed to make contact.

For the next six months, until the end of March 1940, warship losses were as a result of U-boat attack, mines, or, in one case, collision. In April, however, the Germans launched Operation Weserubung, the invasion of Norway, which, though a strategic success, led also to the destruction or at least crippling of most of the major surface units of the German Navy.

The Norwegian campaign has been seen by many experts as the first major test of strength between sea and air power, although the amateurish way in which the Allied operations on land were planned and conducted was probably the deciding factor in the outcome of the conflict. At this point, reference to Map 5 is essential

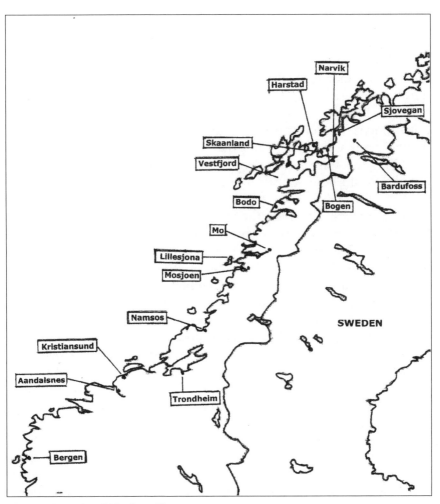

Map 5. Central and Northern Norway.

for following the military and naval operations in detail, although it must be borne in mind at all times that the map cannot convey the often severe weather conditions and the difficult terrain, which both sides encountered.

Operation Weserubung (literally, 'Exercise Weser') required the commitment of most of the large vessels of the German Navy. Although the first major clash took place on 8 April 1940, the events leading to it can be traced back to mid-September 1939. During the winter months, iron ore from northern Sweden, on which the German steel industry depended, was shipped through the

Norwegian port of Narvik, and down to Germany through Norwegian coastal waters. On 19 September 1939, Winston Churchill, then First Lord of the Admiralty, had sought to persuade the Cabinet that Norwegian territorial waters should be mined by the Royal Navy if the Norwegians could not be persuaded to undertake this themselves, as they had done in 1918. The Chamberlain government was reluctant to violate Norwegian neutrality in such a manner, but Churchill, tenacious in this as in most things, was unwilling to let the matter drop, arguing that the loss of the iron-ore supply would have a critical effect on the German ability to wage war.

By December, however, the mining of Norwegian coastal waters had been overtaken by a much greater scheme, involving the despatch of British and French troops to northern Norway, and then to the ore fields around Gallivare in Sweden. The Supreme War Council in Paris, who on 19 December recommended a force of around 4,000 men, even hoped, optimistically, that Norway and Sweden would consent to this action, if the Allies portrayed it as providing support for them against potential Soviet aggression, the Soviet invasion of Finland having commenced on 30 November. However unrealistic this belief might have been, Churchill and the Chiefs of Staff were enthusiastic in their support, although the Chiefs of Staff did not feel that the Allies would be able to land forces in Narvik before late March.

The War Cabinet discussed the matter early in January 1940 and then hesitated for three months or so. On 12 March it finally decided that troops should be landed at Narvik, and subsequently at Trondheim, only to find that on the following day Finland made peace with the Soviet Union. On 14 March, the War Cabinet cancelled the operation.

On the German side, Admiral Raeder had been expounding the virtues of Norway as a base for German naval units since October 1939, and in January 1940 Hitler ordered OKW to begin detailed planning for either a full-scale invasion or a much smaller operation in support of a coup d'etat by a Norwegian politician, Vidkun Quisling. Shortly afterwards, German suspicions that the Allies had their own plans for Norway were heightened when, on 16 February 1940, the British destroyer *Cossack* entered Jossingfjord and rescued almost 300 British merchant seamen from vessels sunk by the *Admiral Graf Spee*, who were being held captive aboard the German supply tanker *Altmark*, which was sheltering inside Norwegian waters.

On 21 February, six divisions were allocated to the operation, which was originally scheduled for 7 April, but was subsequently postponed for two days until the 9th. Between 3 April and 7 April, twenty-six supply ships and tankers sailed from German ports, with a second wave of eleven supply ships sailing on 8 April. The task forces for Narvik and Trondheim sailed early on 7 April, followed on 8 April by three further groups heading for Bergen, Kristiansand and Oslo. On 8 April, there were over one hundred German ships off the Norwegian coast, including two battleships, one pocket battleship, two heavy and four light cruisers, fourteen destroyers and eight torpedo boats, virtually the whole operational strength of the German Navy.

In the light of all this naval activity, the failure of British Intelligence to provide adequate warning was remarkable. In February and March 1940, the British embassy in Stockholm had been receiving reports from Swedish, American and Rumanian sources that a major German operation against Norway was imminent, and both Bomber Command and Coastal Command aircraft had reported considerable activity in German ports early in April. Unfortunately, the Admiralty Naval Intelligence Department at the time had not recovered from years of disorganization and failed to co-ordinate the information being received from various sources. It may even have been possible that intelligence was only believed if it corresponded with the preconceived notions of those interpreting it. Thus, even though Military Intelligence had identified the six divisions in north-west Germany, the idea of an attack on Norway was discounted because six divisions was believed to be too small a force to undertake such a campaign.

This is not to say that, since 14 March, the Allies had been completely inactive. On 28 March, the Royal Navy was finally given instructions to mine Norwegian waters in an operation, code-named Wilfred, which was to take place on 5 April (subsequently postponed to 8 April). Although three separate forces were originally allocated, only the minelaying off Bodø took place, involving four minelaying destroyers escorted by four further destroyers, with the battlecruiser *Renown* and her screen of four destroyers providing cover. At the same time, in an operation named Plan R4, six battalions of troops were to be ready to occupy Narvik, Trondheim,

Stavanger and Bergen as soon as the Germans retaliated to the minelaying, as they would surely do if their supplies of iron ore were threatened.

The troops for Bergen and Stavanger, four battalions in all, were aboard four cruisers held ready at Rosyth, but neither these nor the transports laden with the remaining troops were to sail until a German attack had commenced.

When, on the afternoon of 7 April, twelve Blenheims of Bomber Command attacked part of the German striking force, the information was passed on to Sir Charles Forbes, still waiting at Scapa Flow, by the Director of Naval Intelligence, with the comment that the report was 'of doubtful value', and even then only after a delay of four hours. Forbes did, however, take the Home Fleet to sea at once, although, in common with Churchill and Pound, he believed that the force attacked by the Blenheims constituted a new attempt by *Scharnhorst* and *Gneisenau* to break out into the North Atlantic. Consequently his course was intended to intercept this supposed operation, which meant that the Home Fleet would be unable to challenge the German units heading for central and southern Norway. Indeed, the only Royal Navy surface forces between the German invasion force and Norway were *Renown* and her screen, and the eight destroyers off Bodø.

On the morning of 8 April two events occurred which should have left no room for further doubt: the destroyer *Glowworm*, detached from *Renown's* screen to search for a man overboard, encountered the German Trondheim invasion group and was able to transmit an enemy report before being sunk (but not before she had rammed and damaged the heavy cruiser *Admiral Hipper*), and the Polish submarine *Orzel* sank the German transport *Rio de Janeiro*, whose survivors, many of whom wore German Army uniforms, informed their Norwegian rescuers that they were heading for Bergen to help defend Norway from British attack.

Upon receipt of the enemy report from *Glowworm*, Forbes commenced a redeployment of his forces, sending the battlecruiser *Repulse* (*Renown's* unmodernized sister ship), the light cruiser *Penelope* and four destroyers to the aid of *Glowworm*, but a report from a reconnaissance aircraft catapulted from one of Forbes's ships, received at 1430 hrs, of a battleship, two cruisers, and two destroyers steering west caused him to alter course to the north-west for a time, before turning south. The ships observed by the aircraft were actually *Hipper* and her destroyers, and the westerly course was simply a delaying tactic, so that the attack on Trondheim would take place at the scheduled time.

The cumulative effect of the original wrong interpretation of the available intelligence, resulting in the faulty disposition of most of the Home Fleet, effectively gave the German naval forces a clear run at their objectives. To further compound the errors, the destroyers off Bodø were ordered by the Admiralty to join *Renown*, thus leaving Narvik unguarded, and the four cruisers laden with troops for Plan R4 were ordered, again by the Admiralty, to disembark the troops and join the Home Fleet. Plan R4 was, therefore, abandoned at the very moment when the situation for which it had been conceived came about!

However the strategic situation might have been misinterpreted or mishandled, the reaction of individual units of the Royal Navy when they did come into contact with German forces was aggressive. *Glowworm* has already been referred to above, and Vice Admiral Whitworth in *Renown* also did not hesitate to engage a more powerful force when, early in the morning of 9 April, the battleships *Scharnhorst* and *Gneisenau* were encountered off Vestfjord. *Gneisenau* was hit three times but the German ships were able to escape in the stormy weather conditions.

Nevertheless, German troops had reached their landing areas largely unmolested, including some 2,000 mountain troops landed in Narvik later on 9 April from ten German destroyers. The presence of these destroyers, and the fact that their escape was delayed by their inability to refuel quickly from their oiler, the whaler *Jan Wellem*, led to the first and second battles of Narvik, which were to have a major influence on Operation Sealion. Although these actions do not shed any light on the theme of this and subsequent chapters, which is an assessment of the ability of the Royal Navy of 1940 to operate effectively in the face of air attack, it is difficult to overestimate their consequences, and they deserve at least a brief mention.

The first battle took place on 10 April. The commander of the 2nd Destroyer Flotilla, Captain Warburton-Lee, whose ships had been in company with the battlecruiser *Renown*, was ordered by Vice Admiral Whitworth to establish a patrol line at the entrance to Vestfjord to prevent a German landing at Narvik. In fact, by the time Warburton-Lee had established his patrol line at 0930 hrs on the 9th, the German destroyers had already reached Narvik. Unaware of this, the C-in-C Home Fleet, Sir Charles Forbes, instructed Warburton-Lee to despatch some of his destroyers to Narvik to ensure that no landing took place. Subsequently, Warburton-Lee received a signal direct from the Admiralty, informing him of a small German landing at Narvik from one ship, and giving him the opportunity to use his discretion to sink the ship and recapture Narvik. Warburton-Lee took the four 'H' Class destroyers of his flotilla into Vestfjord and learned from the Norwegian pilot station that at least six German destroyers and a U-boat were at Narvik, and the town was heavily garrisoned with German troops. This was duly reported to the Admiralty at 1751 hrs, and Warburton-Lee stated his intention to attack at dawn on 10 April.

By this time a fifth destroyer from his flotilla (*Hostile*), had joined him, and Whitworth in *Renown*, concerned about the weakness of Warburton-Lee's five destroyers in the face of six larger German vessels, ordered (at 1959 hrs) the light cruiser *Penelope*, together with four powerful 'Tribal' and 'K' Class destroyers, to support him. Unfortunately, this intervention by the Admiralty had, not for the first time and certainly not for the last during this campaign, confused the issue, and Whitworth subsequently, at 2038 hrs, cancelled these reinforcements, fearing that his orders may have conflicted with Admiralty intentions of which he was as yet unaware.

In brief, the British attack began at around 0430 hrs on the 10th. The five destroyers (*Hardy*, *Hunter*, *Havock*, *Hotspur* and *Hostile*) found themselves in action with ten larger and better armed German vessels, but for the loss of *Hardy* and *Hunter* were able to sink one, cripple a second so badly that she sank on the following day, damage three more, and sink seven ore-carriers and a supply ship. Warburton-Lee died aboard *Hardy* and was awarded a posthumous Victoria Cross.

The second battle took place on 13 April. The remaining eight German destroyers, of which only four were operational, the others being either damaged or suffering from a variety of mechanical defects, were either sunk or damaged and forced to scuttle by a powerful task force consisting of the battleship *Warspite* and nine destroyers. In addition, a U-boat, U-64, was bombed and sunk by a Swordfish aircraft catapulted from *Warspite*.

Thus, in two actions, the total operational strength of the German destroyer force had been reduced by 50 per cent. Had these vessels been available to the Sealion planners, then they could have provided at least some sort of credible surface protection for the invasion convoys. Without them, and with the additional losses in larger ships inflicted upon the German Navy during the Norwegian campaign, this possibility was denied to them. It may perhaps be overstating the case to suggest that the Battles of Narvik made Operation Sealion an impossibility, but their effects were very great indeed.

From the point of view of the ability of the Royal Navy to survive and function in the face of German air power, the subsequent land campaign is not directly relevant, but the performance of the Navy in this, its first prolonged encounter with the Luftwaffe, certainly is. Some of the details of the land campaign which involved naval support have, however, been outlined below, and serve to demonstrate the shambolic nature of the whole Allied operation. Although the later stages of the Norwegian campaign overlapped with the evacuations from France, it is easier to look at the two events separately.

When Forbes sailed with the Home Fleet late on 7 April, he chose not to take his only available aircraft carrier, *Furious*, with him, and it was only at 1630 hrs the following day that the Admiralty ordered her to sail from the Clyde, and only at 0400 hrs on the 9th that she flew on her two Swordfish Squadrons (816 and 818), but not her Skua Squadron (801). As a result of this delay, the carrier only met up with the main fleet late on the 9th. By this time, Forbes had ordered an attack on the German force attacking Bergen; four cruisers (*Manchester*, *Southampton*, *Glasgow* and *Sheffield*) and eleven destroyers had been despatched to carry this out. The operation, which had it taken place would almost certainly not only have destroyed the German cruisers *Köln* and *Konigsberg*, but also the supply ships and transports carrying the German 69th Division, was cancelled over the head of Forbes by the Admiralty, who feared (wrongly) that the Bergen shore batteries were in German hands. This decision, taken by an Admiralty remote from the scene of operations, was to have an adverse effect on the conduct and outcome of the campaign.

On the afternoon of the same day, Forbes's forces came under heavy attack by aircraft of Fliegerkorps X, when forty-one Heinkel He IIIs of KG (Kampfgeschwader) 26, and forty-seven Junkers Ju 88s of KG 30 attacked for around three hours from 1400 hrs, just missing three cruisers and sinking the destroyer *Gurkha* when she left the

101

destroyer screen. The shortcomings of HACS were clearly demonstrated in this action – some ships expended more than a third of their anti-aircraft ammunition, whilst only succeeding in shooting down four attacking aircraft. As a result of this attack, Forbes decided that the Home Fleet should not operate within range of shore-based aircraft.

The Allied response to the successful German assault consisted of troop landings at Namsos and Aandalsnes, in order to capture Trondheim by means of a pincer movement, and landings in the Narvik area. The forces involved were poorly equipped and the operations themselves ill-conceived from the start, but their dependence on the Royal Navy for the initial landings, supply and eventual evacuation was absolute, and again brought the clash of air and sea power into sharp focus.

The Namsos operation began on 14 April, when the cruisers *Glasgow* and *Sheffield* supported the landing of 350 marines and seamen from destroyers. The following day the destroyer *Somali* was attacked by the Luftwaffe whilst supporting the landings, but not damaged.

On the morning of 16 April the Hallamshire Battalion of the York and Lancaster Regiment, part of 146 Brigade, a Territorial brigade which had originally been part of the proposed Plan R4, were transferred from the liner *Chobry* at Lillesjona, some one hundred miles north of Namsos, into three destroyers and landed near Namsos. *Chobry* and a second liner, *Empress of Australia*, were bombed whilst at anchor, but not damaged. A second battalion was transferred from *Empress of Australia* to *Chobry*, losing much of its equipment and ammunition in the process, and half of the third battalion transferred into two destroyers.

By the evening of 17 April, the whole of 146 Brigade's three battalions had been landed. In an attempt to close Stavanger airfield, which was in use by the Luftwaffe, the heavy cruiser *Suffolk* was despatched to bombard it. The bombardment was unsuccessful and *Suffolk* was under continuous air attack for seven hours, as a result of which she arrived back at Scapa Flow with her quarterdeck awash. On 19/20 April four French transport vessels, escorted by the French cruiser *Emile Bertin*, the anti-aircraft cruiser *Cairo* and French destroyers, landed 4,000 ski troops of the Chasseurs Alpins, although in keeping with the amateurish nature of the whole campaign, their skis had been left behind, to follow in a later convoy.

This force was also attacked by the Luftwaffe and the French cruiser suffered damage from one bomb. On the morning of 20 April, however, a heavy raid by over sixty aircraft severely damaged the port facilities at Namsos.

On 27 April, the decision to abandon the campaign in central Norway was taken and a force of three cruisers (*Devonshire*, *York* and the French *Montcalm*), together with nine destroyers and three French transport ships, was despatched to carry out the evacuation. On 30 April, the sloop *Bittern*, transferring French troops to Mosjoen, north of Namsos, was damaged by bombing and sunk by torpedo from the destroyer *Janus*. The evacuation took place on the night of 2/3 May, with the destroyer *Afridi* being the last to leave. The squadron came under heavy air attack by Junkers Ju 88s and Junkers Ju 87s from 0800 hrs on the 3rd. At 1000 hrs the French destroyer *Bison* was hit and badly damaged, and the destroyers *Afridi*, *Grenade* and *Imperial* stayed behind to rescue survivors, leaving the scene at 1130 hrs. Just before catching up with the main force, *Afridi* was hit by two bombs and sank at 1445 hrs, survivors being rescued by *Imperial* and *Griffin*. The main convoy, with the troops from Namsos on board, successfully repelled attacks by over fifty aircraft and reached Scapa Flow on 6 May.

The southern part of the Trondheim pincer was equally badly planned. The first troops despatched were 148 Brigade which, like 146 Brigade at Namsos, was a Territorial brigade. Also like 146 Brigade, they were inadequately equipped and poorly trained for the task. One regiment, the 1/5th Leicesters, had embarked in the cruiser *Devonshire* on 7 April, and almost immediately trans-shipped to the liner *Orion*. They then disembarked from *Orion*, and on 16 April half of the battalion sailed for Norway aboard the anti-aircraft cruisers *Curacoa* and *Carlisle*.

The other half of the battalion sailed two days later, aboard the trooper *Magnus*, but lost its transport when the cargo ship carrying it was torpedoed in the same convoy. The second battalion, the 1/8th Sherwood Foresters, suffered similarly, being embarked in a cruiser, disembarked and then split between three vessels (the cruisers *Arethusa* and *Galatea*, and the trooper *Orion*). In their case, however, the *Orion* contingent was transferred over to the cruisers whilst at sea. The result of all this activity was to ensure the loss of much essential equipment and stores, and what remained was hopelessly mixed up.

Before these forces arrived, however, a force of marines and seamen, some 680 strong, had been landed at Aandalsnes from four Royal Navy sloops on 17 April, while the first half of the 1/5th Leicesters and the Sherwood Foresters were landed the following day, their convoy having been attacked by the Luftwaffe without suffering damage. The two anti-aircraft cruisers stayed to provide protection for the base at Aandalsnes and *Curacoa* was damaged on the 24th. The convoy with the remainder of the Leicesters arrived at Aandalsnes on 21 April. On 23 April two battalions of regular troops from 15 Brigade arrived at Aandalsnes in the cruisers *Glasgow* and *Sheffield*, with six destroyers. The third battalion arrived on 26 April.

As already noted, however, the decision to abandon the operation around Trondheim was taken on 27 April, and commenced on the night of 30 April/1 May, when over 2,000 men were evacuated in the cruisers *Sheffield*, *Galatea* and *Arethusa*, with six destroyers. The remainder of the force were subsequently ferried to the cruisers *Manchester*, *Curlew*, *Calcutta* and *Birmingham* by destroyers, with the last to leave being a Royal Engineers demolition party which boarded the sloop *Auckland* early on 3 May. The evacuation had been under sustained air attack throughout, but no ships were sunk or damaged.

Military operations in the Narvik area commenced on 14 April, when Major General Mackesy, with two rifle companies of the Scots Guards and a number of staff officers, arrived at Harstad in the Lofotens in the cruiser *Southampton*. His instructions were to organize his force at Harstad and produce a plan to expel the Germans from Narvik, but consultations with officers of the Norwegian Army persuaded him to land the two rifle companies at Sjovegan, northeast of Narvik, to reinforce the Norwegian 6th Division which was defending the approaches to the airfield at Bardufoss.

At around the same time, the naval force commander, Admiral of the Fleet the Earl of Cork and Orrery, arrived in the cruiser *Aurora*, and received a signal from Vice Admiral Whitworth, commanding the battlecruiser squadron, that the German forces in Narvik were demoralized following the Battles of Narvik, which had resulted not only in the loss of the entire German force of ten destroyers, but also of the ammunition supply and motor transport for the troops on shore.

Cork concluded that an immediate assault by the Scots Guards rifle companies supported by 200 marines could capture Narvik at once, and signalled for Mackesy to meet him. Unfortunately, by the time *Southampton* received the signal, the Guards had already begun to disembark, and Mackesy decided to continue with the disembarkation. This initial disagreement rather set the tone for the whole operation. Having met for the first time at Harstad on the 15th, Cork and Mackesy argued frequently, the situation not being helped by the fact that the two men were in joint command and expected to work together to plan operations.

Also on the 15th, 24 Guards Brigade arrived at Harstad in three liners, escorted by the battleship *Valiant* and nine destroyers. Cork once again argued for an immediate attack, but Mackesy refused. As the Guards' artillery had not yet arrived, the Guards themselves had had no Arctic warfare training and the whole area was under a deep layer of snow, it is surely hard to criticize him!

On 18 April, the training cruiser *Vindictive* transported the Irish Guards from Harstad to Bogen, where they were ferried ashore by Norwegian fishing boats. A Luftwaffe attack caused no casualties but delayed movement for a time. Two days later, Lord Cork was made supreme commander, and an assault on Narvik was planned for 24 April, preceded by a bombardment by *Warspite*, three cruisers and eight destroyers.

Further heavy snow prevented the attack, but the bombardment took place, with limited effect as snow still obscured potential targets. Further troop reinforcements arrived on 28 April, and on 6 and 9 May, in the form of three battalions of French Chasseurs Alpins, two battalions of the French Foreign Legion, and four Polish battalions, together with a French tank company. On 6 May, eight 3.7- inch anti-aircraft guns arrived. Eventually, Allied forces around Narvik were built up to 30,000 men. By this time, however, the evacuations from central Norway had taken place, which enabled both the Luftwaffe and the Royal Navy to concentrate their efforts in the north, and on 4 May the Polish destroyer *Grom* was sunk.

Early on 13 May, the battleship *Resolution*, accompanied by the cruisers *Aurora* and *Effingham*, five destroyers and four assault craft, embarked the two Foreign Legion battalions and bombarded Bjerkvik, after which the Legion landed successfully. As part of a regrouping of the remaining Allied troops in Norway, the decision was made to move 24 Guards Brigade further north to Bodø, some 160 miles from Harstad, and on 11 May 1st Scots Guards were taken to Mo, 60 miles south of Bodø, by the cruiser *Enterprise*. 1st Irish

Guards sailed from Harstad to Bodø in the Polish liner *Chobry* on 14 May, but early on the morning of 15 May the liner was bombed by a Heinkel He 111 and abandoned. The Irish Guards were taken from the liner by the destroyer *Wolverine* and the sloop *Stork*, and returned to Harstad. The third battalion, 2nd South Wales Borderers, sailed in the cruiser *Effingham* early on 17 May. In order to avoid air attack, the cruiser deviated from the usual route and struck a shoal at 23 knots, some 12 miles from Bodø.

As most of their equipment had been lost with the cruiser, however, the troops were returned to Harstad in the destroyer *Echo* and transferred to the *Coventry* to enable *Echo* to return to assist *Effingham*, and to collect her crew. Both battalions were now seriously short of equipment, and although two companies of the Irish Guards were taken to Bodø by destroyer on 19 May, the rest of the battalion took three days to re-equip; the last companies of the South Wales Borderers did not reach Bodø until 25 May.

By now, however, events elsewhere had begun to take ships away from the Home Fleet. On 24 April *Warspite* was withdrawn for service with the Mediterranean Fleet, and by mid-May an anti-aircraft cruiser and seventeen destroyers had followed. Earlier on 7 May, two cruisers were transferred to Sheerness, and a destroyer flotilla to Harwich. After the German blitzkrieg of 10 May, as the crisis deepened, further vessels departed – three destroyers to the Humber on 18 May, and two cruisers to the same base on the 26th. On the same day, the anti-aircraft cruiser *Curlew* was bombed and sunk by Junkers Ju 88s of KG 30 off Skaanland.

By 23 May, evacuation was decided upon, although the final assault on and capture of Narvik still took place on 28 May in order to conceal this, and was supported by the anti-aircraft cruisers *Cairo* and *Coventry*, the 6-inch gun cruiser *Southampton* and five destroyers. *Cairo* was hit by two bombs and at 0630 hrs Lord Cork withdrew the main naval force after receiving assurances from the commander of the assault troops (General Bethouart) that his troops were firmly established. Two destroyers and the *Coventry* were left behind to provide gunfire support if needed, but Narvik was abandoned by the remaining German troops around noon.

The troops in the Bodø area commenced evacuation in destroyers on 29 May, and on the following night the Irish Guards embarked in the destroyers *Fame* and *Firedrake*. The Scots Guards and the South Wales Borderers were embarked in three destroyers (*Echo, Arrow* and *Delight*) on 31 May, transferred to the liner *Franconia* and taken to Harstad. Cork had fifteen troopships, protected by *Coventry*, available to evacuate both Harstad and Narvik, and a convoy of stores and the few French tanks sailed at the end of May.

The main evacuation was in two convoys, the remaining troops at Narvik being ferried to Harstad by destroyers where two troopships at a time were loaded. The first convoy (*Vindictive*, one destroyer and six liners) left early on 7 June, and the second (four liners, three smaller vessels, five destroyers and the cruisers *Southampton* and *Coventry*) on the morning of 9 June. Later on the same day, the aircraft carrier *Glorious*, which had flown on the surviving Hurricanes and Gladiators of 46 and 263 Squadrons, and her escorting destroyers *Ardent* and *Acasta*, were sunk by the *Scharnhorst* and *Gneisenau* after sailing on independently ahead of the main convoy, apparently because *Glorious*'s commanding officer was eager to get back to Scapa Flow in order to court-martial his Commander (Air).

The conclusion commonly drawn from the Norwegian campaign was that it demonstrated the undermining of sea power by air power – the view expressed by, among others, the author of the campaign history, Dr T.K. Derry, the author of *The War at Sea*, Captain S.W. Roskill, and by Field Marshal Alanbrooke.

A paper presented to the International Commission for Military History in 1975 by Professor Riste, a leading Norwegian expert on the campaign, however, argued that the real lesson was not so much the effectiveness of air power against warships, but the speed and mobility which it imposed on and contributed to land warfare. Certainly, the psychological impact of German air superiority was considerable, a typical example being the abandonment of their steel helmets by some of 146 Brigade for fear of being spotted from the air. Lieutenant General C.J.E. Auchinleck, who took over from Mackesy on 13 May, pointed to the effects of German air supremacy in his report of 19 June 1940. It was used not only to support ground troops by low-level and bombing attacks, but also to supply advance units and to land combat troops by parachute.

Liddell Hart was not convinced of the undermining of sea power, but he did believe that the Luftwaffe was the decisive factor in the campaign – by undermining morale, disrupting the flow of supplies along narrow roads and forcing the frequent relocation of battalion headquarters. Actual casualties from the air were, in fact, not great.

The South Wales Borderers, for example, during four weeks in the Narvik area, lost three killed and eight wounded to air attack.

Intriguingly, the German view of the campaign was that the Luftwaffe was less effective against naval targets than had been expected. In contrast, after the first attack by Fliegerkorps X on 9 April, Forbes concluded that the Home Fleet could not operate within range of land-based aircraft. The outline of warship operations given above, however, surely suggests that this was not necessarily the case. On most occasions warships were able to operate successfully, if not always freely, often in waters where their freedom of manoeuvre was seriously restricted. Obviously, the element of risk always existed, but the Norwegian campaign seems not to have demonstrated that air power had superceded sea power, but rather that air power could influence the outcome of a land campaign in a manner that naval operations could not.

In Norway, only sea power, whether British or German, could have transported men and equipment in the quantities necessary, and maintained their supplies. Air power in 1940 could indeed transport troops, but not heavy equipment, weapons or vehicles. It could play an important, possibly even crucial, role in the land battle, but whilst it could harass and impede naval operations, the events of the Norwegian campaign had not demonstrated that it could prevent them.

Perhaps the final words should be the comments made by a Royal Navy destroyer captain after the campaign was over, and quoted by Captain Roskill in *The Navy at War* (Roskill 1960):

It is very far from being a triumph of air over sea. In spite of the total absence of air cover, short nights and perfect weather, I do not think any essential sea or landing operation has not come off. And escort vessels, solitary and stationary in fjords, have been constantly maintained. But of course you can't go on for ever in what amounts to enemy coastal waters if he has all the air; and the wretched and undefended troops can't go on at all.

HMS *Venomous*. During the Dunkirk Evacuation, *Venomous* rescued 4,140 men, making five trips. In September 1940, she was part of the 18th Destroyer Flotilla, based at Harwich. As a 'Modified W' Class destroyer, she was armed with four 4.7-inch guns, two 2-pdr anti-aircraft guns, and six 21-inch torpedo tubes. She was over twenty-one years old by September 1940 but, in common with her sisters, was still a potent weapon against an invasion fleet without surface escorts. *(IWM Neg. No. 56091)*

HMS *Vimiera*. Originally a 'V' Class destroyer, *Vimiera* had been rebuilt between June 1939 and January 1940 as a 'Wair' anti-aircraft escort vessel. The photographs show the extent of the conversion, which involved the replacement of four low-angle, 4-inch guns by two twin, 4-inch, dual-purpose mountings, the removal of both sets of torpedo tubes and the construction of a new bridge. The unsatisfactory HACS control system for the guns can be seen at the rear of the bridge. The only close-range armament consisted of two sets of the ineffective quadruple .5-inch machine guns. In September 1940, *Vimiera*, although part of the Rosyth Escort Force, was actually based at Sheerness. *(IWM Neg. Nos. FL22801 & FL5533)*

Admiral Hipper. During the summer of 1940, *Hipper* was the only major German warship in operational condition. This pre-war photograph shows her before she was fitted with a funnel cap and a lengthened, raked bow. She was an elegant, powerful warship, hindered by unreliable engines. Her role in Sealion would have been to divert the British Home Fleet away from the landings by operating in the vicinity of Iceland. *(IWM Neg. No. HU1009)*

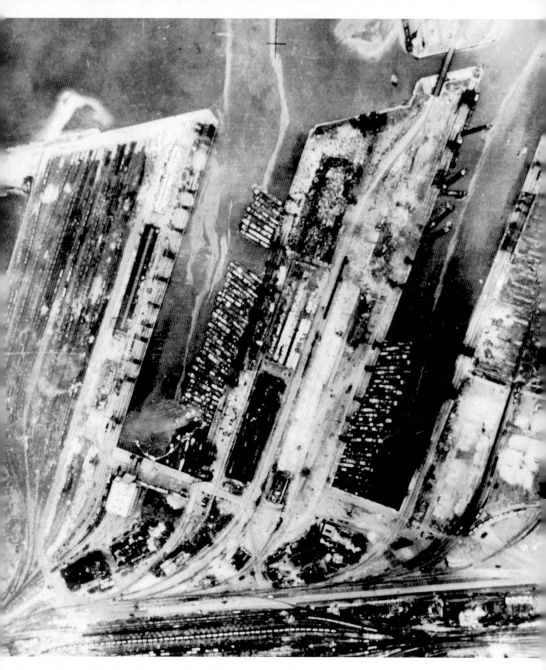

Proof of intent? Aerial photographs of Operation Sealion barge concentrations at Dunkirk. By September 1940 the German naval staff had assembled sufficient shipping to transport the invasion force, and, if Sealion had gone ahead, 150 of these barges would have sailed on the afternoon of 20 September 1940 carrying leading elements of the 17th and 35th Infantry Divisions. *(IWM Neg. No. C1819)*

...nilar concentrations of barges at Boulogne. The largest of the invasion fleets, including 330 barges, ...uld have sailed from here with the 26th and 34th Infantry Divisions, to attack the Bexhill–Eastbourne ...ding area. *(IWM Neg. MH6657).*

HMS *Garth*. One of the first Hunt Class escort destroyers to commission, *Garth*, together with her sister *Fernie*, was escorting coastal convoy CE9 when the Gris Nez battery fired at them (and missed) on 12 August 1940. *Garth* was armed with two twin, dual-purpose, 4-inch guns and a four-barrelled, 2-pdr, close-range mounting. In September 1940, she was part of 21st Destroyer Flotilla, at Sheerness. *(IWM Neg. No. FL13374)*

Two of the motley collection of vessels hastily converted for use as part of the Sealion fleet. The 37mm anti-aircraft gun mounted on the deck of the coaster would have been of little use against a determined attack by Royal Navy destroyers and cruisers. (IWM Neg. Nos. HU72022 & HU72023)

A rare photograph of invasion barges exercising off St Malo. The comparatively crude nature of the modifications carried out to convert these vessels into primitive landing craft can be seen, most particularly the rudimentary ramp cut into the bows which can hardly have improved their already dubious seaworthiness! (IWM Neg. No. HU95927) (Photographs 1 to 10 by kind permission of the Imperial War Museum)

HMS *Winchelsea*, September 1937. *Winchelsea* was a 'W' Class destroyer, completed in 1918 and armed with four 4-inch guns. She had taken part in the Dunkirk evacuation and by September 1940 was part of the 11th Destroyer Flotilla of Western Approaches Command, based at Liverpool. Most of the 'V & W' Class destroyers in 1939–40 would have looked very similar, although some would have had the after set of torpedo tubes removed and replaced by a 12-pdr anti-aircraft gun. This would also have involved removal of the mainmast.

HMS *Verity*, August 1939. Like her sister *Venomous*, *Verity* had been heavily involved in rescue operations prior to Dunkirk and in the Dunkirk Evacuation itself. By September 1940 she too was part of the 18th Destroyer Flotilla based at Harwich. This photograph shows more clearly than that of *Venomous* the general layout of a 'Modified W' Class destroyer, and in particular the greater size of the 4.7-inch guns when compared to the 4-inch mountings of *Winchelsea*.

A typical 'A-I' Class destroyer, HMS *Anthony*, when newly commissioned in 1930. These vessels were the successors to the 'V & W' Class, and both the similarities and the differences are clear from the photographs. *Anthony* rescued over 3,000 troops from Dunkirk before being damaged by a near miss on 29 May. By September 1940, she was part of the 12th Destroyer Flotilla, based in the Firth of Clyde.

HMS *Arrow*, 1938. The photograph shows how little the 'A' Class had changed in the years since their commissioning in 1930. In September 1940, *Arrow*, like *Anthony*, was with the 12th Destroyer Flotilla.

HMS *Greyhound* in July 1939, with Spanish Civil War neutrality stripes painted on the shield of B mounting. *Greyhound* was one of the later 'A-I' Class, only completing in February 1936. Her sisters of the 'G' Class suffered badly at Dunkirk, but she herself rescued 1,360 troops before being damaged on 29 May. Repairs were completed by 17 June, and on 30 July she joined the 13th Destroyer Flotilla at Gibraltar.

HMS *Javelin* in June 1939, when newly completed. In September 1940 *Javelin* was the leader of Captain Mountbatten's 5th Destroyer Flotilla of powerfully-armed 'J' and 'K' Class destroyers, based at Plymouth to counter the arrival on the western flank of the probable invasion area of a German destroyer flotilla. With a maximum speed at full load of 32 knots, and a main armament of six 4.7-inch guns, the vessels of the 5th Destroyer Flotilla were the most powerful Royal Navy destroyers in the area.

The nightmare! HMS *Southampton* in May 1939. The thought of such a vessel, with twelve 6-inch and eight 4-inch guns, breaking into the lines of slow-moving invasion barges must have given even the most optimistic Sealion planner more than one sleepless night. There were six of these Town Class cruisers in Home Waters, as well as several smaller cruisers.

HMS *Revenge*, August 1939. A veteran of Jutland, *Revenge* was a member of the smallest and slowest class of Royal Navy battleship still in service at the start of the Second World War, and had received little in the way of improvement or modernization. She was, nevertheless, the only battleship in the invasion area, and, with eight 15-inch guns, twelve 6-inch guns and eight 4-inch guns, she could bring to bear a formidable weight of high explosive with an accuracy far beyond the capability of Bomber Command in 1940, as Operation Medium, the bombardment of Cherbourg on 10 October 1940, would demonstrate.

Chapter 12

Evacuations Prior to Dunkirk

It takes the Navy three years to build a new ship. It will take three hundred years to build a new tradition. The evacuation will continue.

Admiral Sir Andrew Cunningham during the crisis of the evacuation of Crete, 29 May 1941

Although the German invasion of France and the Low Countries began on 10 May 1940, the Admiralty had begun drawing up contingency plans as far back as October 1939. These involved laying mines off the Dutch coast and sending demolition parties to the Hook, Flushing and Ijmuiden to prevent these ports falling intact into German hands. Similar plans were made for Antwerp, although the Belgian coast was actually under the control of the French Admiral based at Dunkirk. In the event that such actions needed to be taken, the French Admiral (Vice Admiral Abrial) would have four 'Wairs' ('V & W' Class destroyers rebuilt with high-angle guns for anti-aircraft defence) placed under his operational command.

Responsibility for the demolition parties was given to Vice Admiral Sir Bertram Ramsay, Flag Officer Dover, although control of the ships operating off Belgium and Holland rested with the Commander-in-Chief, Nore, Admiral Sir Reginald Plunkett-Ernle-Earl-Drax. With the arrival of spring, anticipation of a German attack had grown and by early May Ramsay was beginning preparations to remove as much shipping as possible from Dutch and Belgian ports should their capture appear imminent, prior to carrying out the proposed demolition work. At the same time, despite the critical situation in Norway, Drax was receiving reinforcements, in the form of the light cruisers *Arethusa* and *Galatea*, which sailed to Harwich from Scapa Flow on 8 May.

On 10 May, the destroyers *Express*, *Esk* and *Intrepid*, which had been laying mines off Heligoland, escorted the minelayer *Princess Victoria* to the Dutch coast, in order to lay a field of 236 mines off Egmond, and similar operations took place on 12 May, 14/15 May, 18 May, 21/22 May, 23/24 May, 25/26 May and 27/28 May.

On 12 May, Drax received further reinforcements from the Home Fleet, when the cruisers *York*, *Sheffield* and *Manchester* joined his command. By 1100 hrs on 15 May, when Holland surrendered, demolition parties had been landed at Ijmuiden, the Hook and Antwerp, and the destroyer *Brilliant* had supervised the removal of twenty-six merchantmen, fifty tugs and some 600 barges from Antwerp.

In accordance with the earlier agreement, six (rather than the promised four) 'V & W' Wairs were placed under the command of Vice Admiral Abrial on 10 May, and remained so until 1815 hrs on 19 May, when the survivors were withdrawn. The six vessels (*Valentine*, *Vimiera*, *Westminster*, *Whitley*, *Winchester* and *Wolsey*) found themselves almost constantly in action, usually under heavy air attack with no air support of their own. *Valentine* was crippled and beached in the Scheldt whilst attempting to protect a large passenger ferry; unable to take avoiding action, *Winchester* suffered hull damage from a near miss off the Dutch coast and on 15 May sailed to Liverpool for repairs; *Westminster* struck a submerged wreck approaching Dunkirk early on 16 May and was towed to Dover for dry-docking; and *Whitley* was dive-bombed and wrecked off Nieuport on 19 May.

As the military situation deteriorated, the Royal Navy could do little more than watch impotently as disaster overtook the Allied land forces. Demolition parties could put ports out of commission for a time, supplies could be transported, supply ships protected and naval gunfire support given near the coast, but such actions could do nothing to avert the approaching collapse. The destroyer force found itself increasingly committed to rescue operations, and on 16 May, for example, *Whitshed* was sent to Ostend to assist in the evacuation of refugees. She was heavily bombed approaching the port, but not hit, and was again bombed on 19 May, fortunately with the same result. By 20 May, Admiral Abrial had decided, in the face of heavy air attack, to withdraw large French ships from the port, and on the same day minesweeping trawlers were attacked between Dunkirk and Ostend. On 21 May three further destroyers were transferred to Dover from the Nore, whilst *Keith*, *Wild Swan*, *Whitshed* and *Venomous* all brought back British civilians from Dunkirk, Boulogne and Calais. Three of these were bombed, but none were hit.

By 19 May, the true extent of the crisis, and the real possibility that the British Expeditionary Force might be lost, was becoming plain. The duty of producing a plan for 'the possible but unlikely evacuation of a very large force in hazardous circumstances' was given by the Admiralty to Admiral Ramsay. Fortunately, Ramsay was a highly capable officer. Although he had resigned from the Navy in 1935, when Chief of Staff of the Home Fleet, in protest at the autocratic style of the then C-in-C, Sir Roger Backhouse, he had considerable staff experience at both the Naval Staff College and the Imperial Defence College – even after his retirement he had been asked to produce a report on Dover as an operational base, and had been given command of Dover in September 1939. He was highly professional, and his personality inspired respect and loyalty from his subordinates. Within days, he would find himself commanding a huge staff, drawn from all three services.

The resources available to him on 19 May were wholly inadequate, consisting of thirty-six personnel craft based at Dover or Calais, and the existing destroyer force which was already fully committed. With these vessels, he would be hard pressed to transport even the 10,000 men per day from each of the ports of Calais, Boulogne and Dunkirk which the War Cabinet proposed on the morning of 20 May. At the same meeting, it was decided to assemble a large number of small vessels to be ready to proceed to the French coast. Fortunately, on 14 May the Admiralty had ordered that owners of pleasure craft between 30 and 100 feet in length should register them, and had received an overwhelming response, so the necessary information to make possible their rapid assembly was already to hand. The vessels available to Ramsay were also increased by the addition of thirty ferries and eighteen drifters and coasters. On the 22nd, forty Dutch schuits (shallow-draft, powered barges of between 200 and 500 tons), which had been brought to Britain when Holland surrendered, were also requisitioned and given naval crews.

Ramsay would have known almost immediately that – references by the War Cabinet to Boulogne and Calais notwithstanding – any major evacuation would have to be from Dunkirk, and he would also have known how unsuitable the Dunkirk area was for such an operation. As previously stated, the main harbour at Dunkirk, which had seven dock basins, had already been heavily bombed, and blocked, on 20 May. As a result, only a jetty west of the harbour, and the east mole, were still available as embarkation points in Dunkirk itself. The mole was a wooden structure, only 5 feet wide, but 1,400 yards long, and it had never been intended that large vessels should attempt to moor against it. The harbour was also subject to strong tidal currents and was therefore difficult to enter, even in ideal conditions. The beaches, stretching for some 16 miles, were gently sloping and, including the sand dunes inland from the beaches, were around one mile wide. As a result, they could accommodate a large number of troops, but transporting them to ships would be a slow and hazardous undertaking.

The destroyer force which would become the heart of the evacuation fleet was already heavily involved in desperate operations to the west of Dunkirk, predominantly at Boulogne and Calais. The 2nd Panzer Division reached the Channel coast at Noyelles late on 20 May, and after waiting most of 21 May for further orders, began to advance along the coast towards Boulogne. British reinforcements, in the form of 20 Guards Brigade and a battery of anti-tank guns, were transported to Boulogne in two channel steamers escorted by the destroyers *Vimiera* and *Whitshed*, arriving early on 22 May. Early on 23 May, 2nd Panzer Division surrounded Boulogne, and the destroyer *Verity* lifted off the Adjutant General of the BEF, Lieutenant General Sir Douglas Brownrigg, and his staff, taking them to Dover. Naval gunfire support was given to the Boulogne garrison by a flotilla of nine French destroyers, supported by the British destroyers *Keith*, *Whitshed* and *Vimy*, but by 1500 hrs on the 23rd the order was given to evacuate the port, and additional destroyers sent by Ramsay had arrived to assist.

The destroyers entered the harbour in pairs, under heavy attack from some sixty Ju 87 Stukas. The first pair, *Keith* and *Vimy*, were not hit by air attack but suffered considerable superficial damage from fire from German ground troops, both captains being killed. The second pair, *Whitshed* and *Vimiera*, embarked a further 500 troops each, being replaced in their turn by *Venomous* and *Wild Swan*. Once again, both vessels picked up around 500 troops, but by now most of the town had fallen and the ships were under heavy fire from both small arms and tanks. A third destroyer, *Venetia*, was hit and badly damaged by artillery fire from a captured French shore battery, and all three ships returned to Dover.

Finally, early on 24 May, *Vimiera* returned and by 0245 hrs had somehow managed to embark around 1,400 troops and civilians. Three hundred Welsh Guards had to be left behind as the destroyer was already filled to and indeed beyond capacity. Throughout the evacuation, destroyers both in and outside the port had been subjected to heavy air attack, but none of the British ships were hit, although the French *Orage* was sunk, *Frondeur* and *Fougueux* damaged, and *Chacal* sunk by shore batteries.

On the same day that 2nd Panzer surrounded Boulogne, 10th Panzer had closed all the land exits from Calais. The small Allied force in Calais, consisting of a French garrison manning the Citadel fortress and a single platoon of the Argyll & Sutherland Highlanders, received reinforcements on 22 May in the form of twenty-seven cruiser tanks of 3rd Royal Tank Regiment, brought over in two transports escorted by the destroyer *Vimiera*, and 30 Brigade, in two transports escorted by *Windsor*, which arrived on 23rd. At 2200 hrs on the same day, *Verity*, having previously delivered General Brownrigg and his staff to Dover, transported Major General McNaughton, commander of the 1st Canadian Division, to Calais, to assess whether the BEF supply lines could be kept open through the port.

His report was such that at 0300 hrs on 24 May Brigadier Nicholson, commander of 30 Brigade, was told that evacuation had been decided upon, and that the transports which had brought his Brigade to Calais were to be used to evacuate non-combatant personnel. These instructions, sent by Major General Dewing, Director of Operations at the War Office, were soon countermanded, firstly by General Fagalde of the French XVI Corps, responsible for all Allied forces in the Channel ports, who forbad the evacuation of Calais and placed the French troops there under Nicholson's command, and subsequently by Churchill, who upheld Fagalde's decision.

On 24 May, Ramsay received reinforcements to strengthen his battered and exhausted destroyer force, in the shapes of *Wolfhound*, *Grafton*, *Greyhound* and the Polish destroyer *Burza*. *Wessex* was sent at 0700 hrs to provide naval gunfire support for Calais, followed three hours later by *Wolfhound* and *Vimiera* with the same orders. *Burza* followed early in the afternoon. At around 1645 hrs, *Wessex*, *Burza*, and *Vimiera* came under heavy air attack by twenty-one Ju87s, during which *Wessex* was sunk and *Burza* heavily damaged. *Vimiera* was nearly hit, but was able to rescue survivors from *Wessex*, whilst *Burza* returned to Dover under her own power and was subsequently towed to Portsmouth for repairs. Early on the morning of the 25th, *Wolfhound* entered Calais with Vice Admiral Somerville, who carried with him a letter from the War Office advising Nicholson that Calais would not, after all, be evacuated. This information did not reach him until most of the surviving tanks of 3rd RTR had been put out of action by their own crews as a result of the earlier evacuation order. Despite the War Office order, in the early hours of the 25th Ramsay despatched a number of trawlers and drifters, escorted by *Verity* and *Windsor*, to be on hand to evacuate 30 Brigade, but in the absence of a change of orders they returned before dawn.

For the remainder of the day, *Grafton* and *Greyhound* bombarded shore targets in support of the beleaguered garrison, until poor visibility and shortage of ammunition forced them to return to Dover just before midnight, and on the morning of the 26th, first the cruiser *Galatea*, and then her sister *Arethusa*, bombarded German positions, escorted by *Grafton* and supported by *Wolsey* and *Wolfhound*. The surviving defenders were subjected to heavy air attack from two Stukageschwader (StG 77 and StG 2), in support of a major assault by 10th Panzer, and organized resistance had ceased by 1700 hrs. Even so, two small Royal Navy yachts, *Conidaw* and *Gulzar*, managed to rescue fifty men early in the morning of the 27th.

Chapter 13

Operation Dynamo, The Dunkirk Evacuation

This is a special job for the Luftwaffe.
Reichmarshall Hermann Göring, 23 May 1940

As the final resistance in Calais was ending, the Admiralty, at 1857 hrs on Sunday 26 May, gave the order to Vice Admiral Ramsay to commence the evacuation of the British Expeditionary Force from Dunkirk, known as Operation Dynamo. Map 6 shows the Dunkirk area, and the evacuation routes followed by Ramsay's ships, as described below.

Originally, Ramsay had planned to use two evacuation routes. The shorter, Route Z, was some 39 sea miles long, from Dunkirk along the coast to Calais and then across to Dover. Almost immediately, however, German control of that part of the coast made this route vulnerable to coastal artillery fire and dangerous to use in daylight. Consequently, there was a concentration on the second route, Route Y, which at 87 sea miles was over twice as long, northeast from Dunkirk, round the Kwinte Buoy, and then west, in order to pass north of the Goodwin Sands, and then south to Dover. (On 30 May, Ramsay introduced a third route, Route X, which required the sweeping of a French minefield, but which was only 55 sea miles long). Obviously, the loss of the quickest route increased transit times and therefore reduced lifting capacity, although Ramsay did receive reinforcements in the form of the anti-aircraft cruiser *Calcutta* and the destroyers *Mackay, Montrose, Wakeful, Worcester* and *Impulsive*.

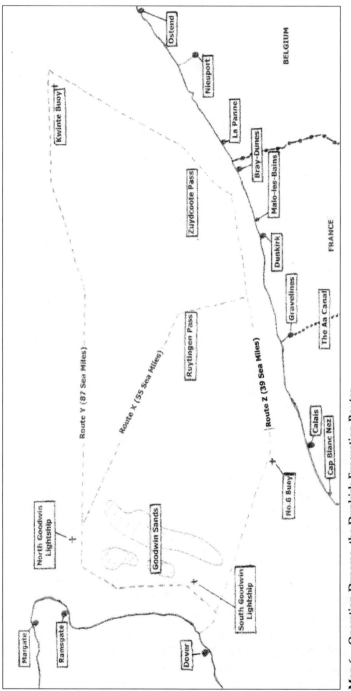

Map 6. Operation Dynamo, the Dunkirk Evacuation Routes.

When Dynamo commenced, the Admiralty believed that, at best, the Navy could rescue around 45,000 men before enemy action ended the evacuation, probably after two days at most. Already worn down by several days of constant action (for example, when on the 24th two of the destroyers which had participated in the Boulogne evacuation, *Vimy* and *Whitshed*, were ordered to change moorings in Dover harbour, the master of the tug *Simla* found their crews to be so exhausted that he moved both ships without waking them), the destroyers which would form the backbone of the evacuation would once again find themselves operating in congested, dangerous waters, whilst often overcrowded with large numbers of troops and unable to use the speed and maneuverability which was their main defence against air attack.

The purpose of the earlier accounts of the Norwegian campaign and the events leading up to Operation Dynamo has been to highlight the major occasions on which the Royal Navy came up against the Luftwaffe in order to try to determine from these encounters what would have been the likely outcome of an attempt by Royal Navy cruisers and destroyers to defeat Operation Sealion in the face of German air superiority. Accordingly, it is not proposed to present a detailed account of the Dunkirk evacuation, as there are already a number of excellent accounts. What follows is, therefore, a brief synopsis of the main events of those nine days, with particular emphasis on the role of the destroyer force and the Luftwaffe.

The first point to make is that there might never have been the opportunity to carry out Operation Dynamo if German forces approaching Dunkirk on the 24th had not been ordered to stop on the line of the Aa Canal. A number of reasons for this halt order have been put forward since the War, the most improbable being that Hitler deliberately gave the BEF an escape route in order to improve the prospects for subsequent peace negotiations with the British government. In fact, the halt order, as the war diary of the German Army Group A, which fell into Allied hands after the War, made clear, was issued by the Army Group commander, von Rundstedt, for what at the time were sound military reasons.

Although the armoured vehicles which had led the advance across France had seen little actual combat since the breakthrough on the Meuse, they had travelled a considerable distance on their own tracks and were in need of maintenance, especially as they would shortly be required for the second stage of the invasion, the drive to the south and to Paris. There may even have been some reaction to a small counter-attack by British tanks near Arras on 21 May, which caused a degree of alarm out of all proportion to the actual achievements of the attack itself. Of course, Hitler could have reversed the halt order, but he chose not to do so when he visited von Rundstedt's headquarters on the morning of the 24th. His own knowledge of the Flanders area from the First World War would have persuaded him that the marshy terrain was unsuitable for tanks, but he had also been assured by Hermann Göring that the Luftwaffe was the ideal weapon to eliminate the encircled armies. For whatever reason, the halt order remained in force until the morning of the 27th.

Perhaps Göring should have consulted his senior commanders before making his boast, as they were far less confident about their ability to make it good. Albert Kesselring, commander of Luftflotte 2, complained that the task was completely beyond the strength of his forces, and the commander of Fliegerkorps VIII, Wolfram von Richthofen, confessed to General von Kluge, of the Fourth Army, that on 24 May his dive-bombers had not even attacked Dunkirk, as their bases were still too far from the front and they were in any case providing close support to the Army. Most of the twin-engined bombers were still operating from bases in Germany. Richthofen even went so far as to ring the Luftwaffe Chief of Staff, Hans Jeschonnek, who was a personal friend, to tell him that the Luftwaffe alone could not stop the British from escaping.

On 25 May, twin-engined bombers from Fliegerkorps I and IV made a few sporadic attacks in the area of Dunkirk, and on the following day similar small-scale raids were made on the town and harbour, although the weather, overcast in the morning followed by steady rain, hampered air operations. On the morning of the 26th, the War Cabinet finally decided on evacuation and informed Gort, whose response was that 'a great part of the BEF and its equipment will be lost.' He then informed his corps commanders. Brooke, in command of II Corps, was of the opinion that even with luck only 25 per cent of the BEF would be saved.

By 26 May, 27,936 men had already been evacuated. On the 27th, the first full day of Operation Dynamo, the Luftwaffe arrived in strength. The first attacks, by aircraft of KG 1 and KG 4, hit the docks area before dawn, and were followed by a further attack at first light by KG 54, resulting in the sinking of a large French freighter, *Aden*, which was berthed on the east mole. At 0720 hrs the Stukas of Fliegerkorps VIII arrived, concentrating their attacks on the ships lifting men from the beaches, as the harbour was unusable.

In all, the Luftwaffe carried out twelve major attacks on 27 May, involving 300 bombers and dropping 15,000 high-explosive and 30,000 incendiary bombs. In reply, RAF Fighter Command carried out twenty-three patrols, of from nine to twenty aircraft, between 0500 hrs and dusk. Air cover for the evacuation fleet during the nine days of Operation Dynamo was provided by 11 Group, commanded by Air-Vice Marshal Park, and thirty-two fighter squadrons took part, although not more than sixteen at any one time; squadrons were sent north for a rest and were replaced by fresh units from 12 and 13 Groups on a regular basis.

Throughout the period, and indeed from as early as 15 May, Air Marshal Dowding had been anxious to conserve his fighter strength, viewing the primary role of Fighter Command as being the close-range air defence of Great Britain, rather than the support of naval forces or the BEF. On the 15th, he had presented to Churchill, Beaverbrook, Newall (Chief of Air Staff) and Sinclair (Minister of Aircraft Production) his case that further Hurricane squadrons should not be sent to France, before a Cabinet meeting which, in the event, decided to send four further squadrons. Also on the 15th, in response to a French plea for a heavy bomber attack on the Meuse bridges and the German forces streaming across them, Bomber Command despatched 100 bombers to attack targets in the Ruhr. This was entirely in accordance with the Air Ministry belief in strategic bombing, but from the point of view of impeding the German invasion of France, unhelpful and largely irrelevant.

On the 16th, Churchill met the French Premier, Paul Reynaud, in Paris, and telephoned London to arrange for six further fighter squadrons to be sent to France. In the absence of the Prime Minister, the Cabinet compromised, agreeing that the six squadrons could operate from French airfields during the day, but must return to the UK each night. As the Air Ministry had estimated that the defence of Britain required fifty-two squadrons, and as Dowding's force had already been reduced to thirty-six before these latest decisions, Dowding was determined to conserve what forces he had left.

He subsequently referred to this period as 'when I was fighting the Germans and the French and the Cabinet and the Air Ministry and now and again the Navy for good measure'. A further problem was the fact that, whereas the Luftwaffe had been trained in the close tactical support of ground forces, the RAF, apart from a small number of slow army co-operation aircraft such as the Lysander, had not. Ramsay was to write critically of the fact that the Navy could not communicate directly with the RAF units allocated to their support, which often resulted in those aircraft being in the wrong place at the wrong time. The inescapable conclusion to be drawn from Dowding's comments is that providing air cover for the evacuation fleet was not high on his list of priorities.

No. 11 Group did, in fairness, face a serious problem. For Park to attempt to provide continuous air cover with the maximum of sixteen squadrons allowed to him (around 200 fighters) would have required frequent patrols by small numbers of aircraft, which would have been overwhelmed by the Luftwaffe, who had some 500 fighters available. The alternative, which is actually the course Park pursued, was to fly 'Squadron Patrols' which involved large numbers of aircraft, often as many as forty, but which were much less frequent and left long periods when there was no air cover at all.

With or without air support, the Royal Navy evacuated 3,324 British troops, together with 1,250 wounded and 4,000 French, on 27 May. As the port had been unusable, the troops had been collected from the beaches, which was a time-consuming process. At low tide, the whalers used by the destroyers (most destroyers carried two oared boats and one motor boat) could take twenty minutes or more to reach the beach, and would then return with twenty-five men. Thus, loading a destroyer from the beaches could take six hours at least, even in ideal weather. Consequently, at 2230 hrs on the 27th, the passenger ferry *Queen of the Channel* was instructed to attempt to berth on the east mole, and succeeded. She was able to load troops and demonstrated that, even though the mole was subject to a tidal range of up to 16 feet, it could be used for embarkation, with as many as sixteen vessels being moored there at one time.

Over the next week, almost 200,000 British and French personnel would use it. The decision to attempt to embark troops from the mole had been taken by Captain William Tennant, who had been appointed (in fact, had volunteered) to be Senior Naval Officer ashore, and who had arrived at around 1800 hrs with a staff of a dozen officers and 160 ratings in the destroyer *Wolfhound*. *Wolfhound* had been heavily attacked by Stukas of Fliegerkorps VIII on her way across from Dover, but had not been hit, and after acting as communications ship for a short time was despatched to embark troops.

On 28 May, the weather was overcast and deteriorated during the day, with the cloud ceiling of around 300 feet limiting the ability of the Luftwaffe to operate, More vessels were being added to Ramsay's fleet, including many of the larger 'A' to 'I' Class destroyers, two 'J' Class, and two 'Brazilian H' Class, six Kingfisher Class corvettes, two gunboats, minesweepers from seven different flotillas, motor torpedo boats from three flotillas and twelve large transports. By midnight 17,804 men had been evacuated. During the morning alone, eleven destroyers succeeded in loading with troops. One, the Scott Class destroyer leader *Montrose*, managed to cram aboard 1,200 troops, and a second, the old 'S' Class *Sabre*, made three trips during the day.

Wakeful, having first offloaded her torpedoes and depth charges, loaded 600 men from the mole in thirty minutes before dawn, disembarked them at Dover and returned to reload. On her way back to Dunkirk she was attacked by Stukas and nearly hit, but was still able to load a further 640 troops from the mole; while returning on Route Y, near the Kwinte Buoy, she was torpedoed and sunk at 0045 hrs on 29 May by a German torpedo boat, S34, with over 700 casualties. A number of vessels attempted to pick up survivors, and one, the destroyer *Grafton*, was torpedoed by a U-boat, U-62, at 0200 hrs, before finally sinking at first light.

Rain and continuing low cloud on 29 May lasted until noon, but by 1400 hrs the clouds had largely dispersed and heavy Stuka attacks involving 180 aircraft of Fliegerkorps VIII, in three waves, began at 1445 hrs. These were followed at 1530 hrs by further attacks by aircraft of KG 30 and Lehrgeschwader I (an operational training unit). In response, 11 Group carried out nine squadron patrols, but were prevented from breaking up the raids by heavy fighter escorts. Ramsay had had seventy vessels operating from the mole and the beaches during the night of 28/29 May, and by the end of the 29th, 47,310 troops had been picked up, more than 33,000 from the mole. The air attacks had, however, caused heavy losses, largely because at the time of their arrival there were eleven ships berthed on the mole. The large 'J' Class destroyer *Jaguar*, just under way when one of the attacks arrived, and carrying a full load of troops, was hit at 1600 hrs and left dead in the water. Her troops were transferred to other vessels and the destroyer *Express* subsequently towed her to Dover.

The destroyer *Grenade*, a stationary target, was hit by three bombs at 1602 hrs and towed clear into open water where her magazine exploded. The French destroyer *Mistral* suffered heavy casualties from a near miss, although her sister ships *Sirocco* and *Cyclone*, carrying 500 troops each, were only slightly damaged. *Verity*, maneouvring to avoid attack, struck a submerged wreck but got clear, *Gallant* was damaged by a near miss and returned to Dover at slow speed, as did *Intrepid* (hit off La Panne at 1830 hrs) and *Saladin*. The losses among the personnel and auxiliary vessels were also heavy, including the large freighter *Clan MacAlister*, paddle steamers *Fenella*, *Crested Eagle* and *Gracie Fields*, and several other transports, trawlers and drifters. In total, fifteen British and four French ships were lost on 29 May.

In the evening, the Admiralty ordered the withdrawal of the seven remaining newer destroyers of the 'I', 'J', and 'Brazilian H' Classes (*Icarus, Impulsive, Intrepid, Ivanhoe, Javelin, Havant* and *Harvester*), which were ordered to sail for Sheerness, leaving only fifteen operational older vessels. Although this measure was intended to preserve sufficient modern vessels for the Home Fleet and for a future anti-invasion force, it seriously reduced the lift capability available to Ramsay, and on the afternoon of 30 May he was able to persuade Pound to reverse the decision.

At 1748 hrs on 29 May, the Admiralty appointed Rear Admiral Wake-Walker in command of vessels operating off the Belgian coast, providing support for Tennant and his hard-pressed shore party. Wake-Walker sailed from Dover in the destroyer *Esk* at 2000 hrs, arriving at 0400 hrs on 30 May. Prior to the arrival of Wake-Walker, however, at 1900 hrs on the 29th, Ramsay had received information from Commander Dove, calling on the direct telephone line from Gort's headquarters, that Dunkirk harbour was completely blocked and that further evacuation must be from the beaches. Quite why Dove made this call is unclear; he was not a member of Tennant's staff and apparently made it on his own initiative, but as it was received just after a signal from the destroyer *Sabre*, at 1825 hrs, that it was 'Impossible at present to embark more troops', Ramsay had no reason to doubt the accuracy of the information.

He did attempt to obtain confirmation from Tennant and Abrial, but received no answer from either. Consequently, he instructed the minesweeper *Hebe*, which was acting as an offshore command ship, to direct personnel ships to the beaches and not to Dunkirk itself. In fact, the harbour was not blocked, although the mole had been broken when the *King Orry* collided with it shortly before she sank. As a result, the whole night was lost, and it was not until 0551 hrs on 30 May that the destroyer *Vanquisher*, having been sent by Ramsay to investigate, reported that the harbour was not blocked. The mole itself was sufficiently repaired to be usable again by 2030 hrs on the 30th.

After such an unpromising beginning, 30 May was a triumph for the evacuation fleet. Fog and rain grounded the 300 Luftwaffe bombers and their fighter escorts, Route X went into operation, the first of the 'Little Ships' arrived, and in the afternoon the bigger, modern destroyers returned. As a result, 53,823 men were lifted, some 30,000 from the beaches. Seven destroyers (*Sabre*, *Wolsey*, *Vimy*, *Whitehall*, *Vivacious*, *Vanquisher* and *Express*) each landed more than 1,000 men at Dover, with the smallest (*Sabre*) actually carrying 1,700, and W*olsey* transporting 1,677 in three trips. In view of this, it was perhaps particularly ironic that Wake-Walker, having transferred his flag to several different ships during the course of the day, should have met Gort and his staff at their headquarters at La Panne at 2000 hrs on 30 May, only to be taken to task about 'the ineptitude of the Navy' by Gort's Deputy Chief of Staff, Brigadier Leese!

Just before midnight on 30 May, Gort was informed by the Chief of the Imperial General Staff, Sir John Dill, over the telephone that the Prime Minister was insisting that French troops be evacuated in equal numbers. Previously, during the morning of the same day, a conference at Ramsay's headquarters in Dover had agreed that the evacuation should seek to reduce the BEF to a rearguard of some 4,000 troops by the early hours of 1 June, and the change in policy would place further strain on the already exhausted evacuation fleet. Nevertheless, 31 May was even more successful, with 68,014 men lifted off.

The weather on the morning of 31 May was still foggy, but it began to clear around midday, and the Luftwaffe carried out a number of small-scale attacks. In reply, 11 Group carried out eight sweeps. The wind had, however, risen to Force 3 and for a time the swell was such that small boats were unable to operate from the beaches. In the afternoon, however, the swell decreased, and many small boats filled with troops departed for England, which though understandable was a course of action Wake-Walker sought to stop, as they were still needed to ferry men to the ships offshore. Navigational difficulties around Dunkirk were increasing, and the fleet was suffering from damage caused by collisions and groundings (often brought about by the exhaustion of the crews) as much as from enemy action. Nevertheless, this day was the high point of the evacuation, with almost 23,000 men lifted from the beaches and 45,000 from the mole.

The morning of 1 June dawned bright and clear, and during the day the Luftwaffe made a final major attempt to disrupt the evacuation. At first light, forty Stukas of Fliegerkorps VIII arrived, protected by Messerschmitt Me 109s and Me 110s, and the captain of the destroyer *Basilisk* later recorded that, of four major air attacks during the morning of 1 June, only the third was opposed by the RAF. The RAF actually carried out eight squadron patrols on 1 June, the first one consisting of forty-eight aircraft, but with sufficient fuel for only about forty minutes over the beaches the aircraft left at 0730 hrs, leaving the fleet without protection between 0730 and 0850 hrs.

There were to be five periods of time on 1 June when the evacuation fleet had no air cover and many of the ships had little or no anti-aircraft ammunition left, the need for a quick turnaround having been given priority over its replenishment.

On 1 June, the evacuation fleet lost thirty-one vessels sunk and eleven damaged. The first destroyer to be lost was *Keith*. She was nearly hit in the first attack, which damaged her hull and steering, and sunk in the second. At 0815 hrs *Basilisk* was hit aft, and, after struggling towards Dover, was hit again and abandoned, the wreck finally being sunk by the destroyer *Whitehall*. The destroyer *Havant* was hit three times and sank at 1015 hrs, and *Ivanhoe* was hit in her boiler room and towed to Dover. At 1300 hrs the French destroyer *Foudroyant* was bombed and sank within three minutes. The last destroyer to leave Dunkirk was *Worcester* at 1700 hrs. She was subjected to attack by thirty-six aircraft, which between them dropped over one hundred bombs, none of which hit, although splinters from near misses killed 46 and wounded 180.

Despite the efforts of the Luftwaffe, supported by an attack by S-boats (motor torpedo boats, generally referred to by the British as 'E-boats'), which sank two trawlers just before midnight, 64,429 troops were lifted off, of which 35,013 were French. At this stage, it was estimated that some 4,000 British troops, and anything from 25,000 to 40,000 French troops, still remained. Tennant, Ramsay and the Admiralty had all agreed that daylight operations should be suspended, and what was intended to be the last lift set out from Dover at 1700 hrs on 2 June, consisting of thirteen personnel ships, nine drifters, six schuits, one gunboat, two armed yachts, a special service vessel, two store ships, eleven destroyers and several small motor boats. By midnight, they had collected 26,256 troops, and at 2330 hrs Tennant, aboard MTB 102 with Major General Alexander, felt able to signal to Ramsay : 'Operation completed. Returning to Dover.'

This was not, however, quite the end. Although the Navy had expected to lift around 40,000 troops on the night of 2/3 June, in the event the French rearguard had been unable to disengage and Ramsay was ordered to undertake a final lift on the night of 3/4 June. He did not feel able to issue an order and so a signal was sent asking which vessels would be prepared to go – 10 transports, 8 minesweepers, 6 destroyers, 4 paddle steamers, 2 corvettes, 10 drifters and numerous small craft volunteered. These set off at 2215 hrs on 3 June and collected 26,209 troops. The last vessel to leave was the old destroyer *Shikari*, at 0340 hrs on 4 June, with 383 French troops aboard, and the Admiralty signal terminating Operation Dynamo was made at 1423 hrs the same day.

For an operation which, the Admiralty estimated, might be able to rescue as many as 45,000 men over a two- or three-day period, the actual statistics of Operation Dynamo are quite remarkable and merit repetition. The following table is reproduced from *The War at Sea, 1939–1945* by Captain S.W. Roskill:

Class or Type of Ship	Number Present	Number of Troops Lifted	Lost to Enemy Action	Lost through Other Causes	Damaged (British Only)
Anti-Aircraft Cruiser	1	1,856	–	–	1
Destroyer/Torpedo Boat	56	102,843	9	–	19
Sloop	6	1,436	–	–	1
Patrol Vessel	7	2,504	–	–	–
Gunboat	2	3,512	1	–	–
Corvette	11	1,303	–	–	–
Minesweeper	38	48,472	5	1	7
Trawler/Drifter	230	28,709	23	6	2

Special Service Vessel	3	4,408	–	–	–
Armed Boarding Vessel	3	4,848	1	–	2
Motor Torpedo Boat	15	99	–	–	–
Schuit	40	22,698	1	3	–
Yacht	27	4,895	1	2	–
Personnel Vessel	45	87,810	9	–	8
Hospital Ship	8	3,006	1	–	5
Cargo Ship	13	5,790	3	–	–
Tug	40	3,164	6	1	–
Landing Craft	13	118	1	7	–
Lighter/Barge	48	4,726	4	8	–
Small Craft	242	6,029	7	135	Unknown
Totals	848	338,226	72	163	45

The 'Little Ships' are included in the 'Small Craft' section, which also includes Royal National Lifeboat Institution lifeboats, naval motor boats and War Department launches.

The crucial role of the destroyers can clearly be seen from the figures, and three of the older vessels may be taken as representative of them all. *Venomous* transported 4,140 troops in five trips, *Worcester* 4,350 in six and *Malcolm* 5,851 in nine.

As the evacuation was ending, just before midnight on 3 June, Nore Command transferred three further destroyers (*Vega*, *Vesper* and *Wanderer*) to Dover, to permit the despatch of damaged vessels for repairs. On 4 June, *Codrington*, *Venomous* and *Shikari* sailed for Devonport, *Malcolm*, *Vanquisher* and *Sabre* for Sheerness, whilst *Esk*, *Express* and *Icarus* returned to the 20th (Minelaying) Flotilla and *Vivacious*, *Winchelsea* and *Whitshed* to the Local Defence Flotilla.

Chapter 14

Operations Cycle and Aerial, the Post-Dunkirk Evacuations

The newspapers have got quite enough disaster for to-day at least.
Winston Churchill, 17 June 1940, when vetoing publication
of the details of the loss of the *Lancastria*.

The evacuations from France did not end on 4 June. There were still around 100,000 British troops in France and Churchill was determined to rebuild the British Expeditionary Force. On 7 June the 52nd Lowland Division began to arrive in Cherbourg, and was due to be followed by the 3rd British and 1st Canadian Divisions. On 10 June, Admiral Sir William James, C-in-C Portsmouth, carried out Operation Cycle, the evacuation of Le Havre. The port was already in ruins, having been heavily bombed for two days, but by the night of 12/13 June, 11,059 British troops were rescued, most of whom were landed at Cherbourg. The only failed evacuation occurred at St Valery-en-Caux, when 6,000 troops of the 51st Highland Division were forced to surrender on 12 June after an evacuation fleet of sixty-seven merchant ships and 140 smaller vessels had been prevented from making a night lift by thick fog, although 2,137 British and 1,184 French troops were picked up from beaches at Veules.

Reality did, however, soon begin to impose itself. On 14 June Lieutenant General Sir Alan Brooke, the recently appointed Commander-in-Chief of what was intended to be a rebuilt British Expeditionary Force, met General Weygand (this was the same day that the German Army entered Paris), and was told that the French Army was no longer able to offer organized resistance. Brooke contacted the CIGS, Dill, and was instructed to evacuate. The 1st

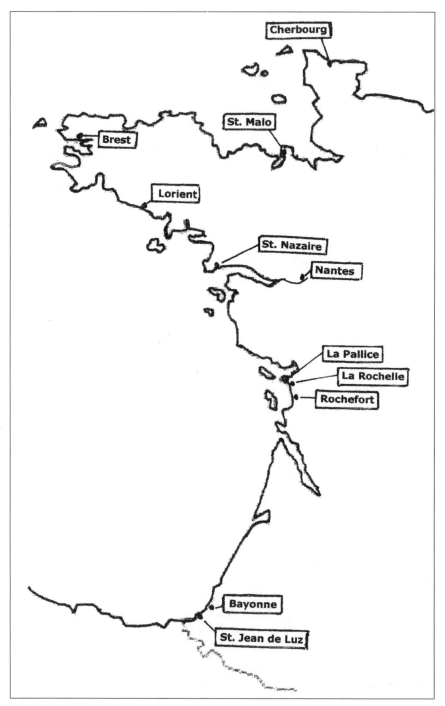

Map 7.   Operation Aerial, the Post Dunkirk Evacuations.

128

Canadian Division, which had just landed, was re-embarked at St Malo, and the 52nd Division returned via Cherbourg, as did the 92,000 troops comprising the base organizations from Nantes, Rennes and Le Mans.

Finally, on 15 June, the Royal Navy commenced Operation Aerial, the evacuation of the remnants of the BEF from Cherbourg and St Malo (by Portsmouth Command), and from Brest, La Pallice and St Nazaire (by Plymouth Command). Map 7 shows the locations of the various evacuation ports used.

The Portsmouth Command evacuations were completed on 18 June, but those undertaken by Plymouth Command lasted until 25 June. The difficulty of these latter operations, largely forgotten by history, should not be underestimated. The distances required the use of large ships and three large liners participated in the lift of 32,584 troops from Brest. Some 36,000 troops were evacuated from St Nazaire on 15 June, and later in a convoy of ten ships at dawn on 18 June, the day after the horrific sinking of the liner *Lancastria*, which was bombed at 1535 hrs and sank with more than 5,000 troops aboard, of whom possibly as many as 3,000 were lost. The Cabinet attempted to keep the disaster secret at the time and the incident is still not widely known about today.

Finally, the last evacuations took place from the Biscay ports of La Pallice, La Rochelle, Rochefort, Bayonne and St Jean de Luz, and the operation terminated on 25 June. In all, 191,870 troops were rescued, together with 310 guns, 2,292 military vehicles and 1,800 tons of stores. One destroyer (HMCS *Fraser*) was lost on the last day, in collision with the anti-aircraft cruiser *Calcutta*.

The figures for troops evacuated during the Dunkirk and post-Dunkirk operations are staggering, totalling over 550,000, of whom over 365,000 were British. In view of the subsequent and enduring belief that control of the air would decide the fate of Operation Sealion, some of the comments made by prominent figures at the time are of interest:

Lieutenant General Brooke, referred to above, had commanded the BEF's II Corps, and wrote in his diary on 23 May that: 'Nothing but a miracle can save the BEF now.'

General Sir Edmund Ironside, the Chief of the Imperial General Staff, wrote on 25 May: 'We shall have lost practically all our trained soldiers by the next few days – unless a miracle appears to help us.'

Viscount Gort, commander of the BEF, cabled the Secretary for War, Anthony Eden, on 26 May: 'I must not conceal from you that a great part of the BEF and its equipment will be lost even in the best circumstances.'

Prime Minister Winston Churchill, in the House of Commons on 4 June, described the Dunkirk evacuation as a 'miracle of deliverance'.

Lieutenant General Henry Pownall, Gort's Chief of Staff, wrote: 'The evacuation from Dunkirk was surely a miracle.'

If the view that, in 1940, warships could not operate within the range of land-based bombers was correct, then Dunkirk must indeed have been a miracle. However, the Norwegian campaign and the subsequent naval operations off the Belgian and French coasts surely demonstrate that this argument cannot be maintained.

Certainly, the exposure of naval forces to heavy air attack without adequate air support for an indefinite period would eventually result in serious losses, but the actual evidence provided by Norway and the evacuations from mainland Europe surely justifies the conclusion that, in 1940 at least, the warships of the Royal Navy could still achieve defined objectives without unacceptably high casualties. Thus, the Royal Navy was able to transport and maintain the land forces in the ill-conceived and badly planned operations in Norway, and subsequently to evacuate those forces, in the face of heavy air opposition with little or often non-existent air support.

Similarly, during the Dunkirk evacuations, the destroyers which formed the backbone of the rescue fleet, and which would subsequently form the cutting edge of the anti-invasion forces, were able to survive heavy air attack for significant periods of time. At least two of the four British destroyers lost to air attack were unable to manoeuvre when they were hit, and it should also be remembered that most of the destroyers (indeed most of the ships generally) at Dunkirk were in positions of maximum disadvantage, in that they were usually manned by exhausted crews, filled to and often beyond capacity with troops, short of ammunition and unable to operate freely in restricted waters.

If the Luftwaffe, with all these factors favouring it, could not hit them with consistency, then it is difficult to justify the claim that that same Luftwaffe would have proved more effective against similar destroyers, operating freely at high speed and with ample room to make drastic course changes, when it sought to protect the slow-moving lines of invasion barges from them. At night, moreover, the Luftwaffe could provide no protection at all. Certainly, at Dunkirk, in addition to those sunk, numerous destroyers were damaged, whether by near misses from bombs, by grounding or by collision, but the often-overlooked fact is that only three of these had not been repaired by 18 June.

That the Luftwaffe should have found ships at sea difficult to hit should not come as a surprise, as most pilots had received no training in the type of precision flying required. Unlike the RAF – which believed that Bomber Command was a weapon capable of winning the war by means of strategic bombing alone, as Douhet and Trenchard had preached, and that Fighter Command's role was essentially defensive, being the air defence of Great Britain – the Luftwaffe in the early months of the Second World War acted in effect as long-range artillery in support of the army. Although Göring too believed in Douhet's theories, the bomber aircraft available to the Luftwaffe were, with few exceptions, capable of carrying small bomb loads only. The Luftwaffe of 1940 (and, indeed, of the whole of the war) was a tactical air force, better equipped to disrupt supply routes behind enemy lines, to destroy defensive fortifications and to hinder the movements of enemy ground forces, than to inflict a crippling, war-winning blow on the enemy by itself.

The Ju 87 Stuka dive-bomber could deliver a small bomb load with considerable accuracy against a static target, but once committed to its dive it was placed at significant disadvantage if the target moved – especially if the target moved at over 30 knots and made violent course alterations! The commander of Stuka-Geschwader 2, Major Oskar Dinort, who had been a famous competition flyer in pre-war Germany and whose Geschwader had had considerable success against ground targets in Poland, recorded the problems he experienced when he led an attack by some forty Stukas against the British naval squadron operating off Calais on 25 May. The reflection of the sun from the surface of the sea made visibility difficult, but, having told his subordinate commanders to select their own targets, he took his section of three Stukas into a dive from 12,000 feet onto the destroyer he had chosen as his victim. Twice in his dive the destroyer made a violent course change, causing him to lose sight of it completely, and the bomb he finally released exploded some 300 feet from the target. The other aircraft experienced similar problems. Dinort concluded that attacks on warships would require a greater degree of expertise than his aircraft had previously needed to demonstrate. The commander of Fliegerkorps VIII, Wolfram von Richthofen, whose dive-bombers would have been at the forefront of any Luftwaffe attempt to protect the Sealion barge trains from the Royal Navy, was adamant that the task was beyond them, and given their lack of success at Dunkirk it is not difficult to understand why.

In conclusion, the Norwegian campaign and the evacuations from mainland Europe demonstrated that, the Luftwaffe notwithstanding, the Royal Navy was still able to undertake its traditional task of transporting the Army to and from overseas campaigns. In the first month of the War it had delivered 161,000 troops, 24,000 vehicles and 140,000 tons of supplies to France without loss, and it subsequently successfully evacuated, under fire, virtually the whole of the BEF. If the bulk of this force had been lost, the political results of such a disaster would surely have brought down the Churchill government and led to peace negotiations. In the event, the Royal Navy won a costly, but vital, victory, whilst the Luftwaffe, whose chief had assured Hitler that it could finish off the BEF alone, failed.

By the last week of June, therefore, the last British troops had been evacuated from mainland Europe, France had concluded an armistice with Germany and Italy was at war with Britain, placing further pressure on the Royal Navy in the Mediterranean. The German naval staff, now faced with the requirement to draw up a workable plan for an invasion of Great Britain, could have seen little in the performance of the Luftwaffe to date to suggest that it could protect whatever invasion fleet they could assemble. From across the Channel, the British, for their part, now needed to decide where and when the inevitable invasion would come, and how best to defend against it.

Chapter 15

'Gunfire and Plenty of It'

I do not say, my Lords, that they will not come. I say only, they
will not come by sea.
John Jervis, Earl St Vincent (First Lord of the Admiralty,
1801–1804) to the House of Lords in 1801.

Immediately after the evacuation from Europe and the capitulation
of France, and throughout the period when the threat of invasion
was perceived to be imminent, the Royal Navy still had other calls
upon naval resources in home waters. It was essential that enough
destroyers were made available to provide a screen for the heavy
units of the Home Fleet, and provision must also be made for convoy escort. The actual dispositions of the available warships would
be the cause of significant disagreement between the Admiralty and
the C-in-C Home Fleet, Sir Charles Forbes.

As early as 28 May 1940, the Admiralty had outlined the strategy
it intended to pursue to defeat an attempted invasion in a directive
to the Commanders-in-Chief in Home Waters. It assumed that the
enemy would accept very heavy losses in order to land the invading
troops, and that early knowledge of the assembly of the invasion
fleet was therefore essential. Once the fleet had been located, the
ports and bases would be mined, shelled and bombed. If this action
was insufficient to prevent the invasion fleet from sailing, then it
would be attacked at its point of arrival. As the Admiralty could not
be sure where this would be, although they assumed the shortest
possible sea crossing, then naval forces must be positioned to cover
the whole of the threatened area, from The Wash to Newhaven.

A third situation might arise, in which reconnaissance was effective enough to make possible the interception of the invasion fleet en

route. If this 'happy possibility' (as the Admiralty described it) occurred, then the Admiralty believed that four destroyer flotillas (i.e. thirty-six vessels), supported by cruisers, would be required to destroy it. These flotillas would operate from the Humber, Harwich, Sheerness and Portsmouth or Dover, which would enable them to cover the entire area under threat. In addition to these forces, the Admiralty intended to concentrate as many smaller vessels as could be released from escort duties to support the destroyers and cruisers, whilst further small patrol craft would also be collected as a mobile screen. In the event, around 400 trawlers and drifters of the Auxiliary Patrol, and around 700 patrol vessels, were eventually to operate right round the British coast.

The Admiralty also expected the German Navy to carry out a diversion in the north, using the two fast battleships (*Scharnhorst* and *Gneisenau*) together with an operation in the southern part of the North Sea by the two old pre-dreadnoughts *Schliesen* and *Schleswig-Holstein*, with perhaps as many as five cruisers in support. In order to combat these, sufficient heavy ships and cruisers must be kept available. In fact, throughout the period of the invasion scare, the Admiralty believed that the German Navy was far stronger than it really was. Both fast battleships had been damaged off Norway and were not available, and only one heavy cruiser, two modern light cruisers, together with the possible addition of an older training cruiser, were actually operational. The Admiralty belief in the possibility of a diversion in the north was correct, however; the German Operation Herbstreise, using their only heavy cruiser, the light cruisers, and several large merchant vessels and liners has already been described.

These dispositions remained more or less unchanged throughout the whole of the summer and autumn of 1940, and were clearly restated in a minute headed 'Defence against Invasion' sent by Churchill to the Chiefs of Staff on 5 August 1940, the first three paragraphs of which read:

1) Our first line of defence against invasion must be as ever the enemy's ports. Air reconnaissance, submarine watching, and other means of obtaining information should be followed by resolute attacks with all our forces available and suitable upon any concentrations of enemy shipping.

2) Our second line of defence is the vigilant patrolling of the sea to intercept any invading expedition and to destroy it in transit.

3) Our third line is the counter-attack upon the enemy when he makes any landfall, and particularly while he is engaged in the act of landing. This attack, which has long been ready from the sea, must be reinforced by air action; and both sea and air attacks must be continued so that it becomes impossible for the invader to nourish his lodgments.

When studied from the viewpoint of the summer of 1940, the emphasis placed by the Admiralty on anti-invasion defences can be understood, but with the benefit of hindsight, the concentration of so many destroyers around the south-eastern coast of Britain (by late July, Nore Command alone had thirty-two destroyers, three cruisers, and seven Kingfisher Class sloops, based at Sheerness and Harwich) can be seen seriously to have weakened the ability both of the Home Fleet, and of Western Approaches Command, which was responsible for providing escorts for Atlantic convoys, to perform their respective roles.

The Commander-in-Chief, Home Fleet, Sir Charles Forbes, had been concerned about the shortage of destroyers and cruisers since the outbreak of war; as early as 27 September 1939 he had written to the First Sea Lord, Sir Dudley Pound, saying that 'I never seem to have any cruisers and very few destroyers to screen the big ships.' The concentration of destroyers in the South-East, together with the transfer south of six cruisers – following a previous suggestion from Pound on 17 May 1940 that the Home Fleet's battleships should be based at Plymouth – must have been viewed by Forbes with considerable concern.

For his part, Forbes was strongly opposed to the serious weakening of the Home Fleet and to the removal of destroyers from convoy escort duties. He agreed with the view expressed by the Chiefs of Staff on 25 May that as long as the RAF remained in being then an invasion was not possible, and that even if the Luftwaffe gained air superiority the Royal Navy could prevent invasion for a time. Had the nature of the ramshackle invasion fleet that the German Navy subsequently assembled been known, the Chiefs of Staff might perhaps have been somewhat more optimistic in their opinion.

Even if the Luftwaffe did secure air superiority, then Forbes believed that there would still be ample time to concentrate the Royal Navy for the attack on the invasion fleet. He successfully fought off the proposal to move the battleships to Plymouth and in July he managed to avoid the transfer of two battleships to Liverpool. He did, however, agree to move the Home Fleet south to Rosyth if an invasion across the North Sea seemed imminent. Eventually, on 20 July, the dispute was resolved when the Admiralty agreed that the heavy ships of the Home Fleet should only enter the southern North Sea if German capital ships were operating there as cover for an invasion force.

Whether the Admiralty's insistence on concentration, or Forbes's belief in rapid redeployment, was the correct approach depended on how much prior warning intelligence and reconnaissance could provide. The crucial factor would be how much notice of an approaching invasion fleet the defending forces could expect to receive.

The first point to make is that many of the conclusions drawn from the available intelligence were wrong. The exaggerated view of the operational strength of the German Navy has already been mentioned, but this did not have a major effect on British planning as even at full strength the German Navy was still inadequate for the task of supporting a major sea landing. However, where that landing would be made was of considerable importance. Some conclusions on the location and timing of the attack could be drawn from the fact that the beachheads would need to be within range of Luftwaffe fighter cover, and the first wave would presumably seek to land around dawn, at or near high tide.

This, combined with the probability that London would be the major target for advancing forces as they broke out, left two options: the South Coast east of Portland, or the East Coast south of the Wash. The Royal Navy had little faith in the reliability of air reconnaissance, as a result of their experiences off Norway where Coastal Command had failed to locate any German warships, although this was probably an unduly pessimistic assessment, given that the aircraft were operating at extreme range in difficult weather conditions. Nevertheless, the Admiralty believed that it was possible that as little as twenty-four hours' notice would be available.

Consequently, deciding which of the two options the Germans would take was vital, if not for the Navy then certainly for the

Army, which would have experienced major logistical problems moving reinforcements from south to east, or vice versa, with the Thames estuary and London in the way, and given the limited mobility of the available divisions.

For what at the time seemed sound military reasons, the British deduced, wrongly, that the East Coast would be the target. The landing beaches were not overlooked by cliffs, for one thing, and East Anglia was far better suited to mechanized warfare for another. By mid-August, only eight divisions were located between Dover and Cornwall, with seventeen between Cromarty and Dover. Only in September, when the barge concentrations in Channel ports became obvious, did the possibility of the South Coast as a target come to be taken really seriously, and even then Churchill and the Chiefs of Staff still believed the East Coast to be the probable main front, with the South Coast as a secondary possibility.

The reason for this erroneous conclusion was not, as might be expected, cunning German concealment of their real plans, but the fact that, for most of the time, the Germans did not have any plans at all, and therefore no preparations were being made. Directive 16 was only issued on 16 July, and it was late in July before Raeder received from Hitler priority for the requisitioning of shipping. Consequently, as there was no evidence to find, it is not surprising that the British air reconnaissance could not find it! The very absence of evidence, however, appeared to point to an attack on the east coast. The reasoning was fairly simple, and seems to have followed the following lines:

1. The Germans must have a detailed plan for invasion.
2. The East Coast and East Anglia are more suited to landings and subsequent tank warfare.
3. Reconnaissance aircraft have not photographed any build-up of shipping in the Channel ports.
4. Therefore the shipping must be in the Baltic ports (beyond aerial-reconnaissance range), and therefore threatening the East Coast, not the South Coast.

The alternative, that there was no German plan in existence as yet, does not seem to have been considered, although in the first week of June reports of German troops in civilian clothes heading for Cadiz, in order to sail to Ireland, apparently were!

At the time, far-fetched and frankly wildly improbable ideas seem to have been given credence. Military Intelligence suggested that tanks might be landed along a wide stretch of coast, rather than the invasion being launched in the conventional manner at all. Whilst the Naval Intelligence Department was sceptical, for the mundane reason that there was no evidence that suitable vessels to carry these tanks even existed, the Naval Staff believed that such an attack was possible. In support of this, the Naval Staff had produced a report (given to Churchill on 10 July) to the effect that 'some 100,000 men might reach these shores without being intercepted by naval forces.' The report had concluded that 25,000 could land on the South Coast (from Channel and Biscay ports), 62,000 on the East Coast (from Dutch, Belgian and German ports), and even 10,000 in Shetland and the north of Scotland (from Norwegian ports), although it then proceeded to point out that these troops once landed could not be supplied.

In late June and early July, the Code and Cypher School at Bletchley Park (which had had some success in breaking the Luftwaffe Enigma cypher during the campaigns in France and Norway) produced decrypts providing information on the deployment of aircraft and referring to long-range guns with which to threaten sea traffic through the Dover Straits; this led the Joint Intelligence Committee, which from 31 May had reported daily to the Chiefs of Staff, to suggest mid-July as the date from which an invasion might be expected. However, even when the Committee received information late in July that the Luftwaffe had been instructed not to attack South Coast ports (Directive 17, of 1 August, did indeed include this restriction) the idea of an attack on the South Coast was still not taken seriously.

Subsequently, even photographs of concentrations of ships and launches in Bremen and Kiel (late in August), and the arrival of large numbers of barges in Belgian ports (early in September), did nothing to disturb their convictions. However, on the basis of aerial reconnaissance on 7 September, which showed large-scale barge movements, the Committee did advise the Chiefs of Staff that an invasion could be expected at any time from 7 September, resulting in Home Forces being alerted on the evening of the 7th.

The conclusion to be drawn from all this is that Forbes was right, and Pound wrong. The Joint Intelligence Committee's initial suggestion of mid-July was not borne out by the information available, and the idea that within a month of the end of the campaign in France the three German armed services could have produced a workable plan for a complex amphibious operation, let alone manage to assemble the necessary shipping from scratch, should have stretched credulity to breaking point. At the time, however, there were so many unknown factors that it is perhaps understandable that those errors which were made erred on the side of safety. Indeed, Forbes's views were not supported by his fellow Commanders-in-Chief at Portsmouth and the Nore. Sir Reginald Plunkett-Ernle-Earle-Drax, at the Nore, was convinced that in order to defeat the invasion force 'we need gunfire and plenty of it.'

In the event, Forbes lost the argument and the destroyers remained tied to the southern ports, patrolling the Channel and the North Sea, but making no contribution to the protection of the convoy routes. As a result, the German U-boat arm experienced its first 'happy time' and six merchant surface raiders (which sailed between 31 March 1940 and 3 July 1940) were able to achieve successes which they would never repeat. On 1 July 1940 Churchill, in accepting the disposition of the destroyer force, stated that 'losses in the Western Approaches must be accepted meanwhile.' The transfer to the Royal Navy of fifty old destroyers from the US Navy in early September 1940 did nothing in the short term to ease the critical shortage of convoy escorts, as virtually all these vessels were in need of refit, and only three had become operational by the end of October 1940.

Quite how serious the losses referred to above were, the following figures from *British Vessels Lost at Sea, 1939–45* (HMSO, 1947) of merchant vessels sunk by U-boats, demonstrate:

Month	Number of Vessels Lost	Gross Tonnage
March 1940	15	47,000
April	6	31,000
May	10	48,000
June	58	284,000
July	38	196,000
August	56	268,000
September	59	295,000
October	63	352,000
November	32	147,000
December	37	213,000

The dramatic increase in merchant shipping losses during the time of the invasion scare is, in fact, probably the single solid contribution that Operation Sealion made to the German cause, especially when it is remembered that the average daily number of U-boats operational between June and October was never more than eighteen, and often as low as eleven or twelve.

However, even though most of the destroyers would probably have been better employed elsewhere, at least until mid-August, from the point of view of the prevention of the invasion, this is not the point. The fact is that the Royal Navy was present in the invasion area in considerable strength.

From late July onwards, in addition to the patrol vessels (over 1,000 of them) there were two cruisers, thirty destroyers and seven sloops in Nore Command, twelve destroyers and a cruiser at Portsmouth, forty small vessels including motor torpedo boats at Dover, and a destroyer division, a cruiser and a battleship at Plymouth. Cruisers patrolled from the Forth to the Humber and from the Humber to the Thames, and the remaining destroyers still on convoy duty did not escort convoys beyond 300 miles west of Ireland. They were therefore available for rapid recall. The Home Fleet at Scapa Flow consisted of three or four battleships and battlecruisers, one aircraft-carrier, two heavy cruisers, three light cruisers and two destroyer flotillas. With such resources waiting to intercept them, the fear permeating German naval planning was surely well founded.

Despite the fact that from as early as the beginning of July 1940 the Royal Navy had more than adequate resources deployed around the South Coast to repel any German invasion force, there still exists the erroneous belief that the Navy was 'kept out of the way' up at Scapa Flow. In fact, the flotillas in the immediate invasion area were extremely active throughout the period during which invasion seemed to be imminent.

Although the Joint Intelligence Committee had suggested mid-July as a possible date when an invasion attempt might be made, it was only from mid-August that invasion preparations were actually detected by the British, and only early in September did aerial reconnaissance reveal the build-up of shipping in the Channel ports. By 7 September, major barge movements had been identified, and as the moon and tides were suitable between 8 and 10 September, British forces were brought to readiness from 2007 hrs on 7 September, when the codeword Cromwell was issued. If Sealion had set sail, the invasion fleet would have had virtually no hope of avoiding detection. A night crossing in moonlight, even though this would increase significantly the navigational problems, would reduce the possibility of detection from the air – but throughout the summer and particularly in September the Royal Navy's flotillas were constantly on patrol, and what follow are examples of some of their nocturnal operations during the first half of September. They are by no means exhaustive.

6 September. The cruisers *Aurora* and *Cardiff* sailed from the Humber to Sheerness at night, escorted most of the way by the destroyers *Wild Swan* and *Wivern*. The 5th Destroyer Flotilla ('J' and 'K' Class destroyers each with six 4.7-inch guns) moved from Harwich to Plymouth in response to the arrival at Cherbourg of four German destroyers.

7/8 September. From Dover, in the early evening of the 7th, some sixty vessels were observed at sea off Calais, and four MTBs (motor torpedo boats) were despatched from Dover, two to operate off Calais and two off Boulogne. The boats for Boulogne withdrew in bad weather, but the other two made torpedo and machine-gun attacks on vessels off Calais. The 1st Destroyer Flotilla (*Atherstone, Beagle, Bulldog* and *Saladin*) from Portsmouth, already at sea, were diverted to support the Calais MTBs in the early hours of the 8th, but returned to Portsmouth without making contact.

8/9 September. MTBs 14, 15 and 17 attacked a German convoy of thirty small vessels near Ostend. Two of the MTBs entered Ostend harbour and launched torpedoes, hitting two vessels. In addition, two cruisers (*Galatea* and *Aurora*), each escorted by three destroyers (*Campbell, Garth* and *Vesper*, and *Hambledon, Holderness* and *Venetia*, respectively), crossed the Channel. One of the groups investigated Calais without being identified, whilst the other entered Boulogne and shelled the inner harbour. The 1st Destroyer Flotilla (*Atherstone, Berkeley, Beagle, Bulldog* and *Fernie*) from Portsmouth patrolled along the French coast from Le Touquet to the mouth of the Seine, and MTBs from Harwich operated in the approaches to Dunkirk. The weather was very poor from around midnight, with heavy rain and a thunderstorm. All vessels involved returned safely, although *Galatea* was damaged by a mine.

141

9/10 September. Six destroyers from the Nore, together with four MTBs, carried out similar operations to those of the previous night, shelling Calais and Boulogne harbours. A further six destroyers from Portsmouth again patrolled the French coast, but this time in the opposite direction to the previous night.

10/11 September. Three destroyers of the Harwich-based 16th Destroyer Flotilla (*Malcolm*, *Veteran* and *Wild Swan*) patrolled off Ostend. *Malcolm* was one of the first destroyers at the Nore to be fitted with radar, and at 0316 hrs on the 11th made contact with surface targets. Several barges and tugs were engaged by all three destroyers, which subsequently were themselves fired upon by shore batteries, but returned to Harwich unscathed.

11/12 September. Destroyers, MTBs, and gunboats, with cruisers in support, operating out of Plymouth, Portsmouth and the Nore, patrolled the Belgian and French coast from the mouth of the Meuse to Cherbourg, entering or examining each port in turn, shelling some where suitable targets presented themselves, and subsequently returning to their own ports unscathed.

12/13 September. Three destroyers of the 16th Destroyer Flotilla from Harwich (*Malcolm*, *Venomous* and *Wild Swan)* sailed at 1700 hrs in order to sweep from Boulogne to Cap Gris Nez. No German shipping was detected.

13/14 September. The same destroyers, patrolling off Boulogne, engaged and damaged a number of German trawlers. During the day of the 13th, Sir Charles Forbes brought part of the Home Fleet (the battleships *Nelson* and *Rodney*, the battlecruiser *Hood*, the new Dido Class cruisers *Naiad* and *Bonaventure*, and eight destroyers) south from Scapa Flow to Rosyth. As already stated, the Admiralty had greatly overestimated the German naval resources available to support Sealion, and had advised Forbes on the same day that the invasion was likely to be supported by *Bismarck, Scharnhorst,* a pocket battleship, the two ancient pre-First World War battleships and several cruisers. In fact, none of the major vessels named here were operational.

Even with part of the Home Fleet now guarding against this (imaginary) threat, Scapa Flow still contained a battlecruiser (*Repulse*), an aircraft carrier (*Furious*), two heavy cruisers (*Norfolk* and *Berwick*), three new light cruisers (*Glasgow*, *Kenya* and *Nigeria*), an anti-aircraft cruiser (*Coventry*) and four destroyers, to guard against the possibility of an attempted breakout into the Atlantic.

With the further option of calling back those destroyers of Western Approaches Command still employed on convoy escort, the Royal Navy had, on 14 September, built up anti-invasion dispositions to their maximum strength.

Quite how strong these dispositions were can be demonstrated by reproducing below a list of the actual vessels which would have sailed to meet Sealion, extracted from the 'Pink List' for 16 September 1940, produced by the Admiralty Operations Division. This details the status (i.e. operational, refitting or repairing, etc.) and location of every major Royal Navy warship. The full document is available as National Archive ADM 187/9, and what is reproduced below is but a fraction of the whole, dealing only with those vessels of destroyer size and above (but including motor torpedo boats), in Home Waters and operational during the week when Sealion might have been launched. Consequently, vessels refitting or repairing and therefore not immediately available have been excluded. Approximate steaming time from the Straits of Dover, assuming a speed of 20 knots, has also been included, in parentheses, after the port. The ports themselves have been listed in terms of their distance from the Straits, with the nearest first, and obviously not in terms of their importance. Destroyers equipped with minesweeping gear are indicated with an asterisk after the name.

The reader may thus be able to judge whether the view remarked upon earlier in this book, 'that the Navy were kept out of the way up at Scapa Flow', is entirely in accordance with the facts!

Dover (1 hour)
2 Motor Torpedo Boats.

Harwich (3.5 hours)
6 Destroyers: *Malcolm, Venomous, Verity, Wild Swan, Wivern, Worcester.*
11 MTBs.

Portsmouth (3.5 hours)
1 Light Cruiser: *Cardiff*.
14 Destroyers: *Beagle, Bulldog, Havelock, Harvester, Hesperus, Highlander, Vanoc, Viscount, Saladin, Sardonyx, Sturdy, Berkeley, Fernie, Mistral* (French).
5 Torpedo Boats: *Branlebas, L'Incomprise, La Cordeliere, La Flore* (all French), *Z7* (Dutch).
6 MTBs.

Southampton (3.5 hours)
2 Destroyers: *Volunteer, Wolverine*.

Sheerness/Chatham (4 hours)
2 Light Cruisers: *Galatea, Aurora*.
18 Destroyers: *Brilliant, Icarus*, Impulsive*, Campbell, Venetia, Vesper, Vivacious, Walpole, Cattistock, Holderness, Garth, Hambledon, Vanity, Vimiera*, Wallace, Westminster, Winchester, Wolsey*.

London (4.5 hours)
1 MTB.

Lowestoft (5 hours)
1 Torpedo Boat: *Draug* (Norwegian).
1 MTBs.

Portland (5 hours)
2 MTBs.

Plymouth (8 hours)
1 Battleship: *Revenge*.
1 Town Class Cruiser: *Newcastle*.
1 Light Cruiser: *Emerald*.
11 Destroyers: *Isis*, Broke, Vansittart, Whitehall, Westcott, La Melpomene* (French), *Ouragan* (French), *Bouclier* (French), *Blyskawica* (Polish), *Burza* (Polish), *Garland* (Polish).

The Humber (10 hours)
3 Town Class Cruisers: *Manchester, Southampton, Birmingham*.
5 Destroyers: *Javelin*, Jupiter*, Jaguar*, Kelvin*, Watchman*.
11 MTBs.

Milford Haven (14 hours)
1 Torpedo Boat: *G.13* (Dutch).

Rosyth (18 hours)
2 Battleships: *Nelson, Rodney*.
1 Battlecruiser: *Hood*.
2 Light Cruisers: *Bonaventure, Naiad*.
1 Anti-Aircraft Cruiser: *Cairo*.
17 Destroyers: *Cossack, Maori, Sikh, Zulu, Jackal*, Kashmir*, Kipling*, Ashanti, Bedouin, Punjabi, Tartar, Electra*, Vortigern, Valorous, Vega*, Verdun*, Woolston*.
1 Torpedo Boat: *Sleipner* (Norwegian).

Liverpool (18.5 hours)
3 Destroyers: *Vanquisher, Walker, Sabre*.

Dundee (19 hours)
3 Torpedo Boats: *Z5, Z6, Z8* (all Dutch).

Belfast (20 hours)
3 Destroyers: *Shikari, Scimitar, Skate*.

Firth of Clyde (21.5 hours)
1 Town Class Cruiser: *Sheffield*.
10 Destroyers: *Keppel, Achates*, Active*, Amazon*, Antelope*, Arrow*, Douglas, St Laurent** (RCN), *Ottawa* (RCN), *Skeena** (RCN).

Scapa Flow (26 hours)
1 Battlecruiser: *Repulse*.
1 Aircraft Carrier: *Furious*.
2 Heavy Cruisers: *Berwick, Norfolk*.
1 Town Class Cruiser: *Glasgow*.
1 Anti-Aircraft Cruiser: *Curacoa*.
7 Destroyers: *Somali, Eskimo, Matabele, Duncan, Versatile, Vimy, Eglington*.

Vessels at Sea on Patrol or Escort Duty
10 Destroyers: *Veteran, Witherington, MacKay, Hurricane, Winchelsea, Warwick, Witch, Wanderer, Vivien, Wolfhound*.
1 Torpedo Boat: *G15* (Dutch).

In addition to the operations of destroyers, MTBs and cruisers, it should also be remembered that further back, from the Wash around the coast to Selsey Bill, were some 700 small patrol vessels, of which almost 300 were at sea at any one time. It was possible that small groups of fast vessels might avoid detection, as the four vessels of the German 2nd Torpedo Boat Flotilla did on the nights of 5/6 September and 8/9 September when they laid minefields in the Dover Straits, but it is surely inconceivable that the vast unwieldy mass of the Sealion fleet could have. Furthermore, whereas the Royal Navy carried out patrols night after night with impunity, the German Navy had virtually no surface vessels with which to oppose them, and the vaunted heavy coastal guns, whilst they no doubt caused anxiety, failed to score any hits. Even the weather conditions – in the words of the German naval staff report of 10 September, 'for the time of year are completely abnormal and unstable, greatly impairing transport movements and minesweeping activities for Sealion' – did not, apparently, hinder the movements and activities of their opponents from Plymouth, Portsmouth and the Nore. Throughout the whole of this period, the British Auxiliary Patrol operated to give advance warning, receiving instructions from the Admiralty concerning weather conditions on a twice-daily basis. The instructions were in the form of a code word, 'Deluge', with 'Deluge 1' meaning that the weather was favourable for small vessel operations, 'Deluge 2' that operations were possible, and 'Deluge 3' that the weather was not suitable.

Finally, it would be wrong to leave the subject of Royal Navy anti-invasion operations without describing the proposed Operation Lucid, which envisaged attacking German barge and shipping assemblies with a weapon Drake or Howard of Effingham would have understood – the fireship! Just as the Armada had been attacked in Calais roads on the night of 7/8 August 1588, so it was planned to send fireships against the ports of Calais, Ostend and Boulogne, on 25/26 September 1940. In this case, the fireships were actually four elderly and decrepit tankers, the *War Nawab*, *War Nizam*, *Mytilus* and *Oakfield*, and the intention was to fill them with a cargo of 50 per cent heavy oil, 25 per cent diesel and 25 per cent petrol, prior to exploding them off the appropriate port when the state of the tide was right to carry the resultant flaming mixture into the assembled shipping.

Perhaps not surprisingly given his enthusiasm for any form of offensive action, the plan had the keen support of the Prime Minister, and on 25/26 September it was intended to carry out the attack. The first group, *War Nizam* escorted by the destroyer *Garth*, left Sheerness at 1830 hrs on the 25th, followed by the rest of her escort (the destroyer *Campbell*, three minesweepers, and several MTBs and motor launches) at 2100 hrs. Unfortunately, the tanker was in such poor condition that her speed gradually dropped below 5 knots, and as the wind direction would probably have carried the blazing mixture away from the intended target, Boulogne, the attack was called off.

The second group, the *War Nawab* escorted by the destroyers *Beagle* and *Wolverine*, did not get even that far. The three sailed from Portsmouth at 0930 hrs on the 25th, heading for Southend, but the old tanker was found to be leaking in so many places that she was declared unseaworthy. A second attempt was made on the night of 2/3 October, but again weather conditions resulted in a 24-hour postponement. On 3/4 October the vessels sailed once again, this time consisting of three forces. Two tankers, *War Nizam* and *Mytilus*, escorted by the destroyers *Campbell*, *Cottesmore*, *Mackay* and *Walpole*, the minesweepers *Salamander*, *Selkirk*, and *Sutton*, and four MTBs and MLs (motor launches), were to attack Calais, whilst the third tanker, *Oakfield*, escorted by the destroyers *Hambledon*, *Garth*, *Venetia*, and *Witch*, the minesweepers *Elgin*, *Hussar* and *Speedwell*, and four MTBs and MLs, were to attack Boulogne. In addition, the whole operation had a covering force of three further destroyers, *Veteran*, *Venomous* and *Wild Swan*.

Once again, weather conditions resulted in a further cancellation, and by the night of 7/8 October, when the final attempt was made, a second tanker, *Mytilus*, had been ruled out as unseaworthy. Yet again, weather conditions resulted in cancellation, but not until after the *Hambledon*, carrying the force commander, Captain Agar, had been mined. Although one more attempt was intended for 1/2 November, this never took place because of deteriorating weather, the condition of two remaining tankers, and the fact that the barge assemblies had started to disperse.

Chapter 16

The Battle of Britain –
the Legend and the Reality

Our fate now depended upon victory in the air.
>Winston Churchill, *The Second World War*, vol. II,
>Chapter XVI

What may well be deemed one of the decisive battles of the world.
>Winston Churchill, *The Second World War*, vol. II,
>Chapter XVI

The introduction to this book explained that it would consist of three sections. The first, and largest, has examined in detail the way in which the German plan for an invasion of Great Britain, Operation Sealion, evolved. It has attempted to view the development of the scheme from the German point of view, highlighting the problems which faced the planners, and looking at how successful, or indeed unsuccessful, they were in resolving these problems. It has then proceeded to describe what may be called the 'nuts and bolts' of the final plan, in order to consider how realistic were the chances of it succeeding, and to ask whether it was ever seriously intended to take place at all.

The second section has, metaphorically, crossed the Channel, in order to look at the way in which the Royal Navy faced up to the challenge presented by Sealion at a time when, many would claim, air power had become the dominating factor in warfare and the Royal Navy could no longer protect Britain from invasion. It has considered how this belief came about, and has assessed how valid it was by concentrating on the effects on the Royal Navy of concentrated air attack during the period from the outbreak of the war until September 1940.

In fact, it is not possible to look firstly at Sealion itself, and secondly at the actual performance of the Royal Navy in the first year of the war, without reaching one inescapable conclusion: The Sealion project failed because of the Royal Navy. When Raeder and his senior staff looked at the problems facing them, the presence of the Royal Navy was the one which could never be overcome. As a result, they shifted, as best they could, responsibility for the conquest of Great Britain onto the Luftwaffe, hoping that by so doing they could avoid the nightmare of attempting an opposed landing. That Göring, with his belief that air power alone could defeat Great Britain, was willing and indeed eager for the Luftwaffe to shoulder this responsibility, actually enabled the German Navy to escape from a potentially catastrophic situation.

The third section of this book, therefore, will question how it came about that the role of the Royal Navy in ensuring that Sealion was never attempted has been largely forgotten. Instead, at least in the United Kingdom, the failure of Sealion has been attributed to the victory of Fighter Command in the Battle of Britain. These two events have since become inextricably bound together in legend. As with many legends, however, the truth is rather different.

Perhaps the most interesting feature of the Battle of Britain/ Operation Sealion connection is the undeniable fact that, in what may for convenience be called the British and German traditions, the two events are viewed from quite different perspectives.

In the British tradition, the two have become inseparable. In simple terms, the Battle of Britain was fought between 10 July and 31 October 1940, and the victory of Fighter Command made Operation Sealion impossible. This is, perhaps, best observed at the end of the 1969 film, *Battle of Britain*, where a scene of massed aerial combat is followed firstly by German troops piling their lifejackets in a heap and marching away, and secondly by a view of a Channel harbour empty of invasion barges. The implication is clear: Britain was saved by the efforts of Fighter Command alone. Sadly, this tradition either denies or is ignorant of the greatest resource available to Great Britain in 1940, the Royal Navy, and still largely accepts the exaggerated importance of the Battle of Britain in the prevention of invasion placed upon it at the time by Churchill for sound political reasons, both domestically and in the United States.

The German tradition is less clear cut. The air battle seems to have commenced with *Adler Tag* in mid-August, and continued until May 1941, when Göring withdrew most of his bomber force from operations over Britain. In other words, the Blitz is part of the battle. In German eyes, the Luftwaffe was not simply seeking to defeat Fighter Command in order to gain a sufficient degree of air superiority to enable the invasion convoys to cross unmolested by a Royal Navy helpless in the face of aerial bombing, but was attempting a much more ambitious task – that of destroying the British will to resist, in accordance with the Douhet theory of which Göring was a fervent disciple.

That the two sides held, and still largely hold, contradictory interpretations of the events of June to October 1940 may be attributed to the effect that these events had on the populations concerned, and these effects greatly differed. In Germany, the possibility that Britain might be invaded came at the end of a period of astonishing success. In less than three months, German armed forces had overrun Norway, Denmark, Belgium, Holland, Luxembourg and France, and had expelled the British Army from mainland Europe. The average civilian would hear speeches about an impending invasion, and after such a run of successes would doubtless assume that it would take place, but he or she would be little affected by it. The eventual postponement and subsequent cancellation would almost certainly be forgotten over time. The Sealion episode did, after all, occupy only some three months of a war which lasted for five and a half years. In the aftermath of defeat, it would come to be regarded, if it was regarded at all, as little more than a flight of fancy.

By contrast, the British saw, and remembered, this period as a time of mortal danger, and subsequently of great triumph. It was 'their finest hour'. They had watched with bewilderment the collapse of the mighty French Army and the German conquest of Western Europe, and the fear that Britain would be next was very real. The threat of invasion, and the various measures taken to prevent it, affected the whole population. In the absence of many of the normal sources of information (newspapers were heavily censored and travel over any distance discouraged and made more or less impossible, even for the small percentage of the population with access to private transport, by fuel rationing), the average person would see the various actions being taken by the authorities and would be obliged to interpret them as best he or she could.

150

Such measures included the erection of concrete pillboxes all over the country, the removal of road signs, the over-painting of railway station names, the dramatic creation, almost overnight, of the Home Guard, and the sealing off of coastal areas in the South and South-East. On 20 June, for example, a 20-mile strip of land between the Wash and Rye was named a Defence Zone, and a permit was required to enter it. Nine days later, the restriction was extended to the whole of the East Coast, and on 3 July beaches from Selsey Bill to Brighton were closed to the public. All these actions led to one inescapable conclusion: that the invasion threat was both real and imminent.

Unlike in Germany, where preparations for Operation Sealion concerned the armed forces without any direct serious effect on the civilian population, virtually the whole of the British population was, to a greater or lesser extent, affected by anti-invasion precautions. Those who thought more deeply how this situation had arisen would doubtless have concluded that, in the words of Winston Churchill quoted earlier, 'There is a plan, perhaps built up over several years, for destroying Great Britain.'

Yet the invasion did not come, and it would be reasonable to conclude that this was because the plan had, at some point, been thwarted. Mr Churchill said it was the Battle of Britain which prevented the invasion. Churchill had his own reasons for saying this, but the statement was accepted at face value, and the Battle achieved the iconic status which, by and large, it still retains today.

The alternative possibility, that no such plan had ever existed, and that the invasion was never attempted because Germany in 1940 did not dare to challenge the supremacy of the Royal Navy in the Channel, would, no doubt, have seemed improbable at the time, and is still viewed with suspicion, despite the overwhelming evidence.

In British folklore, the Battle of Britain has always been perceived as being crucial to the fate of Operation Sealion, both in the reasons why the battle was fought, and in the manner in which the victory achieved by Fighter Command was interpreted. To examine both of these aspects, the obvious starting point is the relevant volume (vol. II) of *The Second World War*, the classic work written by Sir Winston Churchill, and first published in 1949. Chapter XV deals with Operation Sealion, and the following chapter, entitled 'The Battle of Britain', starts with the sentence quoted at the head of this chapter: 'Our fate now depended upon victory in the air.' Even

151

though many since 1949 have uncritically accepted this statement, the actual evidence available demonstrates quite clearly that this was far from being the case.

Churchill subsequently claims that 'The preparation of the embarkation ports, the assembly of the transports, the minesweeping of the passages, and the laying of the new minefields were impossible without protection from British air attack', a view which is, frankly, untenable. It has already been demonstrated that the German Navy had managed to assemble the invasion fleet in time to undertake the operation in mid to late September, and quite how either Bomber or Fighter Command could have hindered the sweeping or laying of minefields is not explained. The fact is that only the Royal Navy could have done this, and it has already been shown exactly how capable the Royal Navy was of fulfilling the task. Indeed, Churchill himself contradicted his own statement in his chapter on Operation Sealion, when he stated that 'the German navy completed the first part of its task' (i.e. the assembly of the invasion fleet in the embarkation ports). Churchill did refer to 'the overwhelming superiority of the British flotillas and small craft' but made it clear that these could not succeed if the Luftwaffe had mastery of the air.

The Battle of Britain was thus seen as the crucial factor in the defence of Great Britain after the fall of France. The assumption was that if the Luftwaffe gained control of the skies, then the invasion fleet would sail. Britain, therefore, was saved from almost certain defeat by the pilots of the Spitfires and Hurricanes of Fighter Command. This appears to be the opinion expressed by Sir Winston Churchill, and it is certainly a widely held view even today. Apparently, as Air Commodore Brothers explained, the Royal Navy 'were kept out of the way up at Scapa Flow' (BBC Radio 4 2005). The popular image is of the supposedly invincible Luftwaffe beaten back, shattered, reeling, and with broken morale, leaving Britain saved from invasion, still in the fight and worthy of the support of the Arsenal of Democracy across the Atlantic. It is a picture of British technological superiority and courage overcoming the odds, and it is evidently far more worthy of remembrance than the dangerous but monotonous nightly operations of elderly destroyers, small gunboats, and converted trawlers and yachts in the Channel and off the French and Belgian coasts.

To assess the validity of this view, it is necessary to look in a little more depth at the Battle of Britain itself. Not at the details on a day-by-day basis, as these have been well analyzed in numerous books, but at the structure of the Battle, at what was achieved, and at what was not.

Subsequently known as 'Battle of Britain Day', 15 September 1940 saw the climax of the daylight air battles, and by a happy co-incidence Winston Churchill was actually present at 11 Group Headquarters in Uxbridge to witness the dramatic events of the day as they unfolded. In his vivid account, contained in vol. II of *The Second World War*, he describes the action that day as 'one of the decisive battles of the war' and remarks that, like Waterloo, it took place on a Sunday. The Waterloo parallel is clearly in his mind throughout and it may not be stretching the analogy too far to suggest that, in the descriptions of the various Luftwaffe attacks as they unfolded one can almost hear the spectral tramp of the boots of the Old Guard as their columns advanced at the climactic moment of the Belgian battle. Nevertheless, it is clear that the announcement to the British and world public of 185 German aircraft lost on that single day, against British losses of less than forty, demonstrated that, like the Old Guard, the Luftwaffe had been beaten – at least as far as its ability to secure air superiority over the invasion area was concerned. As Churchill wrote at the end of his chapter on the Battle of Britain: 'Thus Britain was saved.'

There are, however, a few problems with this view. Firstly, when addressing an assembly of newly promoted Colonel Generals on 13 September, Hitler had already remarked that he did not intend to take the great risk of attempting a landing. Secondly, actual German aircraft losses on 15 September had not been 185, but fifty; and thirdly, the Luftwaffe, since 7 September, had already shifted from attacks on RAF airfields to raids on London, at first by day but later at night. Daylight raids continued into October, but for seventy-six nights from 7 September onwards London was bombed seventy-five times. Göring, as devoted a follower of the theories of Douhet as was the British Air Ministry, now had the opportunity to prove these theories correct.

Those who claim that the Battle of Britain alone prevented the launch of Sealion are presumably unaware of the fact that, almost at the same time as Churchill was broadcasting (on 11 September) – 'the next week or so ... ranks with the days when the Spanish

Armada was approaching the Channel, and Drake was finishing his game of bowls; or when Nelson stood between us and Napoleon's Grand Army at Boulogne' – the German naval staff (12 September) were complaining bitterly that the Luftwaffe was not making any useful contribution to Operation Sealion, and that the Royal Navy was operating almost unhindered in the Channel! The conclusion can only be that, however important 15 September was for the Battle of Britain, for the fate of Sealion it was of marginal importance at best.

The air battle itself is generally regarded as having commenced on 10 July 1940, although the first air attacks on Dover had taken place late in June, and in his account of the battle, Len Deighton identifies four fairly distinct phases as German tactics changed (Deighton 1980). It may now be useful to look at them now in order to determine – or at least try to determine – what the Luftwaffe was trying to achieve, and what relevance these actions had to Sealion.

The opening stage of the Battle of Britain, the so-called Kanalkampf, involved attacks on British coastal convoys by the Luftwaffe in an attempt to draw Fighter Command out into an attritional battle. The effects of these attacks on the convoys and their escorts, and particularly on the destroyers based at Dover, ought to be examined, as the resulting Luftwaffe confrontation with the Royal Navy is relevant to what might have happened when the Navy sought to intercept Sealion, and the Luftwaffe sought to protect it.

The final evacuations from the southern Biscay ports had taken place on 25 June 1940, but at least a week prior to this the Admiralty had begun to rebuild the 1st Destroyer Flotilla, based on Dover, and by 1 July its strength had risen to seven vessels. In addition, the 11th Motor Torpedo Boat Flotilla and ships of the 10th and 11th Minesweeping Flotillas began to arrive from 19 June.

Reconnaissance of most of the major ports, including Cherbourg, Le Havre, Boulogne, Calais, Dunkirk, Nieuport, Ostend, Zeebrugge, Flushing and Ijmuiden on 20 June had revealed no concentrations of shipping, but even so, as has been described earlier, the Joint Intelligence Committee, basing its conclusions on Luftwaffe Enigma traffic decoded by the Code and Cypher School at Bletchley Park, put forward mid-July as a possible date from which an invasion could be expected. In retrospect, removing large numbers of destroyers, escort vessels and anti-submarine trawlers from Western Approaches Command, thereby exposing convoys to heavy losses from U-boat attack was, as Sir Charles Forbes argued, a questionable decision, but its effect was to produce, from late June/early July, a Royal Navy anti-invasion force already more than capable of achieving its objective.

As early as the first week of July, Nore Command already consisted of two modern Town Class 6-inch gun cruisers (*Sheffield* and *Birmingham*) from the 18th Cruiser Squadron, which arrived at Sheerness on 2 July 1940. A First World War vintage light cruiser (*Cardiff*), was based at Harwich, as was the 16th Destroyer Flotilla (*Malcolm, Achates, Amazon, Ambuscade, Antelope, Anthony* and *Arrow*), the 18th Destroyer Flotilla (*Montrose, Venomous, Verity, Veteran, Whitshed, Wild Swan, Wivern* and *Worcester*) and seven Kingfisher Class patrol sloops (*Mallard, Pintail, Puffin, Sheldrake, Guillemot, Shearwater* and *Widgeon*) of the 1st and 2nd Anti-Submarine Striking Forces. In addition, Nore Command included a number of motor torpedo boats and trawlers, minesweepers and light craft of the auxiliary patrol. A number of nightly anti-invasion patrols commenced from 2/3 July onwards, in conjunction with the 21st Destroyer Flotilla based at Portsmouth.

Prior to 28 June, the coastal convoys of the CW and CE series ('W' for westbound and 'E' for eastbound) had come under occasional attack from fast torpedo boats, usually referred to, at least in British sources, as 'E-boats', rather than from aircraft. Indeed, a failed attempt by the destroyers *Vesper* and *Vivacious* to intercept an E-boat force on the night of 18/19 June was probably what led to the transfer to Dover of the 11th Motor Torpedo Boat Flotilla of five boats on 21 June.

The first air attacks on Dover and the destroyer flotilla based there, however, did not begin until 28 June, when a low-level flight of Me 109s machine-gunned Dover harbour and the destroyer leader *Codrington* was attacked near the Folkestone light vessel by a Heinkel He III, but not damaged. Specific responsibility for the conduct of the Kanalkampf was given to the commander of the bomber 'wing' Kampfgeschwader 2, Colonel Johannes Fink. In addition to his own unit, he was also given command of two Stukagruppen, (Ju 87 dive-bombers), and of Jagdgeschwader 51 (Me 109 fighters).

Purely in terms of the battle between the two air forces, there was considerable logic in the German plan. If Fighter Command attempted to protect the convoys, then they would be worn down prior to the main German aerial assault from 12 August, and if they

155

did not then the bombers could attack the convoys and their escorts relatively unmolested. Air Chief Marshal Sir Hugh Dowding had already informed both the Air Ministry and the Admiralty that his planning had not allowed for the protection of coastal shipping, and that any air cover would consequently be minimal. Dowding, indeed, wished to avoid committing his fighters over the Channel because, unlike the Luftwaffe and surely surprisingly for a force specifically created to defend the British coast, the RAF had no proper air-sea rescue organization in place!

The first heavy air attack on a convoy took place on 4 July, when the outward-bound Atlantic convoy OA178 was attacked off Portland early in the afternoon by Stukas under the command of Major Oskar Dinort. Of the fourteen freighters in the convoy, four were sunk and several damaged. The Stukas then attacked shipping in Portland harbour, whilst E-boats sank a further freighter and damaged two more that night. The outcome of this action was a rerouting of Atlantic convoys and an instruction from Winston Churchill that the CW and CE coastal collier convoys, supplying some 40,000 tons of coal per week to the South Coast, should receive an escort of six aircraft.

On the afternoon of 10 July a thirty-coaster CW convoy escorted by the destroyer *Versatile* was attacked by twenty Dornier Do 17s of KG 2, protected by around thirty fighters, but suffered only one loss; the following day Ju 87s of StG 2 and StG 77 attacked Portland harbour, and He 111s attacked Portsmouth. On 13 July Ju 87s of StG 1 attacked a convoy off Dover without success, and on the following day CW6 was bombed by twelve Ju 87s. One coaster was sunk and two damaged, while the escorting destroyer *Vanessa* was near-missed and her engines damaged. She was subsequently towed to port by the destroyer *Gallant*.

The next heavy air attacks in the Dover area took place on 19 July, when some forty or fifty aircraft, both Me 109s and Ju 87s, encountered the destroyer *Beagle*, on patrol off Dover. Despite the numbers involved, *Beagle* had freedom to manoeuvre at speed and was not hit, although near misses caused some minor damage, but no casualties. This occurred at around 1215 hrs, and a second wave of aircraft, nine Do17s, attacked the harbour itself at around 1550 hrs. Again, there were no casualties, but an oiler was sunk, a tug and a drifter damaged, and the destroyer *Griffin* damaged by a near miss.

At 1330 hrs on 20 July, a small formation of nine bombers attacked Dover again, without causing any damage, but at 1800 hrs a much larger force of around thirty Ju 87s with fighter escorts attacked the collier convoy CW7 between Dover and Folkestone. One coaster was sunk, two damaged and one of three escorting destroyers, *Brazen*, was sunk. On the same evening, the destroyer *Beagle*, making her way to Devonport for repairs to the damage sustained on the 19th, was attacked off Portland by ten Ju 87s but again managed to avoid being hit.

Probably the peak of the Luftwaffe offensive against the Channel convoys was reached on 25 July, when convoy CW8 suffered serious losses. This 21-coaster convoy was first attacked off Dover at 1500 hrs by around ninety aircraft, Ju 87s from StG 3 and Ju 88s from KG 4. Five coasters were sunk, and a further five damaged. A flotilla of E-boats despatched to attack the remnants of the convoy was, however, intercepted by the destroyers *Boreas* and *Brilliant*, and forced to withdraw, but both destroyers were themselves attacked by several waves of aircraft and damaged. Three E-boats did, subsequently, attack the convoy off Shoreham, sinking three more ships.

The Dover flotilla had now been under frequent heavy air attack for some fifteen days and, although demonstrating once again how difficult destroyers were to hit, the cumulative effects of one sinking, together with the near misses on various other vessels, had effectively reduced the flotilla to one ship, the leader *Codrington*, and even she was not operational on 26 July, undergoing boiler-cleaning in Dover harbour. Accordingly, Nore Command despatched the destroyers *Vivacious* and *Walpole* as reinforcements. However, at 1430 hrs on the 27th, *Walpole* was damaged by near misses from bombs dropped by Me 109 fighter-bombers, and around three hours later *Codrington*, moored alongside the depot ship *Sandhurst* and unable to move, had her back broken by concussion from a bomb which fell close alongside.

Wisely, but probably belatedly, Dover was abandoned as a destroyer base, when *Brilliant* (under tow) and *Walpole*, escorted by *Vivacious*, departed for Sheerness. The last week of July probably represented the nadir of the fortunes of the Royal Navy in the area – also on 27 July, *Wren* was bombed and sunk off the coast of Suffolk whilst escorting minesweepers, and on 29 July the destroyer *Delight* was attacked and near-missed by fifteen fighter-bombers off

Portland Bill. One of the near misses, however, caused a fire in a fuel tank and the ship was subsequently abandoned.

Finally, one of the Nore-based destroyers, *Whitshed*, was badly damaged by a mine off the Thames Estuary on 31 July. Amidst this gloom, however, the first of the Hunt Class escort destroyers, *Fernie*, arrived to join the 1st Destroyer Flotilla at Portsmouth on 31 July, having passed through the Straits in darkness. Previously, the destroyers in the area had been of the 'V & W', 'B' and 'G' Classes, all of which had low-angle main armaments. *Fernie* carried two twin 4-inch, high-angle guns and, whatever the shortcomings of her HACS control system, was much better equipped to engage aircraft.

Gradually, as more Hunts entered service, they replaced the older destroyers – by the end of December 1940, five of them were based at Sheerness, eight at Harwich and six at Portsmouth.

For a brief period, the Luftwaffe had forced the Royal Navy to withdraw, at least in daylight, from the immediate vicinity of what would become the Folkestone–Hastings landing zone, although at the time Directive 16 was only two weeks old, and was talking grandly in terms of a landing area stretching from Ramsgate to the Isle of Wight. Furthermore, no assault fleet existed as yet, and in any case the destroyer flotillas from the Nore and Portsmouth would still have been able to intervene rapidly.

After the attack on CW8, the collier convoys had been suspended for a short time and new procedures were introduced whereby the convoys would pass through the Straits under cover of darkness, remaining in harbour by day. CE8, which sailed from Dartmouth on 2 August, had been unopposed, but CW9, consisting of twenty-five ships, was attacked by four E-boats off the Isle of Wight at midnight on 7 August. Three coasters were sunk; although the E-boats were driven off by the destroyers *Bulldog* and *Fernie* from Portsmouth, the convoy had lost cohesion and suffered several heavy attacks from Ju 87s on 8 August, during which two further vessels were sunk and three damaged.

This was the last collier convoy to suffer such heavy attack from the air, as the Luftwaffe changed its tactics – the next eastbound convoy, CE9, escorted by two Hunt Class destroyers, *Fernie* and *Garth*, was fired on on 22 August by the heavy coastal guns upon which such great expectations for the protection of Sealion were placed. The guns missed, as they would continue to do, and the collier convoys continued to pass through the Straits until well into 1943.

Kanalkampf demonstrated once again what previous encounters between the Luftwaffe and the Royal Navy had already suggested. Destroyers, when in port or acting as convoy escorts, and therefore subject to restrictions on their maneouvrability, could be vulnerable to air attack, but when free to operate at speed were extremely difficult targets. Destroyer sinkings in the Channel area during the Kanalkampf period, as the above makes clear, were the exception rather than the rule, and tended to occur when lone destroyers were attacked by numerous aircraft. Had the Luftwaffe been called upon to attempt to prevent the Royal Navy attacking the Sealion convoys, they would have found themselves faced, not by individual vessels, but by several flotillas, all moving at speed. In the circumstances, the misgivings Wolfram von Richthofen expressed about the ability of Fliegerkorps VIII to protect the invasion from the Royal Navy can be understood. Even the losses suffered by the collier convoys during the time of the Kanalkampf attacks should be put into perspective. During the last week of July, when the heaviest attacks occurred, no fewer than 103 vessels were safely convoyed through the Straits, and during the whole of the period 10 July to 7 August, the total tonnage lost was, at 24,000 tons, significantly less than that sunk by mines between the same dates.

Directive 17, which gave the order for the main air assault, was issued on 1 August, but adverse weather meant that it was not until 12 August that the second phase, the main attack, Operation Eagle, began, concentrating initially on airfields and radar stations. A large formation of around eighty Ju 88s, with fighter escort, attacked Portsmouth, whilst a further fifteen put the Ventnor radar station out of action for eleven days. The main group, possibly attracted by the battleship *Queen Elizabeth* which was in the final stages of a major modernization, dived on the harbour but failed to hit any warships.

A continuation of attacks on the chain of home radar stations would almost certainly have placed the Luftwaffe in a position of considerable advantage, as these facilities were essential to the Fighter Command network, but as early as 15 August, following a conference chaired by Göring and attended by his three Air Fleet commanders, such raids were abandoned.

For the rest of this period, the Luftwaffe seems to have been attempting to pursue three separate objectives: to wear down Fighter Command and thus draw into the battle what reserves

159

existed; to attack the supposedly-weak left flank from Norway; and to destroy aircraft and aero-engine factories by means of night raids. All this was certainly in accordance with Directive 17, but the effect appears to have caused the Luftwaffe to disregard what was presumably the ultimate objective of the battle, which was to create conditions which would make Sealion possible. Indeed, it is beyond serious doubt that Göring never actually viewed this as the objective at all, but was intent upon proving that Britain could be conquered, or at least brought to terms, by air assault alone.

Certainly, the German naval staff, watching events as they unfolded and seeing nothing in them which contributed towards reducing the main threat to Sealion, the large Royal Navy presence in the area, complained bitterly that paragraph 4 of Directive 17 was being ignored.

The third phase, from 24 August until 6 September, saw the Luftwaffe concentrate attacks on the airfields of 11 Group, and in particular on the seven Sector Stations which actually guided the fighters of 11 Group into battle. During this phase, the Luftwaffe came closest to achieving air superiority over south-east England, and might well have done so had not the attacks on Sector Stations been diluted by the diversion of resources to other targets, mainly aircraft factories. In the event, however, Fighter Command was saved by the unintentional bombing of London on the night of 24/25 August by some dozen Luftwaffe bombers, which was followed by a retaliatory Bomber Command raid on Berlin the following night.

This ushered in the final phase of the battle – daylight and subsequently night raids on London from 7 September onwards. On 8 September, the Luftwaffe informed the German naval staff that their resources would be concentrated on London, and therefore the naval staff were able to comment with some heat on 10 September that, whilst they believed that the Luftwaffe had achieved air superiority over the Channel, they had ignored paragraph 2(e) of Directive 16 which required British naval forces to be attacked in their harbours. The bases of Nore Command, Sheerness and Harwich remained free from air attack, and the nightly naval patrols of the invasion area continued.

Only after the event, when the daylight raids gave way to the heavy night raids on London known as the Blitz, did the idea of the Battle of Britain as a decisive victory take shape, a view enshrined for ever in the epic 1969 film *Battle of Britain*, which wholly disregards the role of the Royal Navy in the prevention of invasion.

The myth that the battle was in some way an aerial Trafalgar is absurd; whereas the Franco-Spanish fleet was virtually annihilated, the Luftwaffe was still very much a major force. Daylight attacks continued well after 15 September, while heavy night-bombing raids on London and other cities were only just beginning, and were largely invulnerable to interception. Sir Alan Brooke was still anxious about British coastal defences well into October, and only late in October were some of the destroyers and cruisers released to other commands.

Obviously, the British could not know that Hitler postponed Sealion on 17 September, reallocated ten of the Herbstreise vessels and six Sealion vessels to Norwegian duties on 19 September, and called Sealion off on 12 October, but the fact that the danger of invasion was still perceived to be real well into October seems to suggest that the victory was not quite so overwhelming, or so clear cut, as legend suggests.

This is not for a moment to suggest that Fighter Command failed. The victory gained was both real and significant. Simply by surviving, they had bought time, and had demonstrated that the Luftwaffe was not invincible. What they had not done, however, by their success was prevent a German invasion, for the simple reason that such an operation was an impossibility unless the Royal Navy presence in the Channel was neutralized, and with the weapons and techniques available to the German armed forces – both Navy and Luftwaffe – in 1940, this was never a realistic possibility.

When questioned during the Battle about the accuracy of RAF claims of German aircraft destroyed, Dowding apparently remarked that if the German figures were correct, then they would be in London in a week! The fact is, both British and German estimates were wildly exaggerated, but in the final analysis this did not matter, as the fate of any German invasion, despite any subsequent beliefs to the contrary, would depend on what happened on the surface of the sea, not on what happened in the skies above it. The Battle of Britain was a notable victory for Fighter Command at a time when Britain needed a victory after six months of defeats, but it did not prevent the launch of Sealion.

Chapter 17

'Be Calm, Be Calm,
He is Coming'

*The true processe of English policy ... is this ... keepe the
Admiraltie; that we bee Masters of the narrowe see.*
                              Libelle of Englyshe Polycye, 1436

Everything which has gone before should surely have demonstrated that Operation Sealion was an unrealistic proposition in the face of the resources the Royal Navy could concentrate to defeat it, but a little harmless speculation might not be entirely out of place. It must be based on the assumption that Hitler, despite the doubts which he had held about the whole enterprise almost from the outset, had had a flash of inspiration and had given ten days' notice for Sealion on 11 September 1940. He had, after all, gone against the advice of his military advisors on other occasions in the first year of the War, and had been successful. Perhaps Sealion could have fallen into the same category.

Before this 'what if' speculation commences, however, the actual dispositions of the naval forces involved during the third week of September 1940 can quickly be described. The Home Fleet, split as it was between Rosyth and Scapa Flow, has already been detailed, so what follows is an outline of the forces likely to be called upon to meet the Sealion vessels once they were reported. The hard-pressed destroyers and escorts still with Western Approaches Command, already struggling to protect their convoys with inadequate numbers, have not been included, but they too could have been called back if the situation had become critical:

Warship Type	Gun Armament & Speed	Base	Number
Battleship (*Revenge*)	8 × 15 inch, 12 × 6 inch, 8 × 4 inch, 21 knots	Plymouth (W. Approaches Command)	1
Town Class Cruisers	12 × 6 inch, 8 × 4 inch, 32 knots	The Humber (Nore Command)	3
Light Cruisers	6 × 6 inch, 8 × 4 inch, 32 knots	Sheerness (Nore Command)	2
Town Class Cruiser	12 × 6 inch, 8 × 4 inch, 32 knots	Plymouth (W. Approaches Command)	1
Light Cruiser (*Emerald*)	7 × 6 inch, 3 × 4 inch, 33 knots	Plymouth (W. Approaches Command)	1
Light Cruiser (*Cardiff*)	5 × 6 inch, 2 × 3 inch, 29 knots	Portsmouth (Portsmouth Command)	1
Destroyers	4 × 4 inch or 4.7 inch, 26–35 knots	Sheerness/Harwich (Nore Command)	24
Destroyers	4 × 4.7 inch, 35 knots	Plymouth (W. Approaches Command)	11
Destroyers	4 × 4 inch or 4.7 inch, 26–35 knots	Portsmouth/Southampton (Portsmouth Command)	16
Destroyers	6 × 4.7 inch, 36 knots	Plymouth (W. Approaches Command)	5

In addition, there were four corvettes and eleven Motor Torpedo Boats with Nore Command, six Motor Gun Boats with Plymouth Command and two MTBs based at Dover. Plymouth, Portsmouth and Dover also contained between them some twenty-five naval minesweepers and 140 minesweeping trawlers, and the numerous small vessels of the Auxiliary Patrol were also available.

To defend the Sealion convoys, Admiral Raeder would have been able to commit five destroyers, supported by four torpedo boat flotillas, based at Cherbourg and Le Havre, and two destroyers and three torpedo boat flotillas based at Ostend, Zeebrugge and Flushing.

Once the go-ahead had been given for Sealion on 10/11 September, the laying of the four mine barriers which must (according to Directive 16) make 'Both flanks of the Straits of Dover, and the Western Approaches to the Channel on a line from Alderney to Portland ... completely inaccessible' would commence in earnest.

163

As previous descriptions of Royal Navy operations in September have shown, the regular night-time sweeps along the French and Belgian coast can hardly be said to have been disrupted, and the likelihood of producing impenetrable barriers in ten days would have been remote.

By September 1940, the Royal Navy were not only sweeping German fields (there were, after all, 698 minesweepers in service), but were also repairing their own fields. Furthermore, the risk of mines breaking loose and appearing amongst the barge fleets, reducing their unwieldy formation to chaos, must have been of serious concern to Raeder and his staff.

Two days before D-Day for Sealion, the attempt to 'pin down' the Royal Navy in the North Sea would begin, when the Herbstreise operation would commence. It was hoped that this force of large vessels, including a number of great German Atlantic liners of pre-war days, sailing from south Norwegian ports in the general direction of the British coast between Aberdeen and Newcastle-upon-Tyne and escorted by the only remaining operational large German warships (*Hipper*, *Nurnberg*, *Köln* and *Emden*) would in some way draw off the Royal Navy from the South Coast. The force would suggest that a landing was planned, but at dusk retreat to the Skagerrak, and repeat the operation the following day if necessary. *Hipper* herself would detach and head north to operate in the area of Iceland.

The problem with this operation, however, was that, by the time Herbstreise was due to sail, much of the Home Fleet was at Rosyth, and the expedition would have been desperately vulnerable. As the Royal Navy dispositions had provided substantial anti-invasion forces around the South Coast without any need to call upon the Home Fleet in any event, there was a real possibility that the German Navy could lose its only remaining large warships whilst failing to draw off any of the anti-invasion flotillas in the south.

At almost the same time as Directive 16 was demanding that the Home Fleet be kept away from the invasion area by a diversionary operation, the Admiralty had decided that their heavy ships would not operate in the southern part of the North Sea in any event unless German heavy units did. Unbeknown to the Admiralty, the German Navy did not have any heavy units serviceable at the time, so the reality was that the anti-invasion deployments already in place would have been unaffected.

On the day before D-Day, Lieutenant Commander Bartels at Dunkirk, Lieutenant Commander Lehmann at Ostend, Captain Kleikamp at Calais and Captain Lindenau at Boulogne would be making their final preparations. The vessels from Dunkirk would take a considerable time to assemble in view of the condition of the port and the locks between the inner and outer harbour, and the Ostend portion of this force would have needed to have sailed at noon in order to meet them. In this 'what if' scenario, one factor over which the Germans had no control would actually have been in their favour. The weather on the morning of 21 September was suitable for the barge trains, with clouds and intermittent rain, although these conditions would certainly have hindered the Luftwaffe. Indeed, for the eleven days from the 21st, the surf was never above moderate. Had it been so, many of the barges would have been swamped.

All this activity, combined with similar preparations in Calais, Boulogne and Le Havre, would have been impossible to conceal, and the British flotillas at Plymouth, Portsmouth and the Nore would have been alerted. There would have been ample time to make preparations for a night attack, when there would have been no risk of intervention by the Luftwaffe.

Thus, by the time night had fallen on 20 September, the Sealion force would have had at least twenty destroyers, together with three light cruisers, approaching from the west, and a similar number, with perhaps as many as five light cruisers, from Nore Command closing from the east. The old battleship *Revenge*, from Plymouth, would doubtless not have been involved; her slow speed would have hindered the much faster cruisers and destroyers, and she would have been unsuited for a night action against light forces.

As a member of the smallest and slowest class of Royal Navy battleship, *Revenge* had received only limited improvements since the end of the First World War, and since October 1939 she had been part of the North Atlantic Escort Force. As Channel Guard battleship, she had undertaken numerous forays into the Atlantic providing heavy cover for convoys including, in December 1939, the first two Canadian troop convoys. She became part of Plymouth Command in August 1940. With her eight 15-inch guns and eight 4-inch high-angle guns, however, she was a powerful asset in the right circumstances, as her bombardment of Cherbourg in October would demonstrate.

Other than the Dora minefield, the only opposition that the Plymouth force might have met would have been the five destroyers and handful of torpedo boats from Cherbourg. Although the advantage gained by the German Navy when B-Dienst had broken the Royal Navy codes had been lost when these were changed in August 1940, these vessels would surely have been despatched to provide some measure of defence for the western flank of Sealion. Quite how much success they would have had is difficult to assess. Even if they had been able to intercept the Plymouth force before it met the larger force from Portsmouth, they would still have been significantly outgunned. Although the modern German destroyers were significantly superior to the older Royal Navy 'V & W' Class in speed and firepower, they would have faced in addition the powerful 'J' and 'K' Class destroyers of the 5th Destroyer Flotilla, which had moved to Plymouth from the Humber earlier in September, and the 6-inch gunfire of two supporting cruisers.

In the past, on numerous night-time minelaying operations, German destroyers had had considerable success, and their high speed had enabled them to avoid action. On this occasion, their speed would be irrelevant – if they were to keep the Royal Navy away from the western flank of the invasion they would have to accept battle. They would probably have inflicted some losses on the Plymouth force, but they would certainly not have stopped it before being overwhelmed.

As the cruisers and destroyers from Plymouth and Portsmouth closed on the western flank, so the powerful forces from Nore Command, mainly based at Sheerness and Harwich, would have been approaching from the north-east. Given the distances involved, and even allowing for the slower speed of the Hunt Class destroyers, there would have been more than enough time to concentrate the whole force in readiness for a night attack. Again, there would have been the Caesar minefield to negotiate, but ships from the Nore had carried out night patrols of the departure ports for Sealion almost constantly for at least the past month, with only one cruiser being damaged. They might have come under air attack before nightfall, but given their freedom to manoeuvre at speed, together with at least the possibility that the Luftwaffe would have had to deal with attacks by Fighter Command, it would have been unlikely in the extreme that the same Luftwaffe which had failed to prevent the

Dunkirk evacuation would now overwhelm the Nore force in the few hours before darkness fell.

Surface protection for the eastern flank of Sealion was minimal: two destroyers and a handful of torpedo boats. If these vessels closed they might well have encountered the heavy ships of Nore Command, the Town Class cruisers. There were ten of these vessels in all, of which eight (*Birmingham, Newcastle, Glasgow, Sheffield, Southampton, Manchester, Belfast* and *Edinburgh*) were in home waters. Of these, *Edinburgh* was undergoing a major refit and *Belfast* was being almost completely rebuilt after mine damage, but three were with Nore Command.

These vessels each carried twelve 6-inch guns and eight 4-inch guns – their power against light surface targets was therefore immense. In the Barents Sea in December 1942, a German destroyer, *Friedrich Eckholdt*, possibly believing she was approaching the German cruiser *Hipper*, actually closed on the cruiser *Sheffield* and was literally blown apart. The captain of *Sheffield* was later to write: 'As we swept down on the target she was disintegrating before our eyes.' The effect of such vessels, together with smaller cruisers and destroyers, sweeping through the lines of small freighters, trawlers, and tugs, all towing barges, can be imagined.

Thus, during the night of 20/21 September, the various Sealion fleets, making their plodding way towards their landing areas, would have found that the impassable mine barriers were nothing of the sort, and the surface escorts totally inadequate. This only left the heavy coastal batteries, which Directive 16 instructed must 'dominate and protect the entire coastal front area'. It should be possible to estimate how effective they would have been in this hypothetical situation by considering their actual performance in 1940, and the result, from the German point of view, is not encouraging. Some of what follows has already been discussed in the chapter dealing with the coastal gun batteries, but it is worth repeating in this context.

The locations of the various batteries have already been described, but the first test firing seems to have been by the Gris Nez guns on 12 August. Ten days later, the slow eastbound collier convoy CE9 came under fire, and between then and December 1940 some 1,880 rounds were fired at convoys – without success. On 29 September 1940, the elderly monitor *Erebus* bombarded Calais and came under fire. *Erebus* dated from 1916, when she had a maximum speed of

167

12 knots; by 1940, the old ship could probably make no more than eight, but she still escaped unscathed.

Subsequently, on the night of 10/11 October, the battleship *Revenge*, returning from the bombardment of Cherbourg, was also engaged. Once again, the great guns missed, as they would continue to do for the rest of the War. The conclusion is clear – if the coastal guns could not hit slow-moving convoys or heavy warships, they could hardly be expected to sink or cripple fast-moving cruisers and destroyers approaching the Sealion fleets from both flanks.

Even in the 'what if' scenario described above, no great powers of imagination are needed to determine what would have happened when the destroyers and cruisers from Plymouth and Portsmouth encountered the 300 motor boats carrying the assault force from Le Havre to the Brighton–Worthing area, or when the Nore forces reached the 157 tugs, trawlers and small freighters, each towing two barges, heading for the Folkestone area from Rotterdam, Ostend and Calais. The close escort, if indeed it could have been so called, would have consisted of minesweepers and armed motor launches which would also have acted as command ships and guides, but these would have been thinly spread and easily overwhelmed.

The outlook for the towing ships and the towed barges would have been even worse. Presumably, those from the nearer ports would have left harbour in daylight on the 20th (the Rotterdam contingent, however, would been at sea for much longer), and cautiously formed up into large blocks of tugs and barges, three or four columns wide and perhaps as many as thirty tug/barge combinations long. In daylight, they would have been able to see the vessels ahead, astern and around them, and navigation would have been simply a matter of following the combination in front. At this stage, the Luftwaffe would no doubt have been prominent, and the tug/barge crews might have taken some comfort from this. Perhaps, after all, it would be all right.

As night fell, however, anxiety would inevitably rise. The Luftwaffe would go home and navigation would become more difficult. It would be essential to keep the next ahead in sight and to watch out for broken towlines which could suddenly place a motionless barge right ahead. In addition, there was the possibility of one of the adjoining tug/barge combinations losing its way and coming too close, making the risk of collision a very real danger, or even of mines breaking loose from the mine barriers and drifting into the formation.

At some stage, however – earlier for the vessels of the outer fleets (the motor boats heading for Brighton–Beachy Head, or the freighters, tugs, trawlers and their barges heading for Folkestone), later for those heading for Rye–Hastings or for Bexhill–Eastbourne, but equally certainly – searchlights, gunfire and explosions would rip the night apart. The vessels in the outer columns would be first to go – possibly the first anyone would know would be the blinding light of a searchlight from a destroyer, followed by the explosion of 4-inch or 4.7-inch shells. The tug/barge combinations, underpowered, many with inexperienced crews, and in their long columns, would be unable to save themselves, or even to man-oeuvre. They would be helpless.

The immediate effect of the attack on the tugs and freighters would probably be twofold. Firstly, barges still attached to their tugs would have been pulled down with them, and secondly other barges, if their tows had parted or been released, would have been left helpless as the formation collapsed into chaos. Quite possibly, smaller barges would have been swamped by the bow waves of destroyers or cruisers passing nearby at high speed, but even the survivors would have been defenceless. By dawn on the 21st, the whole Sealion fleet would have been shattered, but this would not have been the end of the matter.

Given the number of vessels involved, some troops might well have been landed, and as these struggled, with depleted numbers, to establish their bridgeheads, the surviving tugs and steamers would have been required to wait off the beaches until the afternoon of the 21st when they would be expected to re-establish their tow lines and return to their bases to reload with further troops and/or supplies. All this time they would have been under fire from coastal defences and also from Royal Navy warships lying offshore.

This would have been the time when the Luftwaffe would be expected to make a major contribution, providing support for the bridgeheads and sinking or damaging the attacking warships. Quite how this would be achieved has never been made clear – the Luftwaffe had already failed to prevent the Dunkirk evacuation when the only ships present were Allied ones, yet now they would be expected to identify which ships were which among a mass of shipping. In any case, the actual weather for 21 September was 'cloudy, with intermittent rain'. Similar weather had grounded the Luftwaffe on more than one occasion at Dunkirk.

Most critical of all from the point of view of the German naval planners would have been the tug losses. The plan for the initial assault alone had required 365 tugs/trawlers, and the Navy had only ever managed to assemble 386. Although a surplus of some 700 barges existed to replace losses, there were no reserves of towing vessels. Those which did survive the trauma of the initial crossing, the wait for the tide to turn, and the difficulties of re-establishing their towlines would then face further night crossings, and these would, at least in theory, continue for several weeks. In reality, once the full extent of the losses suffered during the first attack had become clear to the German commanders, both Army and Navy, the sheer impossibility of the whole undertaking would surely have become obvious, and the whole operation would probably have degenerated into a desperate attempt to evacuate the survivors.

Sealion, of course, was never attempted, and no doubt this interpretation of what might have happened to it had it sailed will not meet with the approval of those who believe that air, rather than sea, power would have determined its fate. The fact is, however, that on the only occasion when the Germans attempted a seaborne landing by transporting troops in small boats with a weak surface escort across a sea dominated by the Royal Navy – even though the Luftwaffe had air supremacy – the expedition was utterly destroyed. Although the scale of the operation was by no means comparable to Sealion, the outcome is illuminating, and the action took place north of Crete on 21/22 May 1941, by which time the Luftwaffe had become much more skilled at attacking warships.

In order to support the German paratroop and glider landings on Crete, which took place on 20 May 1941, a force of 2,331 men, with heavy weapons and ammunition, was assembled at Milos in twenty-five small cargo steamers with instructions to reinforce the airborne troops who had captured Maleme. This force, escorted by a small Italian destroyer, and moving at 4 knots, left Milos on the 70-mile voyage early on the morning of the 21st. They were intercepted at 2330 hrs on the 21st by a Royal Navy force of three cruisers (*Dido*, *Orion* and *Ajax*) and three destroyers (*Hasty*, *Hereward* and *Kimberley*), and all but three steamers were sunk, despite a brave defence put up by the escorting destroyer (*Lupo*), which survived. Many of the troops and crews were subsequently rescued by Italian fast motor boats, but in terms of the battle for Crete the convoy had been annihilated.

In fact, although Crete eventually fell, no German reinforcements arrived by sea, and some 17,000 troops were evacuated by the Royal Navy, which lost three cruisers and eight destroyers during the operation. The main objective of the Royal Navy, the prevention of reinforcements reaching the German airborne troops by sea, was achieved, but as in the Norwegian campaign, the Royal Navy could not exert any significant influence on the land battle. Once again, German air supremacy was the crucial factor on land; Fliegerkorps VIII, transferred from France and still commanded by the same Wolfram von Richtofen who had been so pessimistic about Sealion, consisted of 716 aircraft, including 433 bombers and dive-bombers and 233 fighters.

To oppose these, the Air Officer C-in-C Middle East, Longmore, had at one stage ninety bombers and forty-three fighters in the whole of the Mediterranean theatre of war, including the Western Desert. This was at a time when the RAF had fifty-six squadrons of fighters and fighter-bombers based in the south-east of England, often carrying out multi-squadron fighter sweeps over France!

Much of the above cannot be anything other than speculative, but the only reasonable conclusion that can be drawn is surely that the Sealion operation as conceived by its planners would have resulted in a disaster for the German forces committed to it. Even if the Luftwaffe had been able to maintain air superiority over the Channel, they would not have been able to defend the invasion fleets from the size of force the Royal Navy would have brought to bear against it; and at night, when these fleets would actually have crossed the Channel, they could have done nothing at all. The impenetrable mine barriers and the dominating heavy guns no doubt read well in the Directive, but they would not have protected Sealion from the cruisers, destroyers and smaller vessels of the Royal Navy from Plymouth, Portsmouth and the Nore, and the greatest fear of the German naval planners, of such vessels rampaging through the lanes of transports, would have become a terrible reality.

When all the myths and legends are stripped away, the actual available evidence suggests that the invasion of Britain was not prevented by the machine guns of Fighter Command, or by the inaccurate bombs of Bomber Command, but by the threat of (in the words of Admiral Drax) 'gunfire and plenty of it' from the Royal Navy.

Although an attempt to carry out the invasion in September would have been doomed to failure, it is difficult to identify any alternative period when an attack might have succeeded. Certainly, it could not have been later, for the weather in late autumn and winter of 1940, and into 1941 would have made conditions in the Channel impossible for the barges; an earlier attack was never a realistic possibility, as neither the plans nor the shipping existed.

The general assumption in the mythology of 1940 always seems to have been that a successful German landing would automatically have led to a German victory, but in fact, other than in the immediate post-Dunkirk period, the evidence suggests that the resources available to the British Army would have been sufficient to provide significant opposition to the initial assault, especially in view of the problems any German forces which did get ashore would have had in obtaining reinforcements and supplies.

Immediately after the conclusion of the Dunkirk evacuation, on 8 June 1940, the War Office identified British forces available in the United Kingdom as consisting of fifteen infantry divisions and one armoured division. One of the infantry divisions was based in Northern Ireland, and the average strength of each infantry division was 11,000 men of all ranks, or approximately half normal strength. In addition, the 51st Highland Division was still fighting (but was eventually lost) in France, and the 52nd and 1st Canadian Divisions were arriving in Cherbourg as part of a 'Reconstituted BEF', which was subsequently withdrawn. The War Office also estimated that it would take around three weeks to reform the troops of the BEF evacuated from France.

An inventory of the weapons available with which to equip the inexperienced divisions in the United Kingdom (seven of which had had little or no training) revealed quite how desperate the situation was, consisting of:

Weapon Type	Number Available
2-pdr Anti-Tank Gun	54
Bren (Machine) Gun	2,300
Armoured Cars	37
Light Tanks	395

Cruiser Tanks	33
Heavy (Infantry) Tanks	72
Field Guns	420
Medium and Heavy Guns	163

Five infantry divisions were responsible for the defence of the coast from the Wash to Selsey Bill. These divisions were seriously short of heavy weapons. Each should have had seventy-two field guns, but the total for all five was only 101, two thirds of which dated from the First World War; instead of the total of 240 anti-tank guns which they should have had, the divisions had a grand total of twelve between them.

The only armoured division (the 2nd) was equipped with 180 light tanks only, and was based in Lincolnshire. By 25 June, a mobile reserve had been established to guard against the feared invasion, consisting of 2nd Armoured Division and 43rd Infantry Division based north of the Thames (to respond to an attack on East Anglia), and 1st Canadian Division, two New Zealand Brigades and 1st Armoured Division (equipped with 81 cruiser and 100 light tanks) based near Aldershot to protect the south-east coast.

In the event, although of course this was not known to the British, no matter how lacking in equipment and trained troops the British Army was in June, the fact is that the Germans were in no position to make any sort of invasion attempt. Furthermore, on 9 July the first arms convoys from America arrived, bringing some 200,000 rifles and ammunition which were distributed mainly to Home Guard units, thus releasing standard .303 Lee Enfield rifles to the Regular Army.

By the middle of August, the situation had improved to such an extent that British home defence forces, excluding the Home Guard, consisted of twenty-nine divisions and eight independent brigades, of which six were armoured. Their dispositions were, however, based on the conviction of the Chiefs of Staff that the German invasion, if and when it came, would be aimed at the East Coast and East Anglia. Consequently, only five divisions were placed between Dover and Cornwall, with a further three in reserve, whilst fifteen and a half divisions, with a further two in reserve, were positioned between Cromarty and Dover.

Only when the barge concentrations in the Channel ports became obvious was the threat to the South Coast fully realized, and by mid-

September the divisions available to meet a South Coast attack had been doubled to sixteen. Impressively, German intelligence (the Abwehr) had estimated that on 17 September Britain had thirty-four and a half divisions, of which twenty were allocated to coastal defence, and fourteen and a half in reserve. The Abwehr had wrongly located some of these forces, but their overall estimate was reasonably accurate. They did, however, believe that it would take some four days for British reserves to counter-attack the bridgeheads, whereas British strategy was based on the number of hours, not days, it would take to undertake counter-attacks.

From 19 July to 21 November 1940, the General Officer Commanding Southern Command was Sir Claude Auchinleck, with Major General B.L. Montgomery as one of his subordinates, in command of V Corps. Auchinleck believed that any German landing should be opposed at the earliest possible opportunity, whereas Montgomery felt that there should be a thin 'screen' of light troops on the coast, with the main strength held in reserve, in his own words, 'poised for counter-attack and for offensive action against the invaders'. This difference of opinion, although not relevant to the main theme of this book, is interesting as it reflects the subsequent conflicts in the German high command towards Operation Overlord, with, in simple terms, Rommel promoting the Auchinleck strategy of coastal defence, and von Rundstedt the Montgomery option of concentrating forces for counter-attack. When planning Overlord, Montgomery had clearly modified his views somewhat, as he assumed that the German policy would have been one of stiff resistance to the initial landings.

Sealion, of course, never took place, but it is clear that, however weak and unprepared the British Army had been in the days immediately after Dunkirk, by the middle of September German troops assaulting the beaches of Southern England would have met stiff opposition, and their need for reinforcement and resupply would have been urgent. Whether reinforcements and supplies could have reached them as they awaited the British counter-attack is, however, quite another matter.

General Gunther Blumentritt, who had been Chief of Staff of Fourth Army from the autumn of 1940, believed, when interviewed after the War, that an attack could have succeeded, observing that 'We might, had the plans been ready, have crossed to England with strong forces after the Dunkirk operation.' This does, however, beg the question. The plans were not ready, the strong forces were not available, unless the second phase of the French campaign was delayed, and in any case there were no suitable transport vessels which could be called upon. Senior German Army officers continually underestimated the difficulty of the Channel crossing throughout the planning of Sealion, and the comment suggests that General Blumentritt was still underestimating it after the War!

There can be little doubt that, immediately after Dunkirk, the British Army was in no state to provide much resistance to strong German forces landing on the East or South Coast. As for the Germans, the fact was that never at any time, whether June or September, were they in any position to ship these forces across, unless the Royal Navy could somehow be removed from the equation, and Germany in 1940 lacked the weapons systems to facilitate this removal.

Chapter 18

Conclusion

Naval power in world affairs still carries the lessons of history.
President Franklin Roosevelt to M. Paul Reynaud,
13 June 1940

When a new Royal Navy ship is commissioned, she inherits the Battle Honours of all previous British warships of the same name. For example, if a new *Orion* were to be built, she would carry five Honours from the seventy-four-gun ship-of-the-line built in 1787 and scrapped in 1814 (including 'The Glorious First of June, 1794' and, of course, 'Trafalgar, 1805'), one from the screw ship-of-the-line built in 1854 and scrapped in 1867, one from the First World War super-dreadnought built in 1910 and scrapped in 1922 ('Jutland, 1916'), and thirteen from the light cruiser built in 1932 and scrapped in 1949.

The earliest Battle Honour is 'Armada, 1588', even though this action took place seventy-two years before the date generally accepted as marking the birth of the Royal Navy. The actual list of awards, together with the criteria which were applied to determine whether an Honour should be awarded, was actually only published as late as October 1954 (a Fleet Order entitled 'Battle Honours for HM Ships and FAA Squadrons'). The Admiralty clearly stated: 'A Battle Honour will be awarded for those actions which resulted in the defeat of the enemy, or when the action was inconclusive but well fought, and in exceptional cases where outstanding efforts were made against overwhelming odds.'

The reason for explaining the above is because, although 146 vessels received the Battle Honour 'Dunkirk 1940', and 432 'English Channel 1939–45', it can be said with certainty that no new warship

176

will ever inherit a specific Battle Honour relating to the defeat of Operation Sealion in 1940, for the simple reason that no such Honour was ever awarded. The fact is that the Royal Navy conclusively defeated Operation Sealion simply by existing, and being present in strength on the flanks of the route Sealion would have been obliged to follow. It would have been an act of almost suicidal folly on the part of the Germans to permit Sealion to sail under such circumstances.

Thus, the anti-invasion dispositions put in place by the Admiralty effectively ensured that any ambitions the Sealion planners might have cherished were thwarted without any need for a naval engagement in the Channel. Indeed, the prospect of such an engagement would have been welcomed by the Royal Navy, as it would have provided the best opportunity for bringing about the wholesale destruction both of the Sealion fleet and the troops it transported. Regular raids by destroyers on the Sealion ports could bring about a few sinkings, and attacks by Bomber Command a few more, but the only circumstances which would render the barges, tugs and freighters open to attack by warships en masse would be whilst they were actually en route, and subsequently as they tried to return and reload, assuming of course that sufficient of them actually survived to reach this stage!

It has been argued that, in fact, the heavy concentration of cruisers and destroyers on anti-invasion duties for much of the latter half of 1940 was a faulty disposition of the resources available to the Royal Navy. Not only did it restrict the operations of the Home Fleet, but it also largely stripped bare Western Approaches Command of the destroyers needed to protect convoys from U-Boat attack. Although, contrary to the popular image, the destroyer of 1940 was not ideal as a convoy escort and anti-submarine vessel, the more suitable sloop was simply not available in anything like sufficient numbers, and the destroyer was the best alternative at the time. The absence of the destroyers held awaiting the invasion from the Western Approaches led to the massive increases in shipping losses already described.

Certainly Sir Charles Forbes was critical of the concentration of resources in an anti-invasion role, and the dispositions can be seen to have restricted seriously that flexibility which has always been a major characteristic of sea power. As the British Army reformed and re-equipped, becoming more able to provide a meaningful defence against a German landing, it seems clear that, at least in retrospect,

Sir Charles's arguments were valid. At the time, however, after the shock of the collapse of France, it would have been difficult to criticize the policy of safety first, and Sir Charles's views were in the minority even among his professional peers.

Moreover, the main criticism of the anti-invasion dispositions – that they tied down a number of cruisers and destroyers to a largely static role, where they were unable to use their major assets of speed and firepower – is not really borne out by events. It has already been shown that these vessels were active throughout the period of the invasion threat, carrying out nightly patrols off the French and Belgian coasts and frequently attacking the various invasion ports. Whilst the Army and Fighter Command both either had to wait, or for sound tactical reasons chose to wait, for the enemy to come to them, the Royal Navy and, later on, Bomber Command, could take offensive action. The naval operations, though rarely finding targets to engage at sea, at least demonstrated to the German Navy what could be expected if Sealion ever sailed.

The fact is that the months from the commencement of the Norwegian campaign in April 1940 to the end of the invasion threat in October of the same year were but a part of that period of the war when virtually the whole weight of the British war effort rested on the Royal Navy, which was often placed in almost impossible situations whilst attempting to turn potential disasters into mere defeats. After Norway, there was a whole series, from Dunkirk, the post-Dunkirk evacuations, Greece and Crete, to Malaya and Singapore. Among these, it is ironic that the prevention of invasion, a vital if unfought victory, has been largely forgotten. The losses for the period are proof enough of the endless challenges which the Royal Navy faced.

From September 1939 to the end of April 1942, or thirty-two months out of the sixty-seven in total between September 1939 and the end of the German war in May 1945, the percentage losses of major warships were as follows:

Warship Type	Number Lost Sept 1939 to May 1945	Number Lost Sept 1939 to April 1942	Percentage of Total
Battleship	3	3	100
Battlecruiser	2	2	100

Cruiser	28	16	57
Fleet Carrier	5	4	80
Destroyer	133	78	59

Thus, in coldly statistical terms, in those months which represented the first 48 per cent of the War, the Royal Navy suffered just over 60 per cent of its total losses in warships of destroyer size and above.

In effect, the Royal Navy found itself holding the ring almost alone until the other two armed services became capable of bearing some of the load. The small Regular and Territorial Army, after the calamities of Norway and France, took time to build up to a size which would enable it to undertake operations against the main German Army. Even the victories it gained during the period (both in North Africa, at Beda Fomm against the Italians in December 1940 to February 1941 under O'Connor, and Operation Crusader against a German/Italian force in November to December 1941 under Auchinleck) illustrate the point, as the sizes of the forces involved were miniscule when compared to the German forces which carried out Operation Yellow, let alone to the numbers which campaigned in Russia.

The contribution to the British war effort during the same period by the Royal Air Force was also, frankly, unimpressive. Fighter Command had, of course, fought and won the Battle of Britain, but the RAF in general had contributed little to the campaign in Norway and had been largely absent from the campaigns in Greece and Crete, despite the fact that, by the middle of 1941, fifty-six squadrons of fighters and fighter-bombers were regularly taking part in offensive operations over France.

In his autobiography, Sir Andrew Cunningham remarked that 'a few squadrons of long-range fighters and heavy bombers could have saved Crete' (Cunningham 1951), and Churchill, in an address to the House of Commons on 10 June 1941, after the battle for Crete had been lost, said, 'There are those who say we should never fight without superior or at least adequate air support, and ask when the lesson will be learned. But suppose you cannot have it ... Must you, if you cannot have this essential and desirable air support, yield important key points one after the other?' In view of these comments, and the fact that that the Royal Navy was once again committed to a desperate evacuation in what amounted to enemy

179

coastal waters, it could surely be asked whether some of the fifty-six squadrons might have been better employed elsewhere.

In contrast to the way the Luftwaffe had been trained to operate in close co-operation with the German Army, the RAF still remained aloof, preferring to act independently and to place its faith in the concept of strategic bombing. Consequently, considerable resources were committed to building up a large heavy bomber force. As a result, not only was Coastal Command starved of aircraft with a range great enough to provide effective air support for convoys, but also British land and sea forces were deprived of the air support which the proponents of air power themselves claimed was essential for success. What is evident from the operations of the Royal Navy in the period between April and October 1940 is that air power, though a potent threat, was not yet as effective against naval forces as its supporters liked to believe – both then and sub-sequently. During the period under discussion, the Royal Navy landed troops, supplied troops and evacuated troops, all in the face of German air superiority and even at times supremacy. Losses, sometimes heavy, were suffered, but objectives were achieved.

Perhaps most important of all, during the critical period from late June until early October 1940, the Royal Navy did indeed 'keep then the seas about in special; which of England is the round wall'. That this victory has never been properly acknowledged should not detract from the magnitude of the achievement.

Bibliography

(Including Broadcast and Internet Sources)

Adams, J., *Doomed Expedition: The Campaign in Norway, 1940*, Leo Cooper, 1989.
Allen, H.R., *Who Won the Battle of Britain?* Panther, 1976.
Ansel, W., *Hitler Confronts England*, Duke University Press, 1960.
Atkin, R., *Pillar of Fire: Dunkirk 1940*, Sidgwick and Jackson, 1990.
Axis History Factbook, Campaigns and Operations (Internet Site).
Barnett, C., *Engage the Enemy More Closely*, Hodder & Stoughton, 1991.
Bassett, R., *HMS* Sheffield, Arms and Armour Press, 1988.
BBC Timewatch, *Sealion* (BBC TV Broadcast).
BBC Radio 4, *The Things we Forgot to Remember: Mers-el-Kebir*, BBC Radio 4, 2005.
Bekker, C., *Hitler's Naval War*, Corgi, 1976.
——, *The German Navy, 1939–1945*, Chancellor Press, 1997.
Bennett, G., *The Battle of Jutland*, Wordsworth Editions, 1999.
Bishop, E., *The Battle of Britain*, Allen and Unwin, 1960.
Blundell, W., *German Navy Warships, 1939–1945*, Almark Publishing, 1972.
Breyer, S., *Battleships and Battlecruisers, 1905–1970*, MacDonald and Janes, 1979.
Brice, M., *The Tribals*, Ian Allan, 1971.
Brown, D. (ed.), *Design and Construction of British Warships, 1939–1945*, Conway Maritime Press, 1995.
Buffetaut, Y., *D-Day Ships*, Conway Maritime Press, 1994.
Bullock, A., *Hitler: A Study in Tyranny*, Penguin, 1962.
Churchill, W.S., *The Second World War*, vols 1 and 2, Cassell, 1949.
Cunningham of Hyndhope, *A Sailor's Odyssey*, Hutchinson and Co., 1951.
Deighton, L., *Fighter*, Triad/Granada, 1980.
Douhet, G., *The Command of the Air*, US Government Printing Office, 1983.
——, *The War of 19–*, US Government Printing Office, 1983.
English, J., *The Hunts*, World Ship Society, 1987.
——, *Amazon to Ivanhoe*, World Ship Society, 1993.
Fairweather, C., *Hard Lying (V & W Class Destroyers)*, Avalon Associates, 2005.
Fleming, P., *Operation Sea Lion*, Simon & Shuster, 1957.
Forty, G., *The First Victory (Beda Fomm)*, Guild Publishing, 1990.
Gordon, A., 'Battle of Britain: The Naval Perspective' (RUSI) (Internet Site).

Grinnell-Milne, D., *Silent Victory*, Bodley Head, 1958.

Grove, E., *Sea Battles in Close Up: World War II*, vol. 2, Ian Allan, 1993.

HMSO, *British Vessels Lost at Sea, 1939–1945*, HMSO, 1947.

Hampshire, A.C., *Lilliput Fleet*, William Kimber, 1957.

Hill, J.R. (ed.), *Oxford Illustrated History of the Royal Navy*, Oxford University Press, 1993.

Hough, R., *The Longest Battle*, Pan Books, 1987.

——, *The Hunting of Force Z*, William Collins, 1963.

Howard, S., *Men of War: Great Naval Leaders of World War II*, Weidenfeld & Nicolson, 1992.

Jackson, R., *Churchill's Moat*, Airlife Publishing, 1995.

——, *Dunkirk*, Cassell, 1976.

——, *The Royal Navy in World War Two*, Airlife Publishing, 1997.

Janes, *Jane's Fighting Ships of World War II*, Bracken Books, 1989.

Kennedy, L., *Pursuit: The Sinking of the Bismarck* , William Collins, 1974.

Lenton, H.T., *British and Empire Warships of the Second World War*, Greenhill Books, 1998.

Lord, W., *The Miracle of Dunkirk*, Allen Lane, 1983.

Macksey, K., *Beda Fomm*, Pan/Ballantyne, 1971.

McIntyre, C., *World War II at Sea*, Bramley Books, 1990.

McKee, A., *The Coal Scuttle Brigade*, Souvenir Press, 1957.

Middlebrook, M. and Mahoney, P., *Battleship (Loss of the Prince of Wales and Repulse)*, Penguin, 1977.

Muggenthaler, K., *German Raiders of World War II*, Pan Books, 1980.

Piekalkiewicz, J., *Sea War, 1939–1945*, Blandford Press, 1987.

Pope, D., *73 North (Battle of the Barents Sea)*, Weidenfeld & Nicolson, 1958.

Raven, A. and Roberts, J., *Ensign 5: Town Class Cruisers*, Plaistow Press, 1975.

——, *Man O'War 2: V & W Class Destroyers*, Arms and Armour Press, 1979.

——, *British Cruisers of World War II*, Arms and Armour Press, 1980.

——, *Man O'War 4: Hunt Class Escort Destroyers*, Arms and Armour Press, 1980.

——, *British Battleships of World War II*, Arms and Armour Press, 1981.

Richards, Denis, *The Royal Air Force 1939–1945*, HMSO, 1974.

Robinson, D., *Invasion 1940*, Constable & Robinson, 2005.

Roskill, S.W., *The War at Sea, 1939–1945*, vol. 1, HMSO, 1954.

——, *The Navy at War, 1939–1945*, Collins, 1960.

Smith, P.C., *Hit First, Hit Hard (HMS Renown)*, William Kimber, 1979.

——, *HMS Wild Swan*, William Kimber, 1985.

——, *Hold the Narrow Sea*, Moorland Publishing, 1984.

Tarrant, V.E., *The U-Boat Offensive, 1914–1945*, Arms and Armour Press, 1989.

Thomas, D., *Crete 1941*, André Deutsch, 1972.

Thomas, D.A., *A Companion to the Royal Navy*, Harrop, 1988.

Thompson, J., *The Imperial War Museum Book of the War at Sea*, BCA/Sidgwick & Jackson, 1996.

Trevor-Roper H.R., *The Last Days of Hitler*, Pan Books, 1973.

Tute, W., *The True Glory*, Book Club Associates, 1983.

——, *The Deadly Stroke*, Pan Books, 1976.

Vader, J., *The Fleet without a Friend*, New English Library, 1971.

Warner, P., *Auchinleck*, Sphere Books, 1982.

Wegener, Wollfgang, *Maritime Strategy of the Great War*, Naval Institute Press, 1989.

West, J.L., *The Loss of* Lancastria, Millgate Publishing, 1988.

Winton, J., *Carrier* Glorious, Leo Cooper, 1986.

——, *Air Power at Sea, 1939–1945*, Book Club Associates, 1977.

Wood, D. and Dempster, D., *The Narrow Margin*, Arrow, 1967.

Young, J., *Britain's Sea War*, Patrick Stephens, 1989.

Index

184

185

192